World
Encyclopedia
of
CATS

To Betty, With All My Love,
December 24, 1979

Pat

World Encyclopedia of CATS

Edited by
Angela Sayer

OCTOPUS

First published 1977 by
Octopus Books Limited
59 Grosvenor Street
London W1

© 1977 Octopus Books Limited

ISBN 0 7064 0586 2

Produced by
Mandarin Publishers Limited
22a Westlands Road
Quarry Bay, Hong Kong

Printed in Hong Kong

Drawings by David Nockels

Contents

Introduction 6

The Care of Kittens
and Cats 9

The Family Cat 21

The History of the Cat 33

The Biology of the Cat 42

Feline First Aid 49

The Mind of the Cat 65

Cat Behaviour 81

Longhairs and
Shorthairs 97

Siamese and other
Foreign Breeds 113

Pedigree Breeding 129

Cats on Show 145

Stars of Television
and Film 155

The Magical Cat 161

The Literary Cat 169

Cat Standards 173

Eastern Magic 177

Index 191

Introduction

Stanley Dangerfield

Once upon a long time ago I interviewed John Freeman on television. At the time I must have been about the biggest dummy ever let loose inside a studio. John Freeman was the total professional, with a string of the most impressive 'face to face' interviews behind him that TV has ever seen.

This was a pet programme and the unaccustomed reversal of roles was accounted for by the fact that Mr Freeman owned two Abyssinian cats. And the fact that I was questioning the arch questioner explained why I was even more clumsy than usual. How else could I have blundered out with my first question? 'Why,' I demanded, 'do you dislike dogs?'

Of course Mr Freeman promptly explained that a love of cats did not necessarily presuppose a hatred of dogs. Mercifully I have forgotten the rest of the programme, except the moment when Pushkin (or was it Dulcie?) bit me. Twice. And hard.

People who associate me principally with dogs often ask me the same question—why I dislike cats. So let it be said that far from disliking them I have a private, as distinct from a public, passion for them. I admire them, respect them, love them. I recognize the many ways in which they are superior to dogs. And at the drop of a hat I will recount to the most hardened dog addict the reasons for such a view, even at the risk of being indicted for treason.

I cannot remember a time when I did not own a cat and I am certain that such a day will never come. A cat is an indispensable member of the family. True, I don't need a large number of cats around me to make the point. One is enough. And that is the size of the Dangerfield cat population, except when a stray temporarily graces the house with its presence.

Currently the cat is a Blue Burmese called—somewhat unimaginatively—Moggie. Of course he is beautiful. Beautiful, that is, if you are prepared to overlook somewhat donkey-like hind legs, a marked tendency to be overweight and a badly battered ear. Maybe the beauty is in his mind? Maybe. But strict regard for the truth forces the admission that, if present, it is well hidden. While he loves all humans, he seems to loathe all animals. Squirrels and baby bunnies which venture into the garden rarely survive to tell the tale. Big dogs pass the house on the other side of the road. Even horses appear to increase their speed as they trot past the front garden which is his stalking ground. And, sad to relate, my bird-loving neighbours once produced a petition requesting Moggie's removal, owing to his systematic and efficient raids on their bird tables. He was not after crumbs!

Yet even a hardened character such as Moggie is not all hostility. To see him with my pet dog is sheer joy. I keep Griffons, which are pint-sized busybodies born to torment and annoy any cat, especially their own. Moggie accepts their antics, suffers the indignities they heap upon him, tolerates even the pulling of his swishing tail. Then, with a pounce, he catches a young one, perhaps a quarter of his weight. Pins it to the ground with a powerful but deliberately harmless paw. And then washes it from head to foot. As I said, he's not all bad. How can he be when for the last twelve years I have never once had to give a pet Griffon a bath?

But that's more than enough about my cat in a book that is supposed to be about yours – about the cat or cats you already have, or the ones you are going to have. Which is as good a starting point as any.

The Care of Kittens and Cats

Stanley Dangerfield

Left
A handsome, confident family cat glistening with health and enjoying an out-door life. Cats so full of character and fun are perfect companions for those who have not set their heart on a pedigree breed.

Below
The Manx is usually a strong character and an excellent companion.

Although at the moment I keep a pure-bred cat, I am not wholly convinced that all pedigree cats are necessarily superior to all moggies, mousers or alley cats – call them what you will. Some pedigree cats are more pleasing to the eye than some cross-breds; but the reverse is also true. Some pedigree cats are better reared and therefore healthier than cross-breds; but once again this is not always the case.

It all adds up to the fact that I would not let breeding or the lack of it deter me from acquiring or keeping a cat that I liked. A good cat, like gold, is where you find it. Character is everything. And the chances are that character owes as much to environment as to heredity.

This admitted, many would still prefer a pure-bred, which means that they are faced with a bewildering choice. Deciding on a breed of dog is easy, because you have a good idea beforehand whether you want a giant or a pygmy, a killer or a softy, a tomboy companion for children or a cosy friend for a maiden aunt. A cat cannot be so conveniently classified.

Summary of the breeds

All cats are roughly the same size and have similar desires, appetites and characters. They do, however, have markedly different types of coat. So an early decision must be made – is it to be long or short? Bear in mind that although a Longhaired cat is fre-

quently prettier it has the disadvantage of moulting more profusely and of requiring more grooming.

The list of the most popular Shorthaired breeds must be headed by the Siamese, Britain's top cat, brought here from Siam some 90 years ago. Most frequently their cream-coated bodies are tipped with seal-brown but the points can also be blue, chocolate, red, lilac, tabby or tortoiseshell. Perhaps the most dog-like of all cats, they love company, enjoy travelling in cars and will go for walks on the lead.

Burmese, either Brown or Blue, are similar to the Siamese in style and temperament but are possibly less vocal and slightly more respectful towards carpets, curtains and other soft furnishings.

Abyssinians are either rabbit-coloured or red and have distinctive ticking on each hair. They are particularly active and normally good-tempered and friendly, although some may be 'one man' cats.

The same can be said of the round-faced, comfortable-looking British Blues. But if you are seeking the unusual, consider the Manx cats. In any and every colour, these characters are unique in having unusually powerful hind legs, a loping gait and, as a rule, an entirely tailless, rounded rump.

Best known of the Longhaired varieties are the Whites, which can have either blue or orange eyes. Although spectacular at their best, regular grooming with powder is necessary to keep them that way.

Blue Persians certainly show the dirt less and have the same 'chocolate-box' appeal as well as a quiet, affectionate nature. They are used with Creams to produce Blue-Creams, looking too elegant to be true but still pure cats when it comes to sharing family life.

If you are looking for even more glamour, give some thought either to the Colourpoint, which has the colouring of the more exotic Siamese in addition to a long coat, or the Chinchilla, with its full, lush silver coat, brick-red nose and emerald-green eyes.

These are only a few of the more popular breeds on offer. I warned you the choice was bewildering!

The right kitten to buy

Being bewildered by the choice of breeds is nevertheless no excuse for losing your wits when faced by the practical proposition of buying a kitten. This needs to be approached with the minimum of sentiment and the maximum of cold, clinical deliberation. You could go to a pet shop and take pot luck. Or you could be smart and visit a couple of cat shows, which would enable you to meet breeders.

I feel quite strongly about seeing all young animals with their mother when making a purchase. It helps you to guess at the youngsters' adult appearance. It provides a guide as to the mother's health and the conditions under which the kittens have been reared. You can reassure yourself about their probable age.

Below
A Seal Point Siamese queen and her four-week-old kittens. Kittens should be around eight weeks old when they are taken away from their mother, and preferably ten weeks old.

And, as a bonus, you might come away with the pick of the litter.

Before making a choice, watch the kittens at play. Then go for one that is sturdy, full of life, with wide-open, bright and sparkling eyes. Never choose a nervous kitten that runs and hides when you go to stroke it. Much better to pick out the individual that is playful and interested in everything that is going on. Kittens vary enormously in temperament and will be little changed in later life. So choose very carefully.

There are health signs which can easily be checked. The inside of the ears should be clean, without any smell or indications of discharge, which may be a form of canker. The nose should feel cool and slightly damp, not hot to the touch. Nose and eyes must also be quite free of discharge. The inside of the mouth should be rosy-pink, the tongue a normal red, and there should be a full set of tiny, clean white teeth.

The stomach should not appear swollen, which could indicate malnutrition or worms. No matter how long the fur, it should not cling, greasy and unkempt, close to the body; nor should there be any black 'coal-dust' specks in the coat, for these are spots of dirt left by fleas. The tail should be lifted up to make sure that there are no signs of diarrhoea.

A kitten should be between seven and ten weeks before you remove it from its mother. This gets the weaning period over but still allows time for social-ization. An older cat which has spent too long in a cattery finds living with humans a rather trying business; and a stray rescued from a cat's home is likely to give even more trouble, perhaps being so set in its unfortunate ways that it never settles down comfortably in the household.

First days at home
When you first get your little blue-eyed innocent home, regard him as a suicidal escape artist. Keep the windows firmly closed and always keep a fire-guard in position. Electric fires are hazards and so too are all types of electric wire. Kittens have been electrocuted by playfully nibbling at wires leading to standard lamps and other electrical equipment.

The most important article to provide at this stage is a sanitary tray, filled with ashes, earth, saw-dust or a proprietary brand of litter. Kitten training must begin here. Cats, regardless of age, are in-herently clean and prefer to relieve themselves out-side when allowed to do so. If you have a garden this will solve hygienic problems but if not the tray will become a permanent fixture. In any event, have the tray available for the first day or two and make sure he is using it. Keep it where the kitten can easily find it, and change the contents whenever they have been soiled. In due course you can start escorting him to the garden at regular intervals, particularly after sleeping, eating and drinking.

A small cardboard box lined with a blanket is an ideal makeshift bed, which can later be replaced. A permanent bed can either be a basket, a type of canvas camp-bed or a wooden bench. Ideally it should be raised from the floor and be equipped with sides to keep out draughts. In my own home a 'dognest' bought for a puppy has proved a sensational success. This is a large loose cushion filled with polystyrene beads which gives way as the cat settles into it, pro-viding both a cosy base and a firm surround.

Now all you have to worry about is feeding. But that will give you more than enough headaches for the first few weeks. It is not so much that a kitten has an enormous appetite, but that it has a small stomach and therefore needs frequent meals. No sooner have you finished one session than it seems you have to begin over again.

There are two stages in feeding kittens. The first is weaning, the second rearing. Since you will probably have bought your kitten fully weaned, the first will not normally apply. But it is just as well to know something about it, in case you later graduate, either by accident or design, to the role of breeder.

Weaning normally commences at around three weeks when the kittens should be encouraged to share their mother's food. A week or so later they should be lapping milk and eating some solid food. After another week they should be getting four meals a day; and at around seven weeks they ought to be fully weaned.

Protein-rich foods such as meat, fish and milk make the best diet, any type of meat or fish being accept-able. Alternatively, tinned proprietary food is suit-able, providing the variety which prevents cats from becoming addicted to one type of food.

Since kittens grow fast and have relatively small stomachs, they require four meals a day when they are two to three months old, and three meals between the ages of three and five months. Milk should be given separately, and fresh drinking water must always be available.

Between six and eight months the period of rapid growth ends. At that point care must be taken, particularly with spayed cats, to avoid over-feeding which results in obesity.

When the natural caution and apprehension caused by the changed surroundings have worn off, the new kitten you have introduced to the household should soon settle. So, for that matter, should you! Then you will remember that your duty is to give him proper attention when he needs it, allow him to sleep when tired, feed him correctly and keep him warm. Nothing here, you will notice, about smothering him with sickly affection. For the moment, training is more important.

From kitten to cat
Keeping a cat in a flat presents an extra problem because there is not always a garden or facility for outdoor exercise. Consequently the cat must be allowed as much indoor freedom as possible; and if

you have a balcony this can perhaps be wired in so that it can sleep in the sun. If there is no balcony, a light wire frame can easily be fixed to the window so that fresh air and sunlight can get in. These precautions are necessary because cats are often seriously injured as a result of falls from roofs or open windows.

If you have a garden, consider fitting a cat-flap, allowing the cat to go in and out at will. But remember that this will also enable him to bring his friends home once they learn how to open the flap!

Regardless of age, never shut a cat out at night. He may be involved in fights and return home injured; or he may get caught in the beam of headlights, being run over or causing an accident. His courting songs may not always be appreciated by neighbours. In inclement weather he risks exposure, perhaps leading to pneumonia. And there is even the chance he may get picked up by cat thieves.

Cats are the most independent of animals, deter-mined only to do things when they are so inclined. Not for them the dog-like desire to please their owners. Although, if they feel like it, they can be trained to perform simple tricks, their cooperation cannot be relied upon. Nevertheless you should insist, right from the start, on certain patterns of behaviour.

Demand, therefore, that your pet does not clean or sharpen his claws on the furniture, curtains or carpet. A firm 'no' is soon understood. In the garden he can be encouraged to use a tree for this purpose. Failing this, buy a scratching post or log from a pet shop and fasten it fairly high up on a kitchen table leg. Once introduced to this, a kitten will quickly appreciate its purpose and use it regularly.

Set your mind firmly against such tricks as jumping onto the table and licking the butter dish or milk jug. Such behaviour may seem amusing when he is tiny, but the joke will soon wear thin. It is also unhygienic, and although you may be prepared to risk this, few

Below
Some cats are incurable thieves and even if you think your own cat would never steal, it is not wise to leave food lying around.

Right
The importance to cats of scratching is often underestimated. They like to flex their muscles and also get rid of old sheaths on the claws. Even if your cat has access to trees a scratching post will save your furniture. This is a Tabby Point Siamese.

of the friends you invite to tea will be as indulgent!

Don't be afraid to talk to your kitten—not such a foolish pastime as it sounds. Cats are great conversationalists and also, being polite, reply when spoken to. Two different sets of vocal chords enable them to produce a wide variety of sounds—some experts say more than one hundred—and very soon you will be able to identify those that demand the satisfaction of basic needs, including one that clearly means 'thank you'. Affection will be shown by a gentle touch of the paw, a lick of the tongue and by placing the paws around your neck. Purring, which seems to be quite involuntary, is a clear sign of contentment.

Provide plenty of playthings, such as rubber mice, pingpong balls or a small teddy bear. Some cats become very possessive over their toys, hiding them away and bringing them out only when they are in a playful mood. Most kittens like hide-and-seek, peering out from under chairs and around corners, scampering away with apparent glee.

By the time your kitten reaches the adult stage, there should be a quiet and satisfying relationship between you. You will have acquired an aesthetically pleasing addition to your household as well as a con-

Previous page
A Siamese kitten having a good kick with his back legs. Notice the top of the sacking is already torn to pieces where he has scratched with his front paws. Posts need to be solid and heavy to take the daily beating.

Left and Right
Two handsome and self-confident tom cats. There are many convincing reasons for not keeping non-pedigree un-neutered male cats. They are untidy about the house and have a tendency to go out and fight with rival males. This means that they can be less affectionate than other cats. Even more important, they produce unwanted kittens which may be uncared for and ultimately stolen for vivisection.

stant companion. Now for a serious word of advice. Unless you intend to go in for breeding, consider neutering. This will stop a male spraying around the house, leaving an unpleasant smell, and will also eliminate the tendency to wander off in search of females and to fight with rival males. Spaying a female kitten is equally important as it stops her 'calling' continually any time from the age of five to nine months onwards. Siamese are particularly noisy. During the mating period females constantly try to get out and neighbours' toms do their utmost to get in. The best person to advise is, of course, your vet, but it is a subject that everyone can sort out for themselves. My own view, however, is that the production of countless unwanted kittens is too serious a risk for any true animal lover to contemplate with complacency.

Grooming

Most cats seem to spend an inordinate length of time washing themselves. Even so, if dirt and dust, burrs, the odd flea, and any loose hair which might cause a furball are to be removed, you will still have to lend a hand. Although often ignored, grooming is a necessary part of daily care and you must certainly devote some time to it.

The tools required are a brush and comb. The brush should not be of wire but one with small, short bristles. The comb should be of the variety made especially for cats, with a wooden handle and metal teeth, the latter being set slightly closer for Short-haired cats. Another comb with very fine teeth will cure the flea problem, should this arise.

The best time to begin grooming is the day after the kitten arrives, because he will then learn from the start to appreciate it as an attention rather than resent it as a punishment. If you also play with him for a

while afterwards he will soon accept, even welcome, the entire routine.

During the grooming session, be sure to examine the ears. If they are dirty, wipe the inside of them with a piece of cotton wool. Should there be an objectionable smell or a discharge, do *not* run to the chemist to buy a canker lotion, which often does more harm than good. Ask the vet to take a look and prescribe the correct treatment for the particular ear infection involved.

A Shorthaired cat is simple to groom. Stand him on a newspaper-covered table, examine the fur for prickles and burrs, then comb thoroughly with the wide-toothed comb. If fleas are present or suspected, repeat with the fine-toothed flea comb. To do his stomach, sit with the cat lying on his back on your lap. Then give a final all-over polish by firm hand-stroking to promote sheen.

A Longhaired cat requires more attention and this,

of course, means more time. The long fur tends to tangle, particularly in spring and autumn, although daily grooming reduces this risk. Tangles must be gently teased out with the fingers or with a blunt knitting needle. Any that have been neglected may have to be cut away with round-tipped scissors although this should not have to be done. The coat will look a bit tatty at first but will recover in time.

A light-coloured cat can be sprinkled with talcum powder, followed by brushing and combing to remove stains. Bad grease stains can be eliminated with surgical spirit on a pad of cotton wool; and butter helps to remove tar from the paws. Tar and paint should never be tackled with chemical cleaners or solvents, some of which cause serious skin complaints.

Food for cats
Feeding, so far mentioned only as a form of 'first-aid' for the new kitten, requires further elaboration, be-

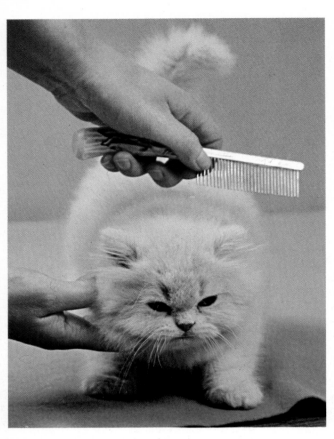

cause only if correct procedures are followed will your cat be able to enjoy a long and healthy life.

A wild cat, being carnivorous, lives by killing, gorging and then sleeping the banquet off for a day or two. A domestic cat could, in theory, do the same, and even the occasional day's starvation would not do much harm. But over the years it has become a nibbler and today it thrives best on two meals every day. Ideally the diet should consist of two-thirds animal flesh (including fish) and one-third cooked carbohydrate. A 10lb cat requires 3–4 oz twice a day.

Vitamins and minerals are also required and, fortunately, these are readily available. The important vitamins for a cat are A, which comes with liver, B1, in cereals and meat which is not over-cooked, and E, again found in liver. Despite its obvious value, however, liver should never form more than one-tenth of the total diet as it tends to promote loosening of the bowels, and in quantity may have a harmful effect, due to an excessive intake of vitamin A. Milk supplies both minerals and calcium and is, therefore, beneficial but can cause diarrhoea.

Tinned cat foods normally contain all the essential requirements of protein and carbohydrates as well as added vitamins and minerals. They are, therefore,

Left and Below
All cats enjoy being groomed regularly if they become accustomed to it when young. Longhaired cats in particular need to be groomed otherwise they may get fur balls from attempting to cope with matted fur themselves. Pedigree longhairs with a possible career in showing need extra attention. Cats particularly enjoy being brushed rather than combed, just as they do rolling in dust.

Right
Cats with silky long hair do seem to be less agile and adventurous than the shorthairs — the stance of this attractive marmalade cat is typical of a longhair — the body shape is clearly very different to that of the Orientals.

*Previous page
Introduction of a Seal
Point Siamese stud to his
queen. This is an
excellent stud house with
a hot pipe running
through it and an
area outside for the stud
to exercise. It is wise
to go and visit the stud
and see the conditions in
which he lives before
sending your own queen
to him. The queen will
stay with her mate for
two or three days and
when she returns you will
have the stud's full
pedigree.*

complete and balanced, convenient to store and simple to serve, as long as your cat will eat them.

Quantities are always difficult to recommend because appetites vary. The following is only a rough guide which should be adjusted if your cat becomes too lean or too fat. The animal's average daily requirement is approximately 200–250 calories, and this can be calculated roughly as follows: small tin of food = 200 calories; milk = 400 calories per pint; white fish and chicken = 500 per lb; liver and rabbit = 600 per lb; lean beef = 750 per lb; herring = 700 per lb. Now you can do your own sums!

Pedigree breeding

Having previously warned about the dangers of indiscriminate breeding, it may seem strange to end this chapter with some hints on how to breed. The difference, of course, is that this has to do with the planned breeding of pedigree cats. The emphasis on pedigree is not mere snobbery. The brutal truth is that far too many cross-bred kittens have brief and

miserable lives simply because they are valueless. The pedigree puss, however, being a very saleable commodity, is carefully looked after from the moment it is born to old age.

Pet males should, in my opinion, be neutered even if they do have pedigrees; but pedigree females can be kept for breeding provided you can put up with all the trouble. They come into season at around five to nine months and stay that way for between two and ten days. Some 'call' only two or three times a year, others every other week. Either way they will mate with any cat, which means constant watching unless you want a mongrel litter.

Prospective mothers should be at least ten months, if not a year old, and are normally sent to the stud for mating, preferably on the third day of 'calling'. The fee is payable in advance.

After returning home the queen, still being capable of mating, should be guarded. Mishaps aside, she carries her young for approximately 65 days, during which time she should lead a normal life. During the

Far left
A family of British Blues and a white stray kitten which the mother is fostering. This family have a good strong cardboard box lined with newspaper which can be changed frequently.

Left
A Seal Point Siamese queen who escaped during her calling period and met a ginger tom. The kittens are two days old and will probably grow into most attractive cats with Siamese and 'moggy' characteristics.

last three weeks, however, she will want up to twice her normal food intake, so meals must be divided.

On the day she is due to give birth, regardless of any plans you may have made, most queens choose their own sleeping quarters. High on their list are wardrobes and, failing these, owners' beds. Sometimes this can be avoided by providing a wooden whelping box a week or so before the event. It should have easy access, be lined with newspapers, and placed in a dark cupboard.

The usual signs of imminent birth are restlessness and refusal of a meal. Soon after this labour will commence, indicated by a heaving of the flanks. Contractions usually follow with ever-diminishing frequency until a liquid discharge heralds the approach of the first kitten. This arrives in a sac, resembling a polythene bag, which the mother instinctively rips open with her teeth.

The mother then massages her kitten into active life by licking it with her rough tongue, after which she eases it towards her teats for suckling. The birth

of this first kitten is usually a slow process and may take up to an hour or more. Thereafter the kittens are normally delivered fairly quickly. The entire process may take from one to six hours, but unless the queen seems unreasonably distressed there is no cause for undue worry on your part. If problems do arise, call the vet promptly.

It is unwise to remove kittens from their box during the kittening process, and the whole family can be left for a few hours of recuperative sleep after it is all over. Then the queen can be given some warm milk, while the opportunity is taken to change the soiled bedding.

A feeding queen produces an enormous appetite and should be given up to three times as much food as she is normally. Quality is as important as quantity and the diet must provide vitamin A and calcium.

The kittens are born blind and open their eyes within a week or so. At three weeks they will be crawling and shortly after that weaning should commence.

The Family Cat

Christine Metcalf

Left
Kittens enjoy each other's company the whole time. When you choose your kitten always consider whether you could not have two,

Below
The coat of a shorthaired black is one of the most striking when it is in top condition. Notice also how bright his eyes are.

The cat is no newcomer to the family hearth. It took up residence centuries ago when man was still a cave-dweller. According to the stories, it was initially attracted by the warmth of the fire—a suggestion that is not difficult to accept as one watches the cat on a chilly evening in a relaxed heap before the fireside or on a summer day basking in a sunny spot in the garden.

The cat is fond of its creature comforts and, where these are provided to its taste, will strike a fair bargain by giving in return loyalty and companionship. However, the cat is both shrewd and discerning, and will rarely stay in a place if it decides otherwise. The fact that you have to earn its affection lends support to the commonly voiced opinion that, far from choosing a cat, it chooses you.

This should not present any problem so long as you observe the code for mutual happiness. Basically, this entails proper care for its physical needs, such as regular feeding, grooming and cleanliness; but there are other considerations to take into account when accepting a cat into your life.

Before acquiring a kitten, it is worth taking a careful look at the characteristics of the different breeds. Apart from the obvious fact that no two cats are alike,

every one having a unique personality, each breed possesses individual features; and if you are attracted to one more than another, it is advisable to consult a reputable breeder. On the other hand, you may have no choice in the matter, simply being asked to give house room to a friend's unwanted kitten. Nevertheless, be it aristocrat or moggy, a cat has basic needs which demand to be satisfied.

The kitten's homecoming

Moving your new kitten from a familiar setting to a strange environment can be very alarming for the small creature. Being cooped up in a basket and taken for a car journey will be brand new experiences. Its mother is no longer there to teach and comfort it, and the brothers and sisters who have been constant playmates are also suddenly missing. When the time comes to sleep there are no other furry creatures of its own kind to form a bundle of warmth. Abruptly it is faced by complete strangers in new surroundings—a dis-

turbing situation at the very least. So the transition from pet shop or cattery to a new home must be handled with the greatest care.

The best time to introduce your kitten is when most members of the family are likely to be around, as during the school holidays. But it must be done by gradual stages. When you first arrive home, take the kitten to a place where it can rest without being disturbed by children or by other animals. A good sleep will help to calm it whereas a boisterous family reception will only frighten it all the more. When it wakes up and has had some refreshment, allow it to explore the house but do not let it out of your sight in case it runs into danger or loses its way.

The shock of coming into a new home can be lessened by providing a close and already familiar companion in the shape of another kitten from the same litter. The little extra expense and effort involved are well rewarded by the friendship you and they will share. Two cats brought up together are never far apart. They can work off all their excess energy by playing with each other, there will be no chance of loneliness during the day if everyone is out of the house, and they can be placed in the same cattery together when the family are on holiday.

Kittens and children

On no account acquire a kitten for your children unless you are willing to take responsibility for looking after it. Youngsters can rarely sustain their interest all the time, becoming so absorbed in other activities such as games, hobbies and homework, that a kitten's mealtime can easily be overlooked. What is more, never give a kitten or any other domestic animal as a gift to a child before first obtaining the consent of the parents. Children often tire of a pet when it loses its baby appeal, and if the adults are not particularly interested either, the pet becomes unwanted. It is sad

when this neglect occurs, as it is not easy to find a new home for a grown animal.

Children tend to love a kitten rather fiercely and must be warned to handle it gently. A tiny bundle of soft fur is very cuddly but the bones are extremely fragile. Avert disaster by teaching them the correct way to hold a kitten, with one hand under the chest while the other goes around and under the back, supporting the weight on the arm. Never allow a kitten to be picked up by the back of the neck as this may cause muscle damage.

A cat loves to play, not only for pure pleasure but also for the exercise. Here too, however, some instructions on do's and don'ts are essential. Simple toys are best. Chasing and retrieving a piece of paper rolled into a ball and thrown across the floor is a favourite game; and a length of string dangled from a height or trailed along the ground is good practice for the hunting instincts. Tying the string to an empty cotton reel will prevent the end from being swallowed.

Pictures in books and papers sometimes show animals wearing clothes—all very charming as entertainment, but liable to put the wrong ideas into the heads of small children. Trying to squeeze a kitten into a doll's dress is a practice to be severely discouraged because the animal's little joints may easily be dislocated.

Like every baby, a kitten tires rapidly and must be allowed to sleep frequently. Its rest should be undisturbed, and it is often necessary to remind children that the time has come to stop playing for a while.

Kittens and other pets

Introducing a kitten into a household where there is already an established pet creates a situation that requires tactful handling but which is basically a matter of applying common sense and diplomacy. An adult cat will not accept a newcomer as readily as will

23

a dog or other animal. The explanation for this is simply territorial ownership. In the wild state a cat has to protect its boundaries in order to safeguard its food supplies. Our domestic pet has inherited this basic instinct from its ancestors, and a newly introduced kitten will possess the same intuitive traits. If challenged, its reaction will be to turn into a ball of spitting, hissing fury. The older inhabitant, accustomed to dispatching all garden intruders in no uncertain fashion, is suddenly faced by a miniscule stranger with the temerity to ruffle its fur and behave aggressively. No wonder it asserts its superiority by cuffing the impertinent little creature's ears. This type of angry confrontation may be amusing for the onlookers but can be distressing and even painful for the participants.

Given prudent handling, such a situation can be avoided and a good relationship allowed to develop naturally. So when you bring the kitten into the home, keep it apart from other established pets in a separate room and make the introduction gradually. All parties must be allowed to adjust to the idea and to settle down to unfamiliar smells before being left together unsupervised. Many unlikely friendships have been forged between cats and other animals (including birds and mice), but you must be around all the time during the early stages to prevent disaster.

In the course of the kitten's many sleeping periods

Above right
A cat door is invaluable. It is easy to fit and once you have taught the cat how to get in and out there is no longer any tie upon you or frustrations for the animal. A flap that is fairly stiff to swing will deter other interested neighbouring cats.

Right
Silver Tabby and Silver Spotted kittens playing around a large kitten pen. A pen is very useful when the kittens are old enough to be away from their mother but too young to be left without surveillance. You can put them out in the sun or confine them indoors.

Far right
A Lilac Point Siamese with powerful paws using a bird table as a scratching post. The kitten will very quickly learn to do the same.

24

you should take the opportunity to fuss and pet the other animals, for this will help them to become reconciled more easily to the presence of an additional member of the household. Animals, like children, crave constant affection and will show jealousy if not reassured.

The self-sufficient cat

Rudyard Kipling wrote of the cat: 'He walked by himself and all places were alike to him.' Folk who do not really know and understand the cat might assume that the writer was describing a single-minded and selfish creature; but those of us who are devoted to the animal know that this very independence is an admirable quality, stemming from the fact that, like its wild relatives, it is a solitary hunter. So when it is out and about it is always alone. This does not mean that it shuns company – on the contrary – but it is selective in choosing friends. The dog will go hunting in packs and leap about the neighbourhood looking for others of its kind to join in play; but the cat enjoys only the company of other cats it knows well – members of the same household.

One great advantage of living with a cat is that it does not need to be exercised, for play is itself the best form of exercise. A garden, affording the freedom to come and go at will, is a great boon but by no means indispensable. If you do have a garden it is a simple matter to fix a cat-flap to one of the outside doors of the house, which will give your pet complete liberty. The opening need not be large (about 6 × 4 inches) but it should swing vertically so that it can be opened from either side. If the flap is fitted with weights it will swing slowly, thus preventing the tail from being trapped. But the opening must be kept well away from bolts and locks so as to deny easy access to burglars.

Daily grooming is necessary to remove loose hair or any odd flea that may have been picked up. In other respects the cat is instinctively a very clean animal, easily house-trained. A garden naturally solves hygienic problems, but for the flat-dweller a litter tray must be provided.

A cat needs to scratch in order to keep claws in trim. The act of scratching removes the outer shell as it becomes worn, leaving new, beautifully sharp claws ready for hunting and climbing. It also enables the muscles and tendons to be kept in good condition. For this reason – and in order to prevent your carpets and furniture from being damaged – a scratching post is an important piece of equipment. Such a post can be bought or made by covering a solid board with a piece of carpet. By holding the kitten's paws and going through the motions of scratching on the post, you can teach it to leave the furniture alone. In this, as in toilet training, there may be the occasional mishap or moment of forgetfulness, in which case just be firm and show it once more what you expect of it. Never become angry, for this will only confuse and

25

frighten the kitten; and on no account strike it, because this may easily cause an injury.

Holiday time

Pets often present a problem for their owners at holiday time and this is sometimes given as an excuse for not keeping them in the first place. It is during the holiday season that animal sanctuaries are faced with a larger than usual number of strays, simply because owners have omitted to make adequate arrangements. Fitting an easy access route such as a cat-flap, putting down a large supply of food and then leaving a cat alone to ration itself to a daily allowance is quite unacceptable. The cat would almost certainly indulge in an orgy of gluttony, leaving none for later. Even catering for its greed by supplying too much food must inevitably result in left-overs that would turn stale or be contaminated by flies. In either case the health and wellbeing of the cat would be bound to suffer.

A useful solution is to arrange with a reliable neighbour to provide regular meals, but it is important to find someone really dependable. Although the cat will miss you, it will remain in familiar surroundings and the upheaval will not be so great. An alternative arrangement is to take your pet to a recognized cattery. There are a number of boarding establishments of this type, some good, others bad. Where possible, personal recommendation is preferable. Advertise-

ments are usually to be found in local papers, and your vet, being familiar with the neighbourhood, should be able to advise.

A visit to the cattery before making a booking is, in any event, well worthwhile. The most important thing to look for is cleanliness, for unless the place is scrupulously hygienic your pet will be at risk. Look particularly at the litter trays, make sure that the house is warm, dry and light, and confirm that there is sufficient space in the pen for exercise as well as a scratching post.

Good accommodation gets fully booked early in the holiday season, so plan well ahead. You will probably be asked to supply a certificate to the effect that your cat is in good health and that it has been inoculated against feline infectious enteritis, so arrange for that as well.

When placing your pet in a cattery it is a good idea to take along its sleeping blanket or a favourite soft toy, for the smell of something familiar will provide a bit of security.

A cattery is especially valuable if you are taking a holiday abroad. Quarantine regulations require that any cat entering this country should spend six months isolated in a quarantine cattery. The fact that an animal may only have been abroad for a short time on a vacation will not affect the ruling, for the restriction is imposed in order to prevent the introduction of rabies. The law does not apply in the United States,

Left
It is rare for cats to enjoy walking on a lead but it is certainly possible to train them to accept a collar and walk calmly on a lead if they are introduced to it as young kittens. This can be very useful at certain times, for instance on journeys and in cars.

Right
Kittens playing. Instinctively they use the fighting technique of all wild animals – the left kitten has forestalled an ambush and promptly caught his ambusher with a paw. He will next go for his neck in playful attack. Only full grown toms actually do each other damage.

but a certificate is required there to show that the cat is free from infection and that it has not been in contact with an animal carrying rabies. Quarantine regulations in Australia are as strict as in Britain.

Travelling with a cat

People who take their holidays in country cottages or in caravans have no such problems. Provided it has been trained to a lead since its early days as a kitten, a cat can be taken along with the family. This type of training should start at about three months. The kitten must be fitted with an elasticated collar to lessen the risk of injury if it is caught up while climbing trees or exploring the undergrowth. It will probably object at first, so the process should be a gradual one—a few minutes each day, increasing to rather longer periods. Once the collar is accepted without fuss, the lead can be attached, initially for a short time and then for progressively longer sessions.

It is essential to keep your cat under control when it is travelling in a car, and a lead is useful for this purpose. There are so many potential dangers if you allow it complete freedom. A sudden noise can alarm the animal so that it impedes the movements of the driver; or the car door could be opened inadver-

tently, causing the terrified cat to leap out in front of passing vehicles, risking its own life and perhaps bringing about an accident.

Another method of transport is in a specially designed travelling basket; but be particularly careful to see that it is securely fastened, for cats can be quite expert at sliding back hinges. The basket should be lined with clean newspaper and a warm blanket. For a short journey a simple hold-all can be used. Place the cat in the bag with the zip fastener closed, leaving only its head free so that he can see what is going on. On all occasions the odd word or caress will have a calming influence.

Moving house will also involve a journey for your pet. It is unlikely to be enthusiastic about the idea but if it has attached itself firmly to the family and if you take pains to reassure it, the change should not be difficult. On arrival, your cat may sulk at first and sit mulishly under the heaviest piece of furniture so that it cannot be reached or coaxed out. It may also refuse to eat and will almost certainly succeed in making you feel guilty for having removed it from familiar surroundings. After a little while, however, it will decide to explore the house, and will be puzzled by discovering new smells and recognizing

smells of carpets and furniture from the old home at the same time.

Reassured, your pet will settle down for a wash, and this is a signal that it is ready to eat. Do not try to hurry the programme but let it follow its course. Like you, the cat has new territory to explore and claim. Provide a litter tray and keep the animal in the house for a day or two until it has adjusted.

One old practice when moving house was to butter the cat's paws, which may have served a useful purpose if only to keep it occupied cleaning the butter off and giving it no time to be nervous. It is doubtful whether there is any other benefit. Should your cat be missing in spite of all your precautions, the first place to look is back at the previous address. Cats have been known to travel considerable distances to return to their old homes.

Safety measures

Cats are all too frequently found lying mutilated or dead by the roadside, for today's fast motoring takes a sad toll of our pets. If you live in a town or near a motorway it is essential to keep an animal under the strictest control and vigilance. If your cat has been trained to the lead it can be taken out under super-

vision. If you have a garden close to a highway a wired-in exercise area should be provided. The wire must, of course, cover the top as well, as a cat is an expert escapologist. In a flat a balcony is not sufficient as a place of exercise nor, unless enclosed, is it safe, because another danger for a cat is height. It is an old wives' tale that a cat always lands on its feet. Certainly it has a well developed sense of balance and can often right itself as it falls. Its natural grace and suppleness will frequently come to its rescue when another animal would meet certain death; but even so, the cat is not immortal and its tiny bones may easily be broken.

Two or three years ago in Glasgow a large number of cats were unaccountably being injured over a short period as a result of falls. The theory put forward by the P.D.S.A. was that during this particular time there was an abundance of thistledown in the air. In their attempts to reach it as it floated high above the city, the playful animals simply tumbled from windowsills. Cat owners were therefore warned to be on their special guard.

Should your cat have the misfortune to injure itself, it must be kept warm and quiet, and veterinary help should be called immediately. My own cat broke

Cats usually know how to make themselves comfortable and these kittens have found an unusual and warm spot to sleep beneath a radiator where they can feel secure and protected.

a leg after falling from an apple tree where she had climbed in pursuit of birds. Fortunately, professional treatment soon put her right and there were no ill effects after the bones had knit.

Town life has many hazards but even the country cat is not entirely without risk, for there is a danger from poison by swallowing weedkiller or by eating a small animal which has itself been poisoned.

The problem of strays

When a hungry, bedraggled waif of a cat appears on the doorstep begging for food, it is hard to resist. But although your instinct is to take it in and cosset it until it looks as sleek and well fed as your own cat, resist the temptation or you may be introducing infection to your family pet. Before inviting the stranger to share your hearth and home you must have it examined by the vet to make sure it is not carrying disease. Meanwhile you can feed it in the garage or somewhere outside the house until you have made the necessary arrangements. If a stray decides to adopt you, do make sure that it belongs to nobody else, for the real owner will obviously be distressed by its absence. It has been known for cats to keep two homes going and even answer to two names, but you must be careful not to fall victim to such a confidence trick!

You can help to make sure that you are not adding to the already serious overpopulation problem by having your own cat altered at a suitable age, assuming you do not want it for breeding. The operation, both for a male and a female, is a simple affair for your vet, and all cats are improved thereby, especially a tom, who will be less likely to want to stay out at night. Rossini wrote a very amusing duet simulating the wailing of courting cats, which, by virtue of considerable artistic licence, was made to sound melodious. It is far less amusing when this caterwauling takes place under your window in the early hours of the morning. Neutering of your male will hopefully dispense with such an experience, apart from bringing other advantages inside the home; and spaying a female may avoid the grievous necessity of having kittens put to sleep.

Having observed the basic rules mentioned in this chapter at the beginning of your new relationship, you will soon discover the many delights of sharing your home with a cat.

Left
An Abyssinian eating grass. It is very important to provide a pot of grass for any cat who is confined to a building.

Below
Comfort and company in front of the fire.

The History of the Cat

Angela Sayer

The cat family may be divided into three sections for classification purposes. These are known as genera or subfamilies and are the *Panthera*, the *Acinonyx* and the *Felis*. The *Panthera* consists of all the Big Cats such as the lion, leopard and panther from Africa and India, the Snow Leopard and Tiger from Asia, and the Jaguar from South America. The Cheetah of Africa and Iran is in the genus *Acinonyx* and is an unusual member of the cat family having only partly rectractile claws. *Felis* is a large group and includes the domestic cat.

The continent of Asia has many small wildcats including Pallas's cat or MANUL, Temminck's golden cat, Bornean red cat, Chinese desert cat, leopard cat, rusty-spotted cat, fishing cat and the flat-headed cat. From Africa comes the caracal, serval, golden cat and the black-footed cat, as well as the sand cat, jungle cat and Caffer cat which are also to be found in Asia. North America, Canada and Northern Europe are the habitats of lynx, puma and bobcat, while in South America live the margay, ocelot, pampas cat, Andean cat, Geoffrey's cat and the little spotted cat.

One of the largest of the *Felis* is the puma, often called the cougar, or the mountain lion. This cat is among the most maligned of all animals and has been accused by ranchers in the United States of the wanton slaughter of calves and other livestock.

In fact the natural prey of the puma is small mammals such as rabbits and rodents, and only in times of extreme hardship will it brave the preserves of man. Unfortunately, just as the fox is becoming urbanized in Britain, so is the puma in the US, as the cities spread, encroaching more and more on the wild areas.

The lynx is an unusual-looking cat with an elevated rump, due to having hind legs much longer than its front ones. Its tail is short and stubby and it has large round paws. The ears of the lynx are pointed and trimmed with tufts of silky hair to match the profuse side whiskers on its cheeks. Found in Northern territories, the lynx is adapted to extremes of cold. A variety of lynx found in the US is known there as the bobcat. A fierce hunter, often lying in wait on a tree branch and dropping on passing deer, the bobcat has nevertheless, been successfully tamed and kept as a pet. An account of a household tabby mating with a bobcat was reported in an American magazine. The offspring favoured their wild father in appearance, but their temperament was similar to that of their mother. One of the male kittens was kept and eventually bred with a neighbour's Persian. Again the kittens resembled their father in looks, but were docile, and were eagerly sought after as pets.

Another lynx is the caracal, slender and reddish-brown in colour with long, pointed and tufted ears. It is a very beautiful cat and is fleet enough to run down gazelle and even to take birds on the wing, leaping into the air to strike them down. The final member of the lynx family is *Felis Chaus* the African wild cat or jungle cat. Almost certainly one of the direct ancestors of our own cats, this animal is rarely to be found in Africa, and never to be found in the jungle! This cat interbreeds readily with domestic cats and the offspring are hardy and fertile, though rather wild by nature.

The serval of equatorial Africa is a short-tailed cat with legs rather like the greyhound. This cat is built for speed and runs down its prey, usually birds, small rodents and lizards, on the open plain. The jaguarundi is quite the opposite with short legs, looking more like a large weasel than a cat. This creature is found in the Americas and is often kept as an exotic pet although its temperament is said to be a little uncertain. The margay and ocelot are on the verge of extinction due to having been hunted persistently for their beautifully marked pelts. Laws are now in existence to protect these cats, and many are kept in captivity where breeding experiments are in operation in an attempt to preserve the species.

Left
Cats love to roll in grass and also eat it — it is a good emetic.

33

It is thought that the Aztecs and Incas had tame margays and ocelots as pets and for hunting. It is recorded that there was a guild of Aztec knights called the Knights Tiger, who were not warriors but initiates in a mystical order. Their 'tiger' was the ocelot, who, they believed, cried each dawn to the rising sun. As the sun was their god, the ocelot became the symbol of their cult. The margay, smaller and more tractable and exceedingly beautiful with its leopard-like pattern and black rimmed, lustrous eyes, was almost certainly kept as a house pet. Even today, they are easily tamed and very playful. Some of the cats look very appealing and are captured as babies and offered for sale in pet stores in some countries of the world. Today, no-one professing to be a cat lover would consider keeping one of these exotic animals as a pet, for docile as they may appear as kittens, they are basically a solitary species, and need their independence as adults.

Other small cats, tabby in pattern, will interbreed successfully with domestic cats and so are most probably responsible for the household cats of today. These include the Caffer cat *Felis lybica* and a closely related wild cat *Felis ocreata*, both of which are native to Africa. Our own cats are designated *Felis catus* whatever shape, size, colour or pattern they may be, having first been given the name by Linnaeus in 1758. Poor communications were possibly responsible for the fact that this was not known by Erxleben in 1777, who decided that domestic cats should be called *Felis domestica*, and so it continued until 1829, when the records of Linnaeus again came to light.

Under taxonomical rules, the first name given to a species must remain, so all the *domestica* had to revert to being *catus*. In the meantime, *Felis catus* had been allocated to the European wild cat, so this, in turn, had to find a new name, *Felis sylvestris*.

In appearance, the small wild cats which most closely resemble our domesticated, non pedigree types are the pampas cat, the jungle cat, the Caffer cat and the sand cat, and it is interesting to try to trace this evolutionary path.

The evolution of the cat

Although very little is known of the exact origin of the ordinary domestic cat, zoologists throughout the world now generally accept that its family tree was established in the *Eocene* period, some 50 million years ago. The members of the cat family or FELIDAE, can be traced back to a common ancestor in a small, weasel-like creature called MIACIS. This long-bodied, short-legged carnivore was also the forebear of several other groups of mammals including the bear, hyena, dog, raccoon, civet, mongoose and weasel. The cat appears to have descended from MIACIS through the civet, while one branch, the civet cat of today, remained almost unchanged. In evolutionary terms, the change from MIACIS to cat was very abrupt, despite the millions of years that passed, and the first cats evolved,

The leopard of Africa and Asia, though similarly spotted to the margay, is much larger. Males may reach almost 2·5 m (8 ft) from nose to tail tip.

The cheetah, classified as one of the Big Cats, is unique in showing certain dog-like characteristics.

The caracal is sand coloured to match its North African desert habitat. It measures 0·9 m (3 ft) from its nose to the tip of its shortish tail.

The margay or American Tiger Cat is about the size of a domestic tabby.

it is believed, at least 10 million years before the first dogs made their appearance.

In the 10 million years following the *Eocene*, MIACIS, a well-developed and highly adaptable animal, prospered, and two distinct groups emerged to be known as HOPLOPHONEUS and DINICTIS. The former had exaggerated canine teeth and a specialized flange on the lower jaw to cover the teeth when the mouth was closed. One species of HOPLOPHONEUS was SMILODON, or sabre-toothed tiger, which although not directly related to the tigers of today, was a very large and powerful cat. This huge beast had six-inch canine teeth and a hinged lower jaw which could open to right angles, enabling it to grasp, stab and kill the giant lumbering herbivores that grazed the forests and plains.

SMILODON was a clumsy creature, the size of a lion and heavily built, his massive strength being necessary to strike down his prey. When the great herbivores began to die out however, SMILODON also met his demise, probably because his bulky fame and very specialized skull structure could not adapt sufficiently fast enough to enable him to capture smaller fleeter animals for food. Fossil remains dating back to the Pleistocene period of $1\frac{1}{2}$ million years ago, including the massive skull of SMILODON, were discovered in a Brazilian cave, showing that the species had survived for several million years before its eventual extinction.

The group known as DINICTIS, on the other hand, flourished and sub-divided during the *Miocene* age of 20 million years ago. In all, some 90 species appeared, all directly related to today's domestic cats, and of which at least 35 species still exist in very similar, recognizable forms. The most successful sub-division of all was that of an animal rather like a lynx, streamlined in appearance and with forward looking sharp eyes set in a small, round head. The long powerful legs had small neat feet in which were sheathed retractile claws. This newly evolved feature enabled the animals to run swiftly and to spring high into the air while the claws were sheathed. With them extended, they could grasp and hold prey firmly, and they also enabled the animals to climb the densely growing forest trees in order to escape from their enemies.

Some species of DINICTIS closely resembled the civet tribe of today, but had rather shorter tails and longer, more pointed snouts. It is interesting to compare other members of the civet family, such as the mongoose and genet, with the fossil remains of DINICTIS from the *Miocene*.

Great changes took place on earth through the following eons. Extremes of climate ravaged the land surface as storms raged and intense rainfall eroded the mountain tops and ridges. In the core the molten rocks stirred and caused intense earth movement, folding and faulting. The *Pliocene* which began 11 million years ago and lasted for 10 million years, saw the oceans and continents assume their present form and the climate become similar to that of today. The giant

sea and land creatures began to die out, while the mammals thrived. The cat-like creatures prospered, multiplied and evolved, and the early ancestors of Man came down from their arboreal homes and began to walk upright on the ground.

After the *Pliocene* came the *Pleistocene* which began 1 million years ago. This was the time of the great Ice Ages which ensured that only the fittest and most adaptable of plant and animal life survived. Many mammals appeared as we know them today, and Man's ancestors developed sufficient intelligence to enable them to make simple stone implements. About 40 species of the cat family emerged, all highly tuned for survival even under the most rigorous conditions.

Ten thousand years ago the *Holocene* age began. The great ice masses retreated and the sea level rose. Mountains, deserts, forests and plains emerged and the climate settled down once more. Man began to cultivate plants and domestic animals for his own use. No cave paintings found to date show any signs of creatures resembling our domestic cats, but it is

reasonably safe to assume that it was towards the end of the Stone Age that the cat first approached Man's settlements, foraging for food scraps and attracted by the warmth of the camp fires. What factor first forged the chains of friendship between cat and early Man, and why this small furred creature was encouraged and fed instead of being clubbed and eaten remains a matter for conjecture. No fossil remains of cats have ever been found near any prehistoric sites however, so we have no record from the years between the authenticated demise of SMILODON and the emergence of the cat as a deity in Egypt 5000 years ago. Certainly through the intervening years, the cat had gradually assumed its place along with other animals we know as 'domestic' and by the time of the Pharoahs, cat and Man had established a firm relationship.

The cat in Ancient Egypt
The Ancient Egyptians domesticated several types of cat, and it is thought that many of our present day breeds and varieties derive from these. Frescoes, tomb paintings and bronzes of Egyptian cats depict tabby

The cat-like animal at the foot of the tree is miacis, *a weasel-sized carnivorous mammal which lived in the Eocene Period, 50 million years ago. From this creature evolved the civets, and from these, hyenas and our present day cats.* Miacis *was also the ancestor of weasels, raccoons, bears and dogs.*

36

patterned, short coated animals of elegant type and conformation. Mummified remains of cats of the period have been identified as two main species, the CHAUS and the GLOVED CAT, species, in fact, which are still found in the wild state in that area. It is the GLOVED CAT which is most likely to have been treated as a housepet, while the CHAUS, a larger, lynx type was probably less easily tamed and so used mainly for hunting and for the control of rats and mice in the immense storage granaries of the cities.

A large wall painting, now in the British Museum, shows an Egyptian gliding in a punt through the tall reeds of a marsh. As the wife and daughter gather lotus blossom, the father puts up several waterfowl which are immediately caught and held by the hunting cat which accompanies them on the expedition. The cat is depicted with small birds in each paw while another, larger bird is firmly gripped between his teeth. Both pet and hunting cats were considered as valuable family assets. House cats were often kept to guard against poisonous snakes in the home, as well as protecting the family larder. Eventually a cult developed in Egypt for the worship of cats, which lasted for more than 2000 years. The cat in all its forms was mummified and considered a God.

Strict laws were drawn up to protect cats and the penalty for killing one of the sacred creatures was death. It is known that a Roman soldier was almost lynched by an enraged mob after having accidentally killed a cat. The incident was taken up in diplomatic circles and was said to have been one of the several provocative actions which started the wars between Egypt and Rome. Earlier, Cambyses, the son of Cyrus the Great of Persia had used his knowledge of the Egyptians' devotion to cats to his own advantage. In order to capture the port of Peluse, garrisoned entirely by Egyptian soldiers, he ordered his troops to carry live cats as they attacked the city walls. Rather than risk killing the cats, the Egyptians capitulated and Cambyses won an easy victory.

At first the Egyptians considered the cat sacred only to the goddess Isis, then gradually the great cat-goddess Bastet emerged. Also known as Bast or Pasht it is from her name that the word 'puss' is probably derived. Bastet's animal incarnation was the cat, and models of the cat were made in every conceivable material. Amulet figures of cats and kittens were worn by everyone, and were made of all types of precious and semi-precious stones, metal, wood and clay. Cat-figures pierced or ringed for hanging on necklets were found in their hundreds in cat graves and under the floors of houses and temples. Carved in gold, silver, quartz, marble, glass, stone and every sort of mineral they portray cats in every mood, and attitude. Cats were also fashioned to decorate rings, brooches and pins and larger figures were made as ornaments for the home.

The earliest portrayal of Bastet as a cat-headed figure may be seen in the museum at Cairo, drawn on a papyrus of the twenty-first dynasty. She took precedence over all other figures of worship at the time, and a centre was built to her glory at Bubastis, just east of the Nile delta, which stood firm for centuries. The Greek historian Herodotus travelled extensively through Egypt in about 450BC and described the temple as a splendid building standing below the general level of all the other buildings, which had had their foundations raised, so that the whole city commanded a view down upon it. It was built of red granite in the form of a huge square encircled by canals, 30·5m (100ft) in width and fed directly from the Nile. In the centre, stone walls surrounded a grove of very tall trees, in the centre of which a shrine held the great statue of Bastet. A relief carved on one of the walls showed the King, Osorkon II, endowing the goddess ''I give thee every land in obeisance, I give thee all power like Ra.''

Holidays, feasts and pageants were held to the glory and honour of Bastet, and her sacred statue was often brought forth from its shrine to be present at the festivities in which she was worshipped. Bastet represented the eye of the God of Light, Horus, and was worshipped as both a solar and a lunar goddess.

It is interesting to note that the Ancient Egyptian word for cat is MAU, which means 'to see' and many legends abound through the ages of links between the movement of the sun and the moon through the heaven and the eye of the cat. Very little is known of the form taken by the rites of Bastet, but it is certain that many live cats were kept in her shrine. These sacred animals were ritually fed and tended by special servants. Wooden figures of temple maidens carrying cats and kittens may be seen in the British Museum. Herodotus reported that one of the most important and popular of all the solemn Egyptian ceremonies was the annual festival at Bubastis, to which thousands of men and women would pilgrimage crowded into barges. Leaving their far-off homes each April or May, they would set sail down the Nile. The long voyages made an excuse for much merrymaking, the men playing flutes and the women banging cymbals. As the barges passed through towns en route, they would draw in to the bank and the voyagers would encourage the townsfolk to begin festivities of their own, drinking, singing and dancing. On arrival at Bubastis, many victims were sacrificed to the goddess and much wine was consumed, followed by feasting and celebrations in the streets. The great statue of Bastet was brought out of the shrine and conveyed by barge to take part in the festival, for it was believed that the goddess was entitled to enjoy the pleasures of a trip such as this from time to time. The worshippers and townsfolk took great pains to ensure that the decorations, singing and dancing were all of the highest order and would thus be pleasing to the goddess.

During the whole of the reign of the cat-headed goddess, every cat was venerated. Housepets were given every care and fed delicacies from their owners' plates. They often had their ears pierced to take jewels and gold rings and were given collars of gold and precious stones to wear. Even stray, untamed cats were cared for and food was left out for them. Sick cats were tended with the attention usually given to ailing children and if one should die the whole family went into mourning, beating their chests and wailing, banging gongs and shaving off their eyebrows as a mark of respect for the dead animal.

When a cat died, its body was rubbed with precious oils and wrapped in layers of fine linen cloth by specialists in enbalming procedures. If the owner was wealthy, the head would be encased in a papier mâché cast and the eyes indicated by circles of carefully painted cloth. Some rich owners had mummy cases carved of wood or fashioned from coloured straw, while others favoured cat-shaped coffins made of bronze. The ears of the cat were always treated carefully, each quite separate and pointing upright, while the legs were bound in with the body.

After the embalming the body would be taken to a special cemetery for cats, while the bereaved family mourned their loss. One such cemetery was discovered at the turn of this century in central Egypt. It was at Beni Hassan, and contained the bodies of more than 3000 mummified cats. The importance of the discovery was not at first realized, and many of the bodies were mechanically excavated and dumped into the holds of ships to be taken to England for use as fertilizer. Luckily, other such finds were made and carefully examined by experts, and it is from such discoveries that much of our present knowledge of the history of the Egyptian cats has been obtained.

Protectors of the grain stores and the home, incarnation of powerful gods, loved and revered by all, it was no wonder that the cat was jealously protected by its Egyptian masters. But although the export of their precious cats was forbidden, gradually, by devious routes, cats were taken by Egyptian monks and Phoenician traders, east to the Orient and westward to Europe.

The world-wide spread of cats

While the cat was being worshipped in Egypt, cats of a similar type were also well established in a semi-wild state in China and India, and trade between Egypt and Rome brought the cat to Italy where, hitherto, the control of vermin had been executed by small snakes and weasels. A curious mosaic depicting a cat with a large bird in its mouth was excavated at Pompeii and has been dated at about 100 years before the Christian era. There is however, nothing to indicate whether this cat was a pet, or merely a wild creature catching its prey. The destruction of Pompeii occurred in AD79 and it was at this time that the history of language was undergoing changes. It is probable that our word *cat* came from the Nubian word *kadis*, for in the early centuries AD, a related word travelled through most of the Mediterranean, Baltic, Slavic and Atlantic

countries, along with the export of the increasingly popular felines. The cat is known by very similar names in these countries, with only minor local modifications in spelling and pronunciation. In Holland and Denmark we find the word *kat*; in Sweden, *katt*; in Germany, *katti* or *katze*; in Poland, *kot*; in Russian, *kots*; in Portugal and Spain, *gato*; in Italy, *gatto*; and so on, including *catt, chat, cath, catus, cattus, cait, katte, kottr, kazza, kattos, kate* and *kotu*. The root word seems to have moved north from the African continent following the paths of the intrepid Romans.

In the writings of the elder Pliny in the first century AD all observations relating to the word *cat* are, indeed, accurate observations of the animal as we know it today, whether wild or domestic, and do not refer to any related species such as mongooses, weasels or civets. It seems safe to assert therefore that our feline friends had become firmly established 2000 years ago.

The Ancient Greeks do not appear to have set much store by the domestic cat, for although there is evidence that cats were kept to take the place of weasels in pest control, they are not depicted in Ancient Greek art. Only one vase shows a small cat being led by a slave, and as it is documented that the Greeks kept dogs and made tiny cages for creatures such as cicadas, it would appear that cats in Greece at that time were merely tolerated for their usefulness and not treated as valued pets. The Romans on the other hand, set great store by their cats, having been impressed by the fact that the animals had been so venerated in Egypt. The Egyptian cults made great impressions on the Romans, and it was perhaps inevitable that the cat worshipped in Egyptian households would be a pampered pet in Rome. Always prolific, it would not have taken many years for the domesticated cat to multiply to such an extent that the common people were able to acquire kittens, as the wealthy households each gained sufficient numbers to protect their stores.

Wherever the Roman armies marched, they took their cats, some of which were left behind in various regions and intermated with the indigenous wild cats. Some places have names which record the importance of the cat. The old Roman stronghold of Cat Vicense, in Holland, is now known as Kattewyk, or Cat's Town. County Caithness, in Scotland is the County of the Cats. Although the Romans carried their cats through all the countries of Europe and into Britain, the first cats in Britain were probably introduced by Phoenician traders, in exchange for Cornish tin.

Cats soon endeared themselves to people, as well as becoming important in their homes, and so established themselves as loyal friends and helpers, while maintaining their qualities of independence. Laws were drawn up for the protection of cats, and a king of Wales, Hywel Dda or Howell the Good, produced a famous piece of legislation in the year 936. The worth of a kitten from the night it was kittened,

until its eyes opened, was one legal penny; from the time its eyes opened until it could kill mice, it was worth two pence; after it was of an age to kill mice it was worth four pence. The qualities, or tiethi of a cat were to see, hear and kill mice, to have claws entire, to rear and not to devour her kittens, and if one was bought and found to be deficient in any one of these qualities, one third of her worth was to be returned.

Howell's laws also stated that if a cat was stolen or killed, its head was to be put downwards on a clean and even floor, while the body was suspended by the tail tip. Thus suspended, threshed wheat was to be poured about it until the tip of the tail was covered, and that was to be the worth of the animal. If corn was not available, a milch ewe, her fleece and her lamb was said to be the value of a cat which guarded the king's grain. The worth of any common cat was four legal pence, and anyone selling a cat was to answer for her caterwauling, to ensure that her ears, eyes, teeth and claws were sound and that she was guaranteed to be a good mouser.

The very first recorded breeding programme for domestic cats dates back to 999 AD when it is documented that a female cat gave birth to a litter of five kittens in the Imperial Palace of Kyoto, Japan. The Emperor was so enthralled with the kittens, born "on the tenth day of the fifth moon" that he ordered special care and attention to be afforded them, and decided to protect them from outside cats in order to breed similar kittens. Cats at that time were valued in Japan as they killed the mice that ate the silkworm cocoons, and it soon became fashionable to follow the Emperor's lead and to keep cats confined for breeding purposes. The cats were tethered on silken leashes and much care was lavished on them. However, this curtailed their hunting activities and the numbers of mice soon increased.

Very soon the silk industry reached the point of collapse, and the grain stores also were overrun with rats and mice. Eventually, in 1602, the government decreed that the cats must be set free, and also imposed a fine on anyone caught buying or selling the animals. The years of confinement had not impaired the Japanese cats' hunting abilities and instincts, and the vermin were quickly brought under control once more.

In 1607, the naturalist Edward Topsell wrote in his Historie of Four-Footed Beastes:
"Cats are of divers colours; but for the most part gryseld like to congealed yse, which cometh from the condition of her meat; her head is like unto the head of a Lyon, except in her sharpe eares; her flesh is soft and smooth; her eies glister above measure especially when a man cometh to see a cat on the sudden, and in the night they can hardly be endured for their flaming aspect. It is a neat and comely creature . . ."
From this we can see that although there were some cats of various colours, in the main they were 'gryseld' or as we would say 'brindled' as the common tabby.

The Egyptian cat-goddess Bast, known also as Bastet or Pasht, was first worshipped as a form of the sun. During the whole of her long reign all domestic and stray cats were regarded as sacred.

39

As various European countries developed their cultures, the role of the cat became rather more than that of a controller of vermin. Many practises and superstitions evolved around the animal and for hundreds of years cats were persecuted in many ways as we shall see later in this book.

While cities developed and people began to live in cramped, over-crowded conditions, the rat population also increased. Wherever man went, the rat followed, its path tracking the routes of invasion,

coated cat is mated to one with a short coat, only short-coated kittens can result. These offspring however, when mated inter se, will produce a proportion of long-coated kittens. It is thought that the Tibetan temple cat came into being this way, starting with a mutant kitten which was treasured for its unusual appearance.

Successive litters produced more and more of the cats with coats very suited to the cold climate in which they lived. The long-coated offspring would have

▲ Cheetah

■ Puma

● Tiger

△ Leopard

□ Jaguar

○ Lion

exploration and commercial trade. The rat devastated the food stores and brought disease, the worst of all being the Black Death that ravaged European and Asian countries in the fourteenth century. In 1660, half the population of London died from bubonic plague, spread by the Black Rat, living and breeding in the sewers of the city. Man's only ally against this menace was the cat, which rose in esteem and value. Despite this, the church outlawed the cat at this time, due to its use in pagan rituals, and for generations the wretched animal was persecuted on the one hand as a devil and encouraged on the other hand as a protector.

Having already brought back plague and pestilence from the East, it was the Crusaders returning from the Holy Wars that brought the first long-coated cats into Europe. How they developed in the first instance is a matter for conjecture. The long-coated effect is the result of a recessive mutant gene, and when a long-

been more likely to survive than the short-coated ones and so the variety probably became fixed after a few generations.

Some zoologists have advanced the hypothesis that the MANUL, also known as Pallas's cat, might be the ancestor of the long-coated breeds. This animal is a very beautiful creature, about the size of a domestic cat and with very long fine hair. The coat is lightly patterned with spots on a grey-brown background, and it has long side whiskers. The MANUL's range is from the Caspian Sea to Tibet and north, to Siberia, and its habitat is in mountain and high plain areas where the temperature is low. The Caspian Sea is the northern frontier of Iran, formerly called Persia and it is also close to Turkey, the capital of which, Ankara was formerly called Angora. Our present-day long-haired cats were formerly called Persians and Angoras and were said to come from those two areas.

The cat today is found all over the world. The map shows the distribution of some of the larger cats.

Although it would be pleasant to build such a legend around the origins of the long-coated breeds, the arguments against the hypothesis must be stressed. First, there are considerable differences in the dentition of the MANUL, and second his ear size and placement is quite unlike that of the domestic cat. Third, and perhaps most important of all, when the pupil of the eye contracts, it does so as a disc, and not with the slit effect as seen in the domestic variety.

Cats purported to have been brought from Angora in the sixteenth century were seen in Europe and were said to have been "Ash-coloured, Dun and speckled cats, beautiful to behold." These cats had long silky fur, and small heads with long noses and pointed ears, unlike the longhaired cats of today. In contrast the cats said to have come from Persia had thicker fur, broad heads and very full, bushy tails. It appears that the two varieties were freely intermated and when this happened, the traits of the Angora were inclined to be overcome by those of the Persian type.

In the eighteenth century, Europe was quietly and methodically invaded by the Brown Rat. This versatile and voracious creature swept across the continent and took over from the indigenous Black Rat. Only the cat was capable of keeping this new enemy at bay, and good ratting cats were at a premium. Cats were employed as rat-catchers in ministerial buildings, stores, shops, warehouses—in fact everywhere where the pests could be found. Gradually the cat population reinstated itself and every farm, bakery and foodstore took pride in its ratters.

The cat gained even more popularity when Louis Pasteur discovered the microbe in the middle of the nineteenth century. Dogs, hitherto allowed to run in and out of the house and to play with the children were suddenly considered far from hygienic. The dainty cat, however, always licking itself so fastidiously, was considered safe to keep in the home. Because of the fear of contagious disease, people opened their homes and hearts to the little cat. The close proximity in which they lived produced a mutual affection and understanding which lasts to this day.

It was perhaps the introduction of cats on board ships that accelerated the spread of the species throughout the world. The holds of the great cargo ships of the past teamed with rats and the only sure way of controlling these pests was to employ the services of ships' cats. The usefulness of cats for rat control was recognized by the courts and some maritime insurance companies would only indemnify for rat damage on a ship if there were cats on board. The absence of cats was held to be negligence on the part of the captain of the vessel, and in such circumstances, the shipping company had to stand the loss. Any merchant seaman, even today, will speak with affection of his ship's cat and tell amusing tales of its excursions ashore in foreign ports of call. Kittens were often born at sea, and when independent, might well disembark far from the land of their conception.

During this century, merchant ships again spread the cat population world-wide. This time, however, the cats were pedigreed prizewinners, transported in the safe confinement of specially constructed kennels. They were potential breeding stock, purchased and transported at great expense, by cat fanciers in many countries from breeders mainly in Britain following the first successful cat shows in the 1890s. Nowadays, transportation of pedigree cats is effected by air, and animals are carried to the opposite sides of the earth in a matter of hours. The modern ease of shipment has meant that the standards of perfection for most breeds and varieties of pedigree cats are very similar throughout the world, and the infusion of new traits—colours and coat patterns, type and conformation has been greatly simplified.

Possibly one of the most expert early naturalist writers on the subject of cats was Pocock (1863–1947) who regarded the study of the domestic cat as a science. He made profound observations which stand up to this day. Pocock considered the type we call *tabby* to be the closest approximation to the earliest domesticated cats, and described two sorts of tabby pattern—the blotched or classic pattern, technically described as *catus*, and the striped or torquata pattern. He regarded the blotched or classic pattern as a mutation that had arisen abruptly and fully developed from the striped or torquata pattern.

In the striped tabby the markings are formed of narrow lines, solid or broken, running transversely or vertically on the sides of the body. Towards the posterior the markings tend to break into shorter stripes or even spots. In the blotched or classic tabby, the broader stripes loop and spiral behind the shoulders and three long stripes run dorsally. In both types the tail is ringed and the face etched with lines. There is often an 'M' marked on the forehead. Pocock explained that the two pattern types are individually variable to a certain extent. Today's exhibition pedigree tabbies have very well defined standards of points which lay down definite patterns of marking which are used in judging. It is generally accepted now that there are four types of tabby pattern in the domestic cat, the classic, the mackerel striped, the spotted and the ticked or *agouti*.

Pocock also listed some of the varieties that had arisen by mutation and cross breeding. He mentioned a tortoiseshell cat from Spain; blue-grey cats from Europe and Siberia; a red cat from the Cape of Good Hope; a Chinese cat, black and yellow and having pendulous ears; a reddish-yellow cat with a long head and sharp nose from New Spain; a Malayan cat with a short, twisted tail; a black cat from South Africa; a greyish coloured animal from Abyssinia; a piebald cat from Japan, a fawn-and-black cat from Thailand, and a jet black cat from Russia. From all these colours, plus the mutation for longhair, it is easy to see how all the beautiful varieties we know today have been permutated.

The Biology of the Cat

Angela Sayer

The cat is a small carnivorous mammal, that is to say that it is a creature that is flesh eating and suckles its young. It is, in fact, the most carnivorous of all carnivores, with specialized dentition highly adapted for stabbing, slicing, tearing and biting, but not for chewing. The cat is designed for survival, an individualist able to run, stalk, climb, leap and hold fast to its prey.

In common with all living creatures, the cat's body is entirely composed of cells which are so tiny that they can only be seen under a powerful microscope. Each cell is a complete, discrete unit of life, but cells are grouped throughout the body and work together to perform different functions and to make different types of body tissues and structures.

The framework of the cat

Although the cat is much smaller than Man, it has more bones in its body and their distribution is different. To be precise, there are 230 bones in the skeleton of the cat, while Man has a mere 206. The skeleton consists of various bony formations that make up a semi-rigid framework to support the other body tissues. The bones of the limbs, spine, chest and pelvis provide a system of levers worked by the pulling power of attached muscles, while other bones protect vital organs. The skull is rigid and designed to protect the brain, while the arched ribcage and pelvis protect other delicate structures.

Four sorts of bones make up the cat's skeleton. These are long bones, short bones, irregular bones and flat bones. The long bones are roughly cylindrical in shape and have hollow shafts in which the bone marrow is found for the manufacture of red blood corpuscles. These bones are known as the femur, humerus and so on, and form the limbs of the body. The short bones are made up of a core of spongy bone surrounded by compact bone, and these are found in the feet and kneecaps. Irregular bones are similar to short bones in structure, but are of varying, irregular shapes and form the spine. Lastly we have the flat bones, made up of two layers of compact bone with a spongy bone layer sandwiched between. These bones are found in the formation of the skull, pelvis and shoulder blades.

The skull is made up of a number of flat pieces of bone fitted together rather like a jigsaw puzzle. In the very young kitten these pieces are not completely joined and, at this critical time, care must be taken to avoid head injury. The flat pieces of bone are pierced by numerous tiny holes through which pass nerves and blood vessels.

A long string of irregular bones make up the vertebral column of the cat, attached to the skull at one end and terminating in the tail tip at the other end. The hollow cervical, thoracic and lumbar vertebrae contain the spinal cord and bony projections on the segments serve as attachment points for the muscles of

The skeleton consists of bony structures which form a rigid framework for the body. It is lightly built with the placement of the limbs adapted for running, jumping and climbing.

(1) Caudal or tail bones (2) Siacra bones (3) Lumbar bones (4) Dorsal or thoracic bones (5) Cervical or neck bones (6) Cranium (7) Scapula or shoulder blade (8) Clavicle or collar bone (9) Humerus (10) Sternum (11) Radius (12) Ulna (13) Carpal or wrist bone (14) Phalanges or toes (15) Pelvis or hip bone (16) Calcis or heel bone (17) Metatarsal (rear), Metacarpal (front) bones (18) Tarsal bone (19) Tibia (20) Fibula (21) Patella or knee cap (22) Costal cartilages (23) Femur.

the back. The design of the connections between the pelvis and shoulder joints with the spine help to make the cat among the most flexible and agile of animals.

Flattened and elongated bones form the thirteen pairs of ribs, and although they are not hollow, these bones do contain a substantial amount of marrow, and so produce some red blood cells. Strong muscles attached to the ribcage vary the volume of the chest cavity, enabling the lungs to fill and empty. The pelvis is also formed of flat bones fused together in pairs to form an encircling structure through which the cat's internal organs pass into the body apertures.

Unlike Man, the cat does not have a collarbone, and as a result there is a degree of free movement in the shoulder. The scapula, or shoulder blade, consists of flat bone roughly triangular in shape, into which fits the first long bone of the arm, the humerus. The end of the humerus joins with the first bones of the forearm, the part of the foreleg which stands free from the body. The two long bones of the forearm are very well developed in the cat, and consist of a thick radius, behind which lies the thinner ulna. The two are united by a very strong ligament. The forepaws are made up of sets of three small bones, each of which forms one digit and corresponds with the finger of the human hand. The tiny end bones articulate so that the claws they contain can be extended or retracted at will. The digit corresponding to the human thumb has no function in the cat and only consists of two bones, forming an appendage known as the dew claw.

In the hindlimb, the femur or thigh bone is very long and rather fragile and fits into the pelvis with a ball-and-socket joint. At the lower end of the femur is another long bone, the tibia, which is jointed. The cat has a kneecap, or patella here, which glides over the smooth end of the femur. A slender bone, the fibula, reinforces the action of the tibia down its entire length to the hock or ankle. The bones of the hind foot are similar to that of the forepaw, but are longer and here, the first toe is absent altogether. From a study of the skeletal structure of the cat, it can be seen that the animal walks on its toes, aiding speed of movement.

Adequate protection and support is provided by the cat's skeleton under normal conditions, but fractures and dislocations often occur as the result of road accidents. Cats commonly jump down from heights too great for them, and so suffer injury. Queens confined in bedrooms have been known to effect an escape from the windows and jump down onto paved areas, resulting in broken bones. With expert veterinary care, fractures of the limbs, and sometimes even of the skull and jaw, heal well and leave no serious after effects.

A dislocation occurs when one or more of the bones making up a joint becomes displaced. The cat is unable to use the affected limb which swells up in an unnatural position, and urgent veterinary treatment is required to reduce the swelling and to set the joint back in position. Some cats have been known to suffer regular attacks of dislocation, which is known as luxation of the patellae, and is thought to be the result of a hereditary condition. Cats suffering from it should be neutered and not used for breeding.

Skeletal abnormalities are not very common in the cat, probably because there has not been the same degree of breeding for exaggerated types, as has occurred in the breeding of dogs. Cats of any breed have the same basic size and shape of their ancestors. Some of the defects encountered are a bent or shortened tail, cleft palate, flattened chest, polydactylism and split-foot. Some cases of bent or kinked tails are due to injury either at birth or later, and are quite common defects in the cat. Other cases however, are hereditary in origin. Shortened tails are due to the presence of a simple recessive gene, while kinked tails are due to a more complicated pattern of inheritance. At the turn of the century, Siamese cats were known for their thickened, short and twisted tails, but this defect has been virtually eliminated by selective breeding methods.

Cleft palate is often associated with harelip and these defects are due to a failure of the two halves of the hard palate and upper lip to fuse normally in the embryo kitten. It is not known how the anomaly is caused, although the condition has been produced in kittens by the experimental use of drugs administered to pregnant queens. Kittens with this defect die soon after birth as they are unable to suckle. A deficiency of Vitamin A in the diet of a pregnant queen may give rise to the birth of kittens with flattened rib cages, and other skeletal abnormalities. Kittens with this deformity have difficulty with breathing, as the lungs are unable to expand fully. Polydactylism is the presence of extra toes on the foot. It is a hereditary defect and surprisingly common in the cat. The number of extra toes varies, some cats may even appear to have a double foot on each leg. In split-foot there is a cleft in the centre of one or both front feet while the toes may be fused together, missing, or possessed of double claws, the defect being inherited through a dominant gene.

Overlying the skeletal framework of the cat is a complex sheath of muscles. These build up the shape and conformation of the animal and afford it movement by contracting and relaxing. Muscles that straighten and extend a joint are known as extensors, while those that bend and flex a joint are known as flexors. There are muscles called abductors which move the limbs from the body, and others called adductors that draw the limbs towards the body. Muscles are composed of specialized fibres able to contract in response to nerve stimuli. Three types are found in the body of the cat. Striped, striated muscle is attached to the limbs and other parts of the anatomy which is under the voluntary control of the animal. Smooth, unstriated muscle carries out the functions not under voluntary control, such as those of the intestinal wall and the walls of the blood vessels.

Finally there is cardiac muscle which is adapted for carrying out the functions of the heart and possesses unique powers of rhythmic contraction.

The circulation

As in other mammals, the blood of the cat is pumped around its body in a typical, double cycle pattern. First the heart pushes the blood around the lung circuit where it is oxygenated, then around the larger circuit which includes all the other organs. The arteries carry blood at high pressure from the heart, pushing it through fine capillaries which pass through the tissues. Here the exchanges of gases, nutrients and hormones occur. Blood at low pressure is collected by the veins and returned to the heart for re-circulation. In the cat, the circulatory system is adapted for rapid change from repose to full exertion. Red blood cells in the cat may be destroyed, and the animal become anaemic, from heavy parasitic infestations. Some drugs can have toxic effects by destroying the bone marrow which manufactures new red blood cells. Aspirin should never be given to cats as this has the effect of destroying the circulating cells in the blood stream.

Skin and fur

Skin is made up of two layers of tissue, each in turn made up of collections of cells. The outer layer of skin is known as the epidermis and the inner layer as the dermis. The epidermis is constantly being replaced as the surface layer dies and sloughs away as dandruff. The skin is often a barometer of the cat's health, being pliable and elastic in the fit cat and stiff and unyielding in the sick animal. A drastic change in the colour of the skin can point to severe illness in the cat. For example, a pallid appearance can mean infestation by parasites, a serious case of shock, or a lack of some vital dietary requirement. A reddening of the skin points to inflammatory disease of the skin or underlying tissues. A bluish effect suggests respiratory disease, heart failure or poisoning, while a yellowish effect indicates jaundice, one sympton of several serious illnesses in felines.

The skin of the cat contains sweat glands, but it is not certain that these are very effective in controlling the animal's temperature, rather they exist to excrete impurities from the body. Sebaceous glands are also present. These open into the hair follicles and secrete an oily, semiliquid substance called *sebum*, which coats each hair as it grows. Skin on the pads and nostrils are free from hair. The nose leather is extremely sensitive to touch, while the pads are more sensitive to pressure. It is through the pads that the cat secretes sweat when hot or frightened. The effective claws grow continuously from the base, like fingernails, and are formed of sheets of hard keratin.

Hair is derived from the outer layer of skin and acts as an insulative layer, keeping the animal warm in cold weather and cool in hot weather. Hair forms a dense pelt over the body and is modified in certain areas such as the whiskers and eyelashes. Each individual hair is a long, thin cylindrical structure, pointed at one end and ending in a tiny bulb at the other, which is embedded in the dermis. Each hair is formed separately in a follicle and pigment cells inject granules of colour into the hair as it grows, giving the coat its genetically determined colour. Special muscles attached to large follicles enable the hairs to stand erect when the cat is angry, startled, or suffering from a low temperature when incubating an illness.

Moulting is the term given to the shedding of dead hairs and usually takes place at certain times of the year. Hair loss also occurs during the course of some illnesses, and in the common diseases of the skin, such as eczema, ringworm and mange, large patches of skin, quite devoid of hair, are seen. Some types of poisoning cause considerable hair loss, and in some neutered cats, a hormone inbalance can cause a form of eczema leading to bare patches along the spine and down the flanks.

Specialized hairs grow in neat rows either side of the cat's upper lip. These are the vibrissae, or whiskers, which are brought into action by the movement of tiny muscles. The whiskers are very sensitive and the slightest touch at the tip transmits a message to a nerve in the upper lip and then through a large nerve directly to the brain. The whiskers are used for touching objects and obstacles, for sensing changes in the environment and also in emotional displays of various kinds.

In laboratory tests, blindfolded cats were observed to walk accurately along narrow ledges and through simple mazes of tunnels and other obstacles, merely by feeling a pathway with their sensitive whiskers. It is probable that cats in the wild use the vibrissae during their nocturnal hunting excursions. In conjunction with their highly adaptable eyes which allow every possible scrap of light to be absorbed, this has probably led to the myth that cats can 'see in the dark'.

Cat vision
The eyes face forward and the fields of view overlap slightly, giving stereoscopic vision. This enables the rather near-sighted cat to judge precisely distances within striking range when hunting.

The parts of the eye (1) Vitreous humour (2) Retina (3) Ciliary processes (4) Ciliary muscle (5) Recti muscles (6) Optic nerve (7) Aqueous humour (8) Iris (9) Cornea (10) Choroid (11) Crystalline lens.

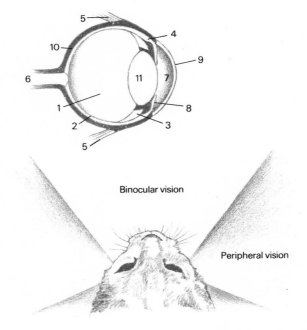

Binocular vision

Peripheral vision

Cats' eyes

Humans have better daylight vision than cats, but after dusk the cat really comes into its own. Although it cannot see in total darkness, it has excellent vision in the dimmest of lights. The ability of the cat's pupil to expand and contract in order to control the amount of light available, explains why the cat's eye looks different each time we look at it. In dim light the iris become relaxed and the pupil widely dilated. The light passes through the curved cornea and lens to the retina at the back of the eye. It is then reflected by a special layer of iridescent cells called the tapetum lucidium, and thus causes the effect of the cat's eyes shining yellow, often seen at night. It is thought that either the tapetum or the retina itself may have a photomultiplying effect on the received light. The delicate mechanism in the back of the eye must be shielded from strong light, and this is effected during the day time by the contraction of the iris, closing down to form a slit-like pupil.

The eyes of the cat face forward, allowing the fields of vision to overlap, and giving stereoscopic vision. This enables the cat to be extremely accurate in judging distances for timing its run or spring in hunting. Large, and set in deep sockets in the skull, the cat's eyes cannot move freely, and the animal has to turn its head, sometimes its body also, in order to bring objects into sharp focus. It is often said that cats are colour-blind, but many cat-owners have noticed a preference in their pets for food dishes, bedding and furniture of certain colours.

An interesting feature of the cat's eye is the presence of a third eyelid, known as the nictitating membrane or 'haw'. This is a sheet of pale tissue situated in the inner corner of each eye and normally tucked away out of sight. The inward movement of the eye within the socket causes the membrane to move diagonally upwards and across the front of the eyeball. The function of the 'haw' is to remove dust and dirt from the cornea and to keep the eye moist and lubricated. When cats are out of condition or incubating an illness, a tiny pad of fat behind the eyeball shrinks and causes the eye to retract a little into its socket. This in turn, allows the nictitating membrane to extend part of the way across the eye, so the appearance of the 'haw' is often taken as an early warning of disease in the animal.

Cat's eyes are useful in diagnosing illness, for a change in their appearance is often the first sign that there is something amiss. Weeping eyes are the first symptoms of illnesses such as pneumonitis, while a distinct change in the colour of the iris indicates jaundice. As we have mentioned, the appearance of the 'haw' across the eye should be followed by a visit to the veterinary surgeon for a check-up. Foreign bodies such as grass seeds may become lodged behind the nictitating membrane and cause intense irritation, inflammation and weeping. Eyes may be injured during fights, and the eyelids, as well as the eyeball itself, may be torn by an opponent's teeth and claws.

The eyes of the cat may be oriental in shape or large, round and lustrous. They may be any shade of yellow from the palest primrose to the deepest copper, embracing all tints of gold and amber. They may be any shade of green from the lightest jade to the darkest emerald. In Siamese cats they range from china blue to bright sapphire, and in some strains even have a violet tinge. Some cats have hazel eyes, and some the tawny shade seen in their larger cousin, the lion. Occasionally a cat may have odd eyes, that is one yellow and one blue or green. These cats are usually white-coated, and the result of crossing blue-eyed with orange-eyed cats. Whatever their colour, cats' eyes are as beautiful as they are functional and possessed of a wealth of expression.

Other senses

In the cat, hearing is exceptionally well developed, and the animal can pick up high-pitched squeaks and rustles, plus many sounds quite inaudible to humans. Research has indicated that the hearing of the cat is superior even to that of the dog. The ear of the cat can be thought of in three sections. Outwardly we see the pinna, or ear flap. This is naturally erect and forward pointing, but is flexible enough to move in order to catch the slightest sounds and to determine accurately the direction of their source. Sound waves are picked up by the pinna which acts as a funnel leading down to the eardrum, stretched across the ear canal. The middle ear is made up of three small bones which transmit the sound waves to the inner ear. Here they are analysed and converted into nerve impulses which are passed along the acoustic nerve to the brain. The auditory cortex of the cat's brain decodes the signals and recognizes them by comparing them with sounds stored in the memory bank. This is how cats learn special sounds and may be taught to respond to their own names as well as to react to simple commands.

The cat's ear can register frequencies some two octaves higher than the human ear, but is less sensitive to lower frequencies. The acuity of hearing diminishes with age, and many old cats are very deaf. Deafness can result from severe ear diseases and may be partial or complete. It can also be hereditary, and is often linked to white coat colour in cats especially when the cat also has blue eyes. In these cats the genetic factor which causes the coat and eye colour is linked with changes in the cochlea, severe enough to inhibit the passage of sound waves.

Very vulnerable to physical injury, the ear flaps are often torn during cat fights. Although they bleed profusely, they usually heal up very quickly, unless the cartilage supporting the ear has also been damaged. Severe irritation can cause the cat to scratch the ear badly, rupturing the blood vessels under the skin and causing a large haematoma or blood blister to form. Unless veterinary treatment is sought for this condition, as the swelling is reabsorbed, the flap crumples, leaving the animal with a collapsed and distorted ear. Having large ears can cause problems, for the canal is open to infestation with tiny mites which live and breed in the moist, warm lining of the ear canal. Cat owners should always be on guard against such pests, and regular inspection of the ear is advisable.

As in most carnivores, the sense of smell in the cat is highly developed. It is stimulated by minute particles of odorous substances in the atmosphere drawn in with the breath, or deliberately sniffed in by the cat. Sensitive nerve endings in the nasal cavities in the form of fine olfactory hairs are linked with nerve cells connected to the brain. Here the olfactory organ is very much larger than would be expected in so small an animal, indicating that the sense of smell is very important in the species. This sense is essential to the animal in its search for food and is also related to its sexual life. In the roof of the cat's mouth is situated a small pouch lined with receptor cells and known as the Jacobson's organ. A cat receiving a subtle or unusual scent will open its mouth and raise its head as if to savour the smell. This strange grimace is called the flehmen reaction, and enables the scent to reach the Jacobson's organ for identification. It is difficult to distinguish between the senses of smell and taste in the cat, but it is true to say that most felines like salt but are impartial to sweet tastes.

Cats do not eat carrion and so find the smell of tainted food highly distasteful. Some cats are very susceptible to perfumes and are attracted to people who use them. The catnip plant exudes a fragrance highly intoxicating to cats, and diluted oil of the plant has been used to trap wild cats such as puma and lynx. How the catnip plant manages to affect cats is a matter for conjecture, but the effect is plain to see. It is almost certain that the plant excites the cat sexually while having a contradictory, soothing effect on the nervous system. Even neutered cats and young kittens purr, growl, roll and rub themselves ecstatically in the plant, given the opportunity.

Cat is carnivore

Moist mucous membrane lines the cat's mouth. The tongue is very specialized and rough, due to large papillae on its upper surface used for grooming the fur, as well as for rasping and softening food. The edge of the tongue is capable of curling like a spoon so that the cat can lap liquids. The mouth is kept moist by the action of the salivary glands, which wash away bacteria and dead cells as well as moistening food to facilitate swallowing. The teeth are highly specialized and an adult cat has twelve incisors, four canines, ten pre-molars and four molars, a total set of 30 teeth. Kittens are born with teeth just visible in the gums. These erupt and are needle sharp at six weeks of age, when the tiny creatures bite on anything they can find and should be given strips of raw meat for 'teething'. Kittens eventually shed their baby teeth as the per-

manent teeth come through. Occasionally, double dentition is seen and the kitten has trouble eating due to having a sore mouth. The veterinary surgeon will quickly ease out the temporary teeth and the condition soon clears up.

Due to the unnatural diet fed to our pets, the condition known as gingivitis is commonly seen these days. This is a severe inflammation of the gums and is seen as a thin, red line along the junction between the teeth and gums. Cats and kittens with gingivitis often drool excessive strings of saliva, and lose condition fast due to the reluctance to eat. Antibiotics and dental hygiene help to alleviate the condition, and then hard foods should be given to keep the teeth and gums in good order.

The teeth of the cat are not designed for chewing. When prey is caught, the cat tears a piece from the carcase and swallows it so the salivary juices in the mouth have little time to start the processes of digestion. The salivary glands of the cat produce little or no ptyalin, the powerful enzyme present in the human mouth which starts the breakdown of starches into blood sugars. This results in the fact that starches present in the cat's diet are relatively untouched by the time they reach the small intestine, so there is little point in feeding starchy foods to your cat. The stomach juices in the cat are much stronger than those in the human stomach. In fact, they are strong enough to reduce hard bone to a soft, cartilagic state. The cat is able to swallow chunks of small rodents and birds, and any parts that are not quickly broken down in the stomach, such as feathers, hair and bones may be regurgitated. In the stomach, proteins start the long process of reconversion into the amino acid building blocks needed to regenerate the cat's body.

From the stomach, partly digested food is passed through the pylorus, a valve to the small intestine, where further digestive changes take place aided by secretions from accessory glands such as the pancreas and liver. It is here that fats are broken down and extracted, sugars are changed structurally ready for storage, and minerals are absorbed. From the small intestine the fluid contents pass into the large intestine and are acted upon by the specialized bacteria living there. Water is drawn off and finally the waste material is passed into the colon to be voided.

Eating habits of cats and kittens are not always very hygienic, and they do not always eat sensibly. They also keep their coats clean by grooming with their rough tongues, ingesting loose hair, dust and grease. It seems inevitable therefore, that they suffer from digestive upsets now and again. The most common cause of trouble in the digestive tract is stale or tainted food. Cats given their freedom often scavenge in neighbours' dustbins, eating things that they would regard with horror if offered at home. Cats are also fond of drinking from garden pools, and the greener they are the better they like the water. They will also drink from water vases, goldfish bowls and oily puddles, all with dire results. Time and again bouts of diarrhoea and sickness can be traced to this craving for drinking quite unsuitable water. To guard against this, clean, fresh drinking water should be provided at all times.

Other causes of gastric upset in the cat can be traced directly to infestation with intestinal worms, and from feeding a quite unsuitable diet. Feeding too much fish can result in great ropes of the food being returned almost as soon as it is swallowed. Too much milk can cause persistent diarrhoea. Whole minced poultry may cause problems when tiny slivers of bone

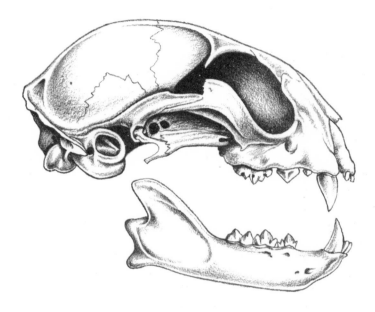

The skull is the bony structure which encases the delicate brain and has specialized areas for eyes, ears and nose. The jaws are strong, with hinged mandibles, enabling the mouth to open wide for gripping prey. The teeth are specialized for gripping its prey, stabbing and tearing, rather than chewing and grinding.

damage the lining of the bowel, giving rise to blood in the motions. A cat that has a long, loose coat may ingest so much hair during grooming operations that it forms a fur ball in the stomach or intestines. Fur balls in the stomach are usually vomited up after a few days of dullness and lethargy, when the cat is hungry and 'asks' for food but is unable to eat it.

Fur balls sometimes move down to the bowel and cause the cat some sickness, complete loss of appetite, indigestion and constipation. The veterinary surgeon will prescribe some form of laxative in these cases and suggest special care of the cat's coat. The coat should be kept as free from loose hair as possible by regular, thorough grooming. This is carried out by first massaging the skin with the fingertips against the growth of the coat to loosen the dead hairs, then a fine comb is employed to remove them. Finally, a damp cloth is passed over the cat to ensure that every loose hair is collected, and this whole procedure is repeated daily. The secret of keeping the cat's digestion in good working order is to feed a sensible diet, change its content as little as possible, and ensure that the food is prepared and served in hygienic conditions.

Cat chat

No animal on earth expresses itself as well as the cat, which can emit a variety of sounds. The nature of the function of its vocal cords is not thoroughly understood, but it is known that there are superior or false cords, as well as inferior or true cords. It is most probable that the various cries emitted by the cat are produced by the true vocal cords, while the false cords are responsible for its purr. All cats purr, although in some no sound is emitted, but the vibrations can be felt by touching the animal's throat. Cats purr with contentment, with affection and even when in pain. Bereaved owners have been comforted that their pet has purred even with its last breath. Purring can begin in the kitten as early as one week of age, and usually starts when it is contentedly nursing from its mother. Young cats purr in a monotone, while older animals purr on two or three notes.

Cats' calls are even more varied than their purrs. Different sounds are made to express different emotions. Cats communicate with each other and with humans by means of various cries. There is a whole language of love between a queen in oestrus and her suitors, and another between a mother cat and her litter. Growls are also varied and meaningful, ranging from growls of anger to those of fear. Cats also spit, scream and hiss. Most vocal of all cats are the Siamese, which have loud, harsh voices, loved by their fans and loathed by their enemies. The cry of a Siamese queen in mid-oestrus is exactly like the wailing cry of a new-born baby.

The tail and paws are also used by the cat to communicate with humans. The attitude of the tail is most expressive. Carried erect it means that all is fine and the cat has a sense of well-being. The tail-up posture is also a welcoming gesture. Even if the tip waves gently from side to side, the cat is still feeling benign. Flashing the tail from side to side is a different matter. It expresses extreme annoyance and often pre-warns of an attack. A cat standing stock still with the tail held stiffly behind in a straight line is certainly about to attack. The hairs on the cat's tail are capable of erection, causing the appendage to look like a bottle brush. A scared cat will hunch its back, erecting the hairs on its tail and spine and turn sideways on to whatever is threatening it, presenting itself as a much larger adversary. It will usually accompany such a threat display with much growling, blowing out its cheeks and smacking its lips menacingly.

A contented cat, sitting on a comfortable lap, will purr and will also often start to knead gently with the forepaws. This action replicates that of kittens while suckling, which knead their paws on either side of the teat. A cat performing this action is consumed with a sense of well-being and love. The cat also bestows its mark of affection on humans, other animals and inanimate objects by rubbing the scent glands of its lips, chin and tail-root against them.

The fertile cat

The cat has a typically mammalian reproductive system, with a few feline modifications. The male cat has paired testes which produce the sperms and the male hormone, testosterone. The testes descend from the abdominal cavity into the tiny sacs of the scrotum, either when the kitten is still within the uterus of its mother, or shortly after birth. Occasionally, one or both testes fail to descend in the normal way, resulting in a sterile, or partially sterile male cat. A cat with only one testicle is known as a monorchid, and a cat without descended testicles is known as a cryptorchid. If such cats are fertile, they can be a menace, for they pass on their condition to their offspring. Monorchids and cryptorchids should be neutered when old enough, as they have all the normal characteristics of the tomcat including the pungent odour of their 'spray'. The neutering operation can be complex and veterinary advice should be sought as soon as the defect is noticed in a young, male kitten.

Male cats become sexually mature at about nine months of age, unless under-developed or raised in poor conditions. If not neutered, they begin to wander abroad and may start to become involved in fights with other cats. The habit of 'spraying' begins when the cat deposits a small spray of urine on points he wishes to mark, usually shrubs and corners of buildings. About this time a subtle change is noticed in his aroma as a chemical substance is produced in the urine, ensuring that the odour clings to everything it contacts.

In the female cat, paired ovaries lie on either side of the vertebrae, just behind the kidneys. The ovaries produce the female hormone oestrogen, and, following the stimulus of mating, shed several ova. These pass down the fallopian tubes where they are fertilized by the sperm from the male. Fertilization can occur up to three days after mating, then the egg cells spend another five days in the fallopian tubes before passing into the uterus. This is a very critical stage in the development of the young kittens, for at this time the ovaries of the mother secrete another hormone, progesterone. This substance is necessary to allow the tiny embyros to implant in the uterine wall. If the queen is taken ill or suffers an accident at this stage, implanting does not take place and the egg cells are passed from the body or resorbed.

Female cats can become sexually mature from the age of six months, but usually have their first period of heat at nine or ten months. The first heat is often determined by the season of the year. The queen can often be in heat for up to five times a year. The heat lasts for about five days during which the queen emits a distinctive call. Many female kittens start their distinctive 'calling' in the early weeks of the first February following their birth. Even though they may not be fully grown or mature, it is quite possible for them to be mated, and to produce a litter, though obviously not advisable. Having a litter too early in life may seriously deplete the young queen's calcium reserves at a critical stage in her development.

Gestation is 65 days in the cat, and kittens born before the fifty-seventh day are unlikely to survive. Queens sometimes go over term and live kittens have been known to arrive up to 72 days after mating. An average litter consists of four kittens, which are born fully-furred, but deaf and blind. They feed from their mother for about eight weeks, although they are capable of eating solid food from the age of four weeks. As the litter becomes independent, the queen spends less time with them and soon her hormones ensure that she starts another breeding cycle.

The colourful cat

As we have seen, the original domestic cats were tabby, and then a very few mutations occurred. The permutations of these provide us with the spectrum of coat colour and the miscellany of coat pattern that we find in cats today. Coat colour in the cat depends on the presence of granules in cells of the skin's epidermis. Complete absence of these granules results in whiteness of the skin and coat. The granules consist of melanin, present as two compounds, eumelanin and phaeomelanin. The first gives rise to black and brown pigmentation while the second produces red or yellow. Variation in colour in each hair is due to the way in which the pigment is distributed in the hair cells. Tabby hairs are characteristically banded yellow with black tips.

Melanin is produced by melanocytes, special cells which form the pigment, passing it to the skin, the hairs of the body and the eyes. The amount and distribution of the melanocytes is determined genetically. The cells are formed in the embryonic kitten and spread over various areas of the body at this stage, when the colour of the adult animal is thus determined. It is the way in which the melanin clumps together that forms the various colour effects that we perceive in the cat's coat. Basically these are black and its derivatives brown and blue, which together in double doses, give lilac. Banding of the hair produces the same colours in tabby form, and the addition of the genetic factor termed Himalayan, restricts the colour to the extremities, as in the Siamese.

Phaeomelanin is responsible for the production of lighter coloured pigment granules for infusion into the hair shafts. This causes the coat colour to be orange, or, as is commonly known—ginger. If this colour is genetically diluted, the effect seen is the lovely buttermilk colour known as cream. Cats can also have white patching where the melanin is missing, and so can be of any of the basic colours, plus white. If the gene for silver is also present in the animal, this causes the basic colour of the hair shaft to disappear, leaving only the black areas. In longhaired cats with this gene, the result is dramatic for it produces the Smoke Persian. The full range of colour in cats will be seen in later sections of this book.

Feline First Aid

Michael Findlay

Of the many species that have been domesticated over the years, the cat is, in many ways, one of the most complex. Brave and fearless, as befits its wild ancestry, the popular household pet retains the habits and behaviour of its jungle relatives. As a result, veterinary treatment of the cat poses a number of specific problems.

Day in, day out, the veterinarian hears from his clients the well-worn cliché, '. . . but they can't talk!' This remark misses the point completely—of course cats cannot talk in the human sense, but they *can* communicate to a surprising extent to an experienced person. To the veterinary surgeon, who is trained to diagnose, administer to, treat and nurse 'dumb' patients on the premise of acting basically on facts gleaned from keen observation and questioning of the owner, this is of paramount importance. Experience may, therefore, give the vet a pretty good idea of what is wrong with a sick cat; but obviously other aids (such as X-rays, tests on blood, urine, etc) will be employed, in addition to routine clinical examination, before a diagnostic conclusion is reached and suitable treatment chosen.

The cat as patient

Carrying the analogy between cats and human patients a stage further, what is of far greater practical importance is the absence of co-operation. The average cat tends to dislike examination and treatment, for it cannot comprehend that what is being done is for its own good. Its instinctive reaction, when being forced to do something undesirable, is to resist. Even the most compliant domestic pet is, potentially, a well-equipped 'fighting unit'. In addition to a battery of fearsome teeth, the average cat has four lethal claws on each hind foot and five on each front foot. It also possesses a loose-fitting coat which enables it to swivel through wide angles within the skin itself, so

Right
This cuddly kitten looks as if butter wouldn't melt in its mouth. However at the merest suspicion of 'treatment' he will move like lightning and his loose fitting coat will make it very difficult for you to hold on to him at all.

Following page left
A patient green-eyed Tabby wrapped up in a towel which is a good way of restricting the cat's movements if you have to treat him on your own.

49

that the handler is often at risk. Although the paws can be immobilized, there is little to prevent a cat biting. So it may be necessary, both in the veterinary surgery and the home, to employ custom-built methods for restraining the feline patient for purposes of examination and treatment.

For the single-handed operative, the best method is to wrap the body of the cat, including all four limbs, in a large blanket or towel. Alternatively, the animal can be enclosed, except for the head, in a zip-up bag. If an assistant is present, the task is, of course, much easier. The cat is placed on a table or on the knee of the assistant who holds the front legs, allowing the vet control of the animal's head. But with a really difficult patient two assistants may be required to keep the cat under sufficient restraint for the surgeon to go about his work without fear of being molested.

An additional problem is the natural inclination of

the cat to interfere with surgical procedures and thus undo whatever good has been done. The patient obviously cannot be kept under observation day and night, nor can it be expected to respond to human words of advice. After all, even a child will pay heed to the warning, 'Don't pick it, or it will never get better'. Yet considering the number of operations performed daily on cats, they are, on the whole, obliging patients. Probably only one cat in fifty removes its stitches a few hours after they have been carefully inserted.

Because of the cat's shape and suppleness, it is almost impossible to bandage it in such a way that it cannot interfere with a wound, but there are three useful tips that may avoid yet another telephone call to the vet. Firstly, a bland, safe but unpleasant-tasting lotion, such as oil of citronella, can be painted *around* a lesion or wound, and this may discourage the cat

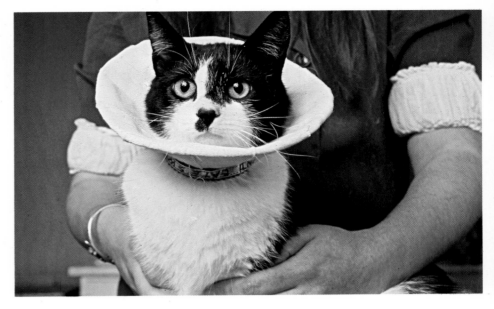

from licking it; but it is not foolproof, for the cat, being fastidiously clean, may be spurred to rid its skin of the noxious material. Secondly, bandaging the back paws with children's socks, for example, will, if the cat is detained indoors, lessen the risk of claws scratching out stitches or dressings applied to any point from the chest forward—and hence within reasonable range of the rear limbs. Thirdly, there is the classic 'Elizabethan collar'—a cone of cardboard or other suitable material around the neck, ensuring that the scratching *and* licking capabilities of the patient are severely restricted. Take care that this is the right size and not too tight—if in doubt seek advice from your vet or from his nursing staff.

A cat recovering from a broken limb, however, presents rather more of a practical problem. Whether the limb has been treated by means of an external plaster cast or with a stainless steel pin inserted through the bone itself, damage rarely occurs and the cat seldom interferes. Furthermore, being a sensible creature, the cat will bear little or no weight on an uncomfortable or painful limb—such as might be expected in the first stages of healing—and will

Above
Cat in an 'Elizabethan collar' which prevents him from licking a wound and also from biting and scratching you.

Right
The cat is potentially 'a well equipped fighting unit'. This comical Silver Tabby illustrates this perfectly:— a fine set of teeth and four sets of claws all at the ready, although he is so held as to be off balance. A blow from a cat's front paw can be very powerful.

Below
The country cat is exposed to barbed wire, drains and even dead branches in trees, and accidents can occasionally happen.

resume normal mobility only when discomfort ceases and the limb has mended.

Home nursing

The most important role that an owner will occasionally be asked to play is that of home nurse. This may involve administering medicines, as directed by the vet. As a general rule, it is not advisable to mix medicines with food, in the hope that the patient will swallow it down unnoticed. The cat, being a fastidious and cautious feeder, is extremely suspicious of 'doctored grub' and unlikely to take all or indeed any of a treated meal or drink, so that the dosage, often critical, cannot be calculated with accuracy. For this reason drugs are rarely given now in powder form. Tablets or pills must be given exactly as instructed,

a wound in this manner.

Any cat with an orthopaedic complaint, a highly infectious condition, or in a generally weakened state, should *not* be allowed outdoors, or at least only if accompanied, for obvious reasons. If in doubt, ask the vet whether it is necessary to impose house arrest in the course of treatment; and if the answer is yes, do remember to provide an indoor litter tray.

As with human nursing, you will be expected to keep an eye on the patient and report progress. Obviously you will get in touch with your vet should there be signs of complications or deterioration; but do so, if only to obtain reassurance, should you be in the slightest doubt.

A word about force-feeding. It is far better for a cat to eat of its own free will than have to be forcibly

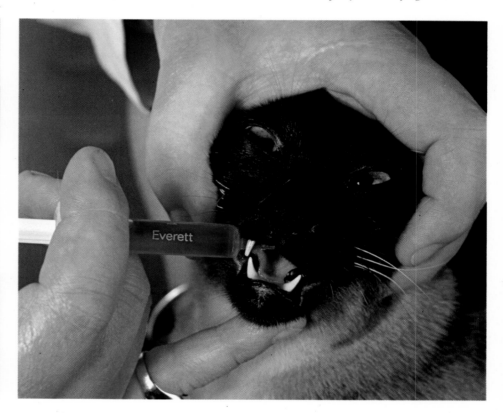

with regard both to intervals between dosages and to feeding times. Provided the cat is satisfactorily immobilized, it is not difficult to administer them, although it is important to see that the cat has finally swallowed the pill and not hidden it under his tongue.

Liquid medicines may be given in drop form with an eye-dropper (fountain pen filler) or the barrel of a hypodermic syringe, which can be obtained from your vet. The principle is the same as with pills, and it is reassuring to know that, given the cat's very strong throat reflexes, neither solid nor liquid medicines are likely to go down the wrong way.

Ointments, creams and the like may be applied, under suitable direction, but do remember that these can easily be licked off during the normal cleaning process. So try to prevent your pet doing this by keeping it under observation for a while after treating

fed. Not only will force-feeding create resentment and antipathy, but it must be done frequently and regularly. At best it will merely sustain life and energy, and it is impossible to force enough food down to build up the patient's strength. It is much preferable to encourage the cat to eat tasty, strongly flavoured foods, such as tinned sardines, salmon and tuna, raw liver and scraped raw beef—perhaps with a pinch of salt as an additional spur. Invariably, when a cat starts to eat following surgery or illness, it will go from strength to strength.

If, however, it proves necessary to force-feed for a temporary period, the vet will suggest appropriate foods. These may include essence of beef or chicken, glucose and milk, proprietary dried milk for cats, beef tea, human invalid diets and tinned baby foods. They should be given in fluid or paste form by the methods previously suggested.

Below
All catteries should be scrupulously clean and all the occupants should have been vaccinated against feline infectious enteritis, and recently wormed. These are three young Abyssinians.

Below right
It is important to see that collars fit a cat comfortably and do not rub. Cats can easily pick up lice, worms and fleas from long grass; but all these can be treated quite simply and should not cause any trouble.

Opposite page below
Shorthaired Brown Tabby sunbathing.

A comfortable environment, airy but draught free, and including direct heat by any safe method, is also an invaluable aid to nursing the really sick cat.

Finally, some warnings for the home nurse. On no account use old medicines unless sanctioned by your vet. Never use human medicines—even a minute dose of aspirin, for example, is enough to kill your cat. Be very cautious indeed about disinfectants, for a cat may die if it comes in contact with strong phenol preparations, which have little or no effect on other animals. Do not use insecticidal powders on a cat, unless specifically prescribed and guaranteed to be safe; insecticides containing DDT—much used until recently—can again prove fatal. And if you have access to morphine—a strictly controlled drug for human use—keep it well out of reach for this is an immediate killer.

Early visits to the surgery
It is probably true to say that the cat is one of the healthiest domestic species, particularly when treated with some knowledge, respect and forethought.

If you want a thoroughbred kitten, buy from a reputable breeder and try to see its first home and, if possible, its parents. Bear in mind the hidden extras to the purchase price, such as feeding, boarding, inoculations, neutering and possible veterinary fees (which can be cared for by taking out an insurance policy). Even when acquiring an ordinary 'moggie', go for one that is apparently healthy, playful, clean and alert. In either case you are within your rights to make your purchase conditional on a veterinary 'all-clear' within the first few days of acquisition.

Although always available to tender advice about buying kittens, a vet will normally see them for the first time at about nine weeks old, when they should be checked from head to toe and any minor problems remedied. At this stage we commonly give advice about exercise, grooming (at least once a day for *all* cats) and diet. It is important to remember that no cat in the wild ever lived on a staple diet of milk and fish, and that the same applies to the household pet. As with babies, the greater variety of food, the better, for this ensures that all essential vitamins, minerals,

etc are provided, with special supplements prescribed if and when they may be necessary.

One of the very common problems detected at this early stage is **parasitic otitis**—an inflammation of the ear canal caused by tiny parasitic mites. It is characterized by a copious amount of dark, crumbly wax, easily visible inside the ear flap and rather resembling peaty soil. Although of uncertain origin, the condition can be readily and permanently cured by means of specific ear drops, usually combined by cleansing of the ear by the vet. Parasitic otitis may be suspected if the kitten scratches its ears continuously. A healthy cat should have absolutely clean ears, with a slightly oily film, and if this is not the case, a visit to the vet is advisable. Do not, under any circumstances, poke any object into a cat's ear.

From about nine weeks of age kittens can, at the moment, be vaccinated against only one disease—**feline infectious enteritis**. This disease is not very common, but when it does occur it is highly infectious and, despite early diagnosis and speedy treatment, almost invariably fatal. It is caused by a virus which

attacks the lining of stomach and bowel, resulting in vomiting, diarrhoea, dehydration (loss of fluids), collapse and death, often within a matter of hours. It is therefore recommended that all cats should be vaccinated, especially those attending cat shows, where a large number of animals are confined within a small area. All good boarding catteries will also refuse to accept a cat which has not been vaccinated against this disease. One or two injections may be required; they are painless and usually without side-effects. They should be boosted from time to time, as advised by the vet.

Treatment for roundworms, discussed later, should also be given at this stage.

Neutering and breeding

The second visit to the surgery, from five months onwards, is most frequently for the purpose of neutering the kitten. The operation of castrating a male kitten is straightforward—a form of routine surgery which most vets undertake daily. It involves a brief stay in the surgery, a short period under anaesthetic, and usually no return visit for stitch removal. There are three good reasons for recommending this operation on the male cat—to minimize the risk of battle scars and possible infections, to reduce the chances of road accidents in the course of sexual forays, and to modify the habit of spraying urine around the house.

Female cats should also be neutered (spayed) in order to prevent unwanted kittens. Cats rarely reach sexual maturity before the age of six months, so the operation can be planned in advance. Again it involves a short period in the surgery and under anaesthetic, although the operation (quite safe) is slightly longer and more complex than in the case of the male. The kitten will come home with some stitches in her flank or on her stomach, and these may, if not self-dissolving, have to be removed in the surgery a week later.

In neither case does the operation cause any discomfort to the tiny patient, there is little if any risk, and there is emphatically no cruelty involved. If done at an early age, there will be no change in the cat's temperament.

If you intend to breed from your queen kitten or if you are certain of being able to care for 'accidental' offspring, you must be aware of the cat's sexual cycle. From the age of about five to six months (but often not until eight or nine) a female cat is receptive to the male, will permit mating and will conceive. When in season she will 'call' (emitting a peculiar, low, throaty growl), show excessive affection both to humans and to other cats, and roll on her back, in addition to displaying other characteristic symptoms. It is unwise to allow a mating before the kitten has matured—say at one year old—for otherwise there may be kittening problems, draining the immature, growing queen of body reserves. Pregnancy varies within normal limits from 60–70 days, a convenient average for calculation being exactly nine weeks.

58

Left
Shorthaired Odd-eyed White.

Right
Shorthaired Blue with very clear yellow eyes. Cats rarely experience eye trouble but when they do it should be promptly treated.

Below
Healthy Chocolate Point Siamese kittens in a strong, draught free basket.

Kittening is rarely complicated, but the owner should be well acquainted with normal behaviour so that veterinary help may be summoned should anything go wrong. Cats are generally very natural, attentive mothers, and it may be necessary to wean the kittens, so that they feed independently, if they have not volunteered to do so by the age of six weeks.

Standard health care
It is important to keep an eye on your cat's teeth after the age of, say, seven years. A hard chalky coating called tartar (or calculus) is deposited from the saliva, especially among cats that are given food they do not need to chew. This alone is probably responsible for more misery (in the form of mouth pain) than any other disease. It is a simple job for your vet, if necessary, to crack off the tartar deposits or thoroughly scale the teeth, dressing the raw gums underneath the tartar and tidying up the mouth. Bad teeth, as such, do not often occur but it is essential to be aware of this particular contingency and all the distress it can cause.

Although cats do not often experience eye trouble, no risks should be taken where vision is concerned, and any ailments that do occur must have prompt treatment. **Conjunctivitis** (pink-eye) is encountered in cats that 'fire-gaze' on the hearthrug, lie in draughty places or simply have irritant dust blown into the eyes. Fortunately, this condition is easily resolved, but it cannot always be differentiated from **corneal ulcers**

59

or scars, although the latter usually occur only in one eye, frequently as a result of a cat fight when a claw may scratch the clear front covering of the eye. This can be difficult to detect without special surgery tests and requires effective and urgent treatment. Symptoms shared in common with conjunctivitis are closure of the eye(s), watering, reddening and pain. It is possible to bathe with cold tea or water on a pad of cotton wool, but inadvisable to use boracic and the like until your vet gives the go-ahead.

Cats often appear at surgery with their 'haws up', when the fine membrane at the inner corner of the eyes covers part of the front of the eye. This is not a specific disease, but may ensue from some other debilitating disease, from parasitic infestations or simply from lack of tip-top condition. The answer is, of course, to diagnose and treat the underlying cause, when the symptom will automatically rectify itself.

Another cause of trouble in cats is the common **abscess**. While this may be acquired as a result of a scratch from a rose thorn or from a cut, the most frequent cause is attack by another animal—usually a

tial to health as well as to looks. If not attended to at least once daily, the coat will mat up to the consistency of carpet felt, removal of which will entail a general anaesthetic at the surgery and probably a semi-bald cat, for it is often necessary to cut and thin fur forcibly to remove all the tufted mats.

In the process of washing their fur, cats—especially Longhaired types—tend to swallow sizeable quantities of hair. Small amounts may pass through without interruption but larger amounts collect in the stomach. While food and fluids can bypass this natural obstruction, the fur is regurgitated from time to time in the form of large sausage-like strings. This is a perfectly natural function, not to be confused with true vomiting, and, in most cases, requires no medication.

Cat claws grow continuously and are kept short by nibbling and scratching. Cutting of claws is necessary, therefore, only in old, infirm cats, or those kept exclusively indoors. Surgical removal of claws is deprecated by vets and is considered inhumane.

Skin disorders also account for a large number of cats attending veterinary surgeries. Characterized by

Below
Grooming all cats is essential and longhairs in particular need daily attention.

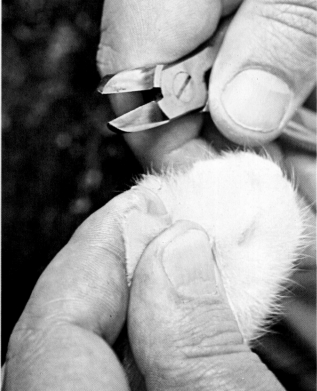

cat, but sometimes a rat, mouse or squirrel. The loose skin of the cat permits infection to drain from the point of injury downwards, so that the abscess is commonly found some distance from the site of the original wound, which may have healed some days beforehand. Emergency home treatment should be aimed at cleansing and applying frequent hot fomentations to the swelling. If serious, however, the abscess may have to be professionally drained and antibiotics prescribed.

Grooming, especially of Longhaired cats, is essen-

irritation to the cat or by hair loss from areas of the body, a clear diagnosis must be established before commencing treatment.

Skin disease in the cat is a vast subject and can only be touched upon here. Initially it may result from parasitic infestations—in order of frequency, **fleas**, **mites** and **lice**. Safe and effective insecticides will quickly rid the cat of its 'visitors' and clear up these conditions. Rather more perplexing, for the cure can be very slow, is **ringworm** or other fungal infection, which requires intense and prolonged therapy to clear the patient. Human contacts may also be at slight risk from such cases, transmission having been known between cat and owner.

Probably the commonest skin disorder, non-infectious in nature, is **military eczema**. This condition is exhibited as scab formation with hair loss down the back from neck to tail, occasionally involving head and belly. There is probably no single cause, but factors that must be eliminated are fleas, dietary imbalance, allergies, excessive or prolonged exposure to hot environments, and hormonal contributions (the disease being most frequent in neutered cats). As for treatment, new drugs have recently made a great difference, so that the condition is no longer the problem it once was.

Internal disorders
Cats of any age may suffer from two quite distinct types of worms which inhabit the bowel. **Tapeworms**, the commoner, are probably less serious and are contracted by the cat swallowing, in the course of grooming itself, a flea or louse which carries the in-

fection. Tapeworms may grow to several feet in length and can cause loss of condition, especially in the coat. They can be detected by inspection of the cat's droppings or of the fur around the anus, where segments of the 'tape' are visible, resembling grains of rice.

Roundworms may pose some threat of infection to humans and should be treated promptly. They may be passed in motions or vomited. Unlike tapeworms, they are usually present in large numbers so that when voided they resemble piles of white earthworms— 2–6 inches long–with an overall appearance of spaghetti. It is advisable to dose a cat with separate preparations, depending on the type of worm, for there is some doubt as to the effectiveness of medicines claiming to rid the cat of both types of worm in a single dose. The simplest doses are in tablet form. Follow instructions on the packet or as given by your vet; and *never* worm a sick cat, a kitten under six weeks of age, or an aged cat, without veterinary advice. While it is wise to worm a new kitten for roundworms, it is unnecessary to give regular doses unless the presence of worms is seen. Cats with tape-

Left
A cat's claws should not have to be clipped as they keep them at a comfortable length themselves by scratching. However, in old age it may be necessary to do it for them.

Right
A beautiful healthy cat on the alert in long grass. A cat's hearing is extremely sensitive, perhaps even more so than that of a dog. Inside the ear there are semi-circular canals on which the cat depends for its balance. It is these that help the cat to right itself when it drops from a height.

worms should be examined for the presence of fleas or lice and, if detected, these should be eradicated in an effort to prevent reinfection of the worms.

Vomiting and **diarrhoea** are not infrequent complaints in the veterinary surgery. While it is obviously important for the vet to diagnose the symptoms and treat them accordingly, it would be fair to say that most may be attributed to chills of dietetic origin or to gastro-enteritis infections quite unrelated to the acute viral enteritis mentioned earlier. As a general rule, initial home treatment should be complete fasting for up to 24 hours. Small amounts of fluid—ideally boiled tap water with a little dissolved glucose—may be permitted if a thirst is apparent. The recovering patient also benefits from dietary consideration, and the best regime is to offer daily four to six small meals of light, easily digested foods, such as cooked eggs, grated cheese, and cooked fish, rabbit or chicken, depending on the cat's preference.

Kidney disease is a common cause of death in older cats. It is nowadays doubted whether the kidneys are actually infected, as was once thought, for it is more likely that death is due to sheer age degeneration of the complex tissues comprising the vital excretory organs. Possibly a malignant cancer condition accounts for a proportion of cats diagnosed as having this terminal **nephritis**. The picture is one of progressively increasing thirst, loss of weight, eventual failing appetite, tendency to vomiting (especially of food), collapse and death. Palliative treatment, if commenced early, will help to prolong life, but the end, regretfully, is inevitable; and it is much less selfish to put an ailing cat out of its misery before the distressing final stages of the illness are reached.

A particular problem, most common in neutered cats, affecting the urinary system, is the acute affliction of **urolithiasis**. This is the building-up in the bladder of fine, gravel-like particles which aggregate to form a complete blockage of the fine urethra through which urine is passed from the bladder to the exterior; this will result in total inability to pass urine and demands immediate attention and skilled veterinary treatment. The cat, often living outdoors, may not show symptoms to its owner unless its predicament is demonstrated by fruitless manoeuvres in a litter tray indoors. This condition may be linked with **cystitis** (inflammation of the bladder), and other factors, such as diet and fluid intake, are regarded as being contributory. Prompt surgical remedy is needed and strict attention should be paid to veterinary advice in order to prevent recurrence, which is always considerably more serious than the first attack.

Finally, a brief mention of four conditions almost specific to the feline species.

Viral respiratory infections are extremely common. They are airborne in droplet form and vary in type from a mild snuffle and sneeze (like the human cold) to a full, serious pneumonia, with dehydration, weakness and lack of appetite. As, at time of writing, there is no effective vaccine available against this generalized infection, speedy attention should be paid to the obvious symptoms which herald this type of disease. It is highly infectious to other cats and great importance can be placed upon home nursing, for the currently available antibiotics used by the vet will only go part-way towards resolving the infection.

Feline infectious anaemia is a slow and progressive loss of circulating red blood cells, as a result of their destruction by a microscopic parasite which may well be transmitted by biting insects such as lice and fleas. Though not thought to be highly infectious to other in-contact cats, it is a long, slow disease, and difficult to diagnose (even from blood smears which *may* show the parasite) until its severest stages have been reached. Fortunately, treatment with specific antibiotics is usually effective, but the one great problem is that the cat may be beyond hope by the time the disease is definite. Suspicious signs are scanty appetite and loss of weight over a period of weeks, visible pallor of gums, lips and eye-lining, and apparent weakness.

Feline infectious peritonitis is another fatal condition of variable course, affecting cats of all ages. It is thought to be caused by a virus and rarely, if ever, responds to treatment. It is usually an acute disease, accompanied by a high temperature and a progressive swelling of the abdomen, due to accumulation of dropsical fluid from the peritoneum which lines the abdomen and its contents. This infection may progress to a pleurisy-like chest involvement, with resultant difficulty in breathing. In the first stages the patient is obviously extremely ill and veterinary diagnosis must be sought immediately.

Lymphosarcoma is a leukaemia-like malignant or cancer condition, affecting cats of all ages, sexes and types. It is known to be caused by a virus and may be transmissible to humans, who would then display symptoms of leukaemia. In its early stages it is impossible to be certain about diagnosis, and confirmatory steps are not always easy. Initially the cat exhibits listlessness, poor appetite and possibly vomiting. Weight loss and a 'haggard' look are also typical. The disease progresses to one of three forms, one attacking the bowel, one the chest contents and one the superficial lymph nodes just underlying the skin in various parts of the body. Symptoms are of a general fast wasting and vary according to the form or site of growths. Any form of treatment to delay the disease, once diagnosed without doubt, is strongly to be condemned. Apart from increasing the risk to human contacts, the outcome of this horrible disease is invariably fatal, and mercy must be shown to the suffering cats.

While it is obviously impossible to cover many aspects of cat ailments, disease and accident in this short space, it is to be hoped that the simplified account given above of the commoner veterinary aspects may be a useful guide to all cat owners.

It is not difficult to recognize when a cat is in peak condition: the eyes, the coat, the activity and general liveliness all indicate how healthy a cat is.

The Mind of the Cat

Angela Sayer

The cat has played a prominent role on the stage of human history. Apart from being cherished as a pet and companion, it has been worshipped as a deity and persecuted as an ally of the devil. Poets, painters and sculptors have paid it honour. It has posed for photographers, starred in films and romped through the pages of fiction, legend and fairy-tale. Quite a tribute, all in all, to an animal with a most singular personality.

What is the reason for man's preoccupation through the ages with this enigmatic little creature? Could it be that he sees something of his own nature mirrored in the moods of his pet? As a species, high on the evolutionary ladder, the cat has amply proved its capacity to adapt successfully to any environment; and this has ensured it of a place in man's affections all over the world.

It is, of course, a mistake to talk of owning a cat; rather the cat consents to live with, and be fed by, its human slave. You cannot punish a cat and get away with it, for the cat will neither forget nor forgive; nor can you force a cat to do anything it has decided not to do, at risk of receiving painful proof of its strength, quite out of proportion to its size!

Maternal devotion

The domestic cat is indeed a formidable adversary, and a mother will nurture and defend her young even at the expense of her own life. A pregnant cat, searching for a suitable nesting niche, was once inadvertently imprisoned in a crate containing engine parts which was subsequently loaded into the hold of a freighter for a long sea voyage. When the crate was broken open at its destination some six weeks later, the little female was discovered in an emaciated condition, but still alive, with two kittens that were blooming and bouncing with health. Evidently she had provided milk for them by licking the protective grease from the machinery in which she was en-

tombed, depleting her own body reserves to the point of near-death. Happily, with loving care from a stevedore's family, she eventually made a complete recovery.

There are many stories of mother cats which have fought to the death against marauders trying to rob them of their kittens. Dogs and feral toms will occasionally attempt to destroy young kittens, and distraught owners have returned home to find the mutilated, dying mother still overlying the babies that she has battled so fiercely to save. Owners of show dogs have had seasonal prospects ruined by allowing their exhibit access to a cat's nest box, the raking claws of an irate little queen having temporarily scarred the inquisitive snout.

A mother cat often has the urge to move her litter to another nest when they are about three to four weeks old. The interesting point about such behaviour is that this is just about the time when the nest or burrow of a wild cat would begin to be soiled by the young kittens. Although the nest box in the home is kept fresh and clean, with newly washed blankets or paper, the cat evidently feels an instinctive need to carry the members of her little family, one by one, to a new abode.

I once had a Lilac Point Siamese queen who always moved her family from the comfort of the warm kitchen to the large, airy bedroom in the attic. Her fourth litter attained the age of four weeks while the attic staircase was being renovated and so blocked off. That did not deter Laretta, however, and when we found the kitchen maternity box empty we started a long search for the missing litter, disregarding the attic, to which access was closed. After a fruitless afternoon, we removed the barricade from the attic stairs and climbed up. To our astonishment, the five little babes were asleep on the bed, but there was no sign of Laretta. We called repeatedly and at last she appeared at the open attic window, thus giving away

her secret. She had carried her kittens, one by one, through the house and up the main staircase, along the hall and out of the landing window, across a sloping roof to the dormer window, and finally into her selected place of refuge!

Early lessons

A mother teaches her kittens to eat solid foods, to play, to fight and to hunt. If she is given a mouse-sized piece of meat, she will proudly take it to her litter, put it down in front of them and give a short, sharp 'prrrp', which encourages the youngsters to emerge from the box to investigate the 'kill'. They may even lick or taste the meat, although not old enough to chew it. Then the queen will pat the morsel, so that it skitters a few inches across the floor. The babies' eyes follow it with interest and some of the bolder ones will perhaps toddle after the meat and place a possessive paw on it.

As the kittens grow, the queen will flash her tail from side to side, prompting the youngsters to pounce on 'prey'. She sets the example by tossing small pieces of meat or balls of paper into the air and then diving upon them as they land, 'prrrping' to the kittens all the while, until they follow suit. When she feels they should be weaned, she will settle down, concealing all her teats and not adopting the characteristic nursing pose which enables them to suckle. If they nuzzle and push at her, trying to nurse, she will eventually jump up onto a chair or shelf, well out of their reach.

Purring, weaving, rubbing and kneading are all signs of contentment and relaxation. The kitten begins to purr while still suckling, the sound being continuous as it breathes in and out, stopping momentarily as the milk is swallowed. As the cat grows, purring is retained as a friendly, contact-establishing sound and is often accompanied by the kneading movements of the front paws which the young kitten adopts while nursing.

The domestic cat frequently rubs lips and body against human legs, and weaves past in such a way that the tail comes in contact with the side of a table or the legs of a chair. In performing these commonplace actions the cat is, in fact, marking its territory in a very subtle way. A number of scent glands are present on various parts of the cat's body, and although such scents cannot be detected by the human nose they provide identification signals for other cats. When the cat rubs and weaves, it deposits odours from the glands on all points of contact, serving to warn off strange cats in the area. It is interesting to see how the cat rubs and weaves possessively around its owner's legs, especially when food is being prepared.

A friend's cat, renowned for these habits, decided to claim ownership to a new electric fire by rubbing his lips and flanks along the teak surround. As he turned to repeat the procedure, his tail tip flicked between the safety bars and immediately ignited, causing him to flee from the room, tail ablaze. Fortunately he was quickly wrapped in a towel and the

only injury was to his pride in sporting a blackened, brush-like appendage where his beautiful fluffy tail had been. He spat and growled at the fire for several weeks, until his new hair grew through, and never again tried to put his mark in that vicinity.

Territorial sense
Entire male cats have the habit of marking out their territory distinctly by spraying urine against any conspicuous object encountered in a daily constitutional stroll. The scent of the urine is most distasteful to humans and it is for this reason that the majority of pet males are neutered. The operation effectively removes the odour from the urine and decreases the need for the cat to spray when marking its possessions. Pedigree males, having once marked the outdoor accommodation in which they are confined (usually a large, heated hut with an attached, wired-in run) will stop spraying until visitors arrive. Many a stud owner has been embarrassed or amused, depending on his

nature, when a beloved male has abruptly turned its back on a visitor, lifted its tail and directed a well-aimed jet at knee level.

A cat investigating the scent trail left by another cat will exhibit a strange and very noticeable reaction. Its eyes half close, its mouth opens and it raises its head as if carefully savouring the scent. This, in fact, is literally what is happening. Such behaviour is known as the flehman reaction and allows the scent to be drawn up to a special olfactory organ in the upper palate. The organ connects with a part of the brain which flashes back the vital information as to whether this particular scent has been experienced previously, and whether it has been left by friend or enemy.

Contrasts in play
Playing is a pastime that brings pleasure both to cat and owner; but different breeds seem to have their individual preferences for certain types of game. Longhaired cats have a particular fondness for

Cats and kittens spend a great deal of time washing and cleaning themselves. The first lesson kittens learn from their mother is how to wash and how to do it thoroughly. They also enjoy washing each other and deliberately choose places where they can never reach to wash themselves. A cat's tongue is rough and suited to going to the roots of even a long coat, and sometimes the cat is quite wet after a long and concentrated washing session.

squeezing into small boxes, usually a size smaller than would comfortably fit their ample frames. They also love to sit on chairs pushed snugly under the table, and to crawl into any object that is rolled up, such as a carpet or a length of linoleum. British Shorthairs derive special enjoyment from playing with pingpong balls and shuttlecocks, becoming adept dribblers and batsmen. They also love playing a game which the owner has to initiate by covering them gently with a large open sheet of newspaper. Then, with body crouched, they will dash from side to side, creating draughts that lift the paper up and bring it floating down again. Only a paw or tail tip shows from time to time as the paper flutters and bounces around the room.

Siamese cats clearly prefer some human participation in their games. One favourite pastime is to lie on their back and allow themselves to be propelled across the floor. A slippery linoleum surface is ideal for this game, for having slithered across to the other side of

There is very little kittens and cats do not know about charming their owners; by one means or another they end up having their own way.

the room, they will tear back to the starting point and demand another go. The Foreign breeds also enjoy playing with a large paper bag which has a small tear in one corner. When the edges of the bag are pushed together so that the back is held open, and it is placed on the floor, the cat will fling itself from the opposite side of the room headlong into the bag, attempting to leap through the slit at the end. The pointed nose sticks fast and there will be several minutes of rolling and cavorting before the cat reduces the bag to shreds.

Most cats love pipe-cleaner 'spiders', made by twisting together four pipe-cleaners and securing them with a piece of wool. In order to avoid scratching the cat's eyes, the end of the 'feet' should be turned back and then the 'legs' can be bent into a hooked shape so as to give a chillingly realistic appearance. I have known Siamese cats to keep such a plaything for years, taking it to bed each night and away on holiday to the boarding cattery.

One of my early Siamese, Rosie, had a series of spiders and would play at retrieving them until we were exhausted. She would give us a short recovery period, then thrust the soggy object into the nearest palm and wait expectantly for it to be thrown, preferably onto a bookshelf or behind the settee so that she could spend some time searching before pouncing for the kill. Alternatively, we would hide the spider under a rug or behind a cushion while she was out of the room. It was fascinating to watch her methodical search, using sight and smell, until she found her favourite toy.

Once, when Rosie was very ill, not having eaten of her own free will for several weeks, the vet told us that there was nothing more he could do for her. Desolate, we carried her around the garden, trying to arouse her interest in life and persuade her to fight back, but to no avail. As I sat nursing her in a shawl beside the fire, I absentmindedly picked up her old toy. 'Spider, Rose!' I said, and immediately her eyes opened, her ears pricked and she made an attempt at her juddering, bird-catching cry. I gave her the spider and she settled into a normal sleep. When she awoke she ate a small meal, and from that day gradually recovered her health and spirit.

The hunter

Nothing in the wild rivals the cat for the deadly accuracy and speed of its hunting; and no other species appears to take such delight in tormenting its prey. These ancestral instincts clearly emerge in the daily activities of the domestic cat. Play teaches the cat to think fast and to develop quick reactions which, in turn, train him to be a skilful hunter. Unfortunately, the victims are often beautiful garden birds, and it is virtually impossible to convey to your pet cat that although you approve of him keeping the rat and mouse population under control, you do not appreciate being presented with a mangled mass of feathers while you are busy grilling the breakfast bacon.

A bird, however, represents a real challenge to the cat's ingenuity. After the first few failures have at last

Left
Two Siamese-Rex kittens – a Tortie Point and a Red Point. All cats do a lot of rubbing and weaving, particularly when asking for food.

Below
The same Red Point Siamese-Rex and a smiling red self Rex.

Right
A handsome Tortoiseshell defying anyone to disturb him.

convinced him that the prey can fly up and away, he will develop a special technique for the final pounce. After the long, careful stalk, he will so judge his run and culminating leap as to compensate for the bird's take-off and trajectory. Lucifer, our large Foreign Red cat, had worked out this technique so accurately that he could sit on the outhouse roof and take the starlings in mid-air as they left their nests in the eaves.

It is not only the svelte Shorthairs that are so agile and cunning in this respect. We had a Longhaired Tortoiseshell, Coppapoppett, whose mouth would water whenever she sighted moorhen chicks on our small lake. The birds wisely nested on the little island in the centre of the lake and the nestlings took to the water as soon as they were hatched. Poppett would judder and drool as soon as the first fluffy little coal-black chicks appeared. We had to confine her to a wired run for three or four weeks until the young birds learned the meaning of fear, fleeing for the safety of the water at the least sign of danger. Not in the least deterred, the cat would lie in ambush for the half-grown chicks as they wandered onto the lawn, soon realizing that, rather than fly off, they preferred to scuttle along on their lanky legs back to the water. One day, I watched her getting into position at an angle between a solitary, grazing bird and the water's edge. As the moorhen saw its danger and scampered off to safety, she ran, not directly at the bird, but along a carefully planned tangential path so that they met with an audible thud on the bank. Luckily I was able

to rescue this particular bird, but of the seven chicks hatched, only one lived to maturity.

In order to warn birds of her approach, we hung a couple of bells around Poppett's neck. This worked very well for a fortnight or so, until we found a dead thrush on the doormat. Poppett dashed past us indoors, bells still intact but not jangling. The mystery was solved when the builders working in the yard told us that they had seen her systematically rolling her neck from side to side in their sand heap. Sure enough, she had so jammed both bells with damp sand that the strikers could not function!

Curiously, although Poppett was so fond of fresh bird meat, she never attempted to stalk or catch any of our fantail pigeons. On the contrary, she would sit in the middle of some twenty or so of the birds, crunching up their meal, and they would show not the slightest sign of being afraid of her.

The developing brain
Recent research into the cat's brain development has shown that slight stress during early kittenhood helps to develop more active brain cells at a critical period in life, and also that frequent handling from the age of six to twelve weeks can determine the temperament of the adult cat. Involved as I am in the forming of new varieties of cats, I have had experimental litters over the years and had often noticed that the 'unusual' kittens in the family would grow up to be more friendly and intelligent than their 'ordinary' litter-

Right
Even if you are an experienced cat breeder or a prospective cat owner with pre-conceived ideas, it is still easy to underestimate the appeal of a very young kitten such as this. If you are not ready to have a cat with you for years to come, you must resist the temptation.

Below
A Burmese 'talking' as he walks through the grass. He is probably complaining about the unco-operative behaviour of the local mice.

mates. I had always wondered whether this was due to some kind of hybrid vigour; but in the light of the new evidence, I now realize that it was always the 'new' kittens that were carefully checked several times daily and given extra handling at the critical period. Genetically, they were no cleverer than their litter-mates, but the early stress of prolonged handling and the later additional handling had clearly developed their full brain potential.

Jackie was the seventh kitten in a Siamese litter. He was born almost hairless and half the size of his brothers and sisters. Weak and weedy, he could not fight his way to the nipple, and by rights he should have died. Instead, I hand-reared him, feeding him every two hours, day and night, from an eye-dropper with evaporated milk and glucose. He grew into the strangest kitten I ever saw—all tummy, eyes and voice—and he could not bear to be left alone. I took him everywhere with me in a pigskin shoulder-bag, almost zippered across, and occasionally he would push his sooty little nose out and announce that it was mealtime.

At thirteen weeks of age, the litter was sold and Jackie, half normal size and still virtually hairless, was even now spending most of his time in my bag. We eventually asked my mother, who lived in the country, surrounded by the paddocks of a vast stud farm of thoroughbred horses, to give him a home. Nobody thought that Jackie would thrive or even live for long, but he surprised us all. On his first birthday he weighed in at a lusty nine pounds, his coat silky and immaculate, his points a dense, glossy seal-brown, and his sapphire eyes sparkling with health. He came up the path to the door, swaying importantly from side to side, the muscles in his neck standing up with the strain of carrying a large hare straddled between his legs. From that day Jackie decided that his purpose in life was to be a mighty hunter.

After one Sunday lunch, we washed up and put out the scraps, including half a Yorkshire pudding, into the pig-pail. About half an hour later we saw Jackie dragging the Yorkshire pudding onto the lawn, placing it carefully on the ground by a circular rose-bed. We watched incredulously as he settled down behind the screen of roses and waited until the starlings came down to the bait, when he began picking them off one by one.

Jackie's favourite pastime was to go on country walks with us, but he hated wet grass. So while we walked the rides between the oak-fenced paddocks of the stud farm, Jackie kept pace, treading sedately along the top rails, growling with annoyance each time he had to jump down to cross a ride or traverse some rough ground or grass.

The language of cats

Of all animals, the domestic cat surely least deserves the designation 'dumb'. Not only does it use its voice most expressively to communicate with other cats and with human companions, but it also employs a complex system of facial attitudes and bodily postures to convey very clearly and unmistakably its every wish and intention.

It expresses fright in several ways—its pupils dilate, its eyes flick rapidly from side to side, its coat and tail fluff up, and it turns its body, similarly ruffled, sideways so as to appear as big as possible, hoping thus to conceal fear. Warnings to would-be intruders are conveyed by the lashing of a tautly held tail, a withdrawal of the ears, a narrowing of the eyes and perhaps a menacing growl or two. The cat shows indifference by holding the tail straight up but in a relaxed state, usually following this by turning deliberately back and possibly undertaking a perfunctory grooming session. Extreme agitation is indicated by the tail in a rigid horizontal position, ears flat to the head and back slightly arched. This may be accompanied by muttered growls and much licking of lips and salivation.

The voice of the cat can be very expressive indeed. Each has its own unique range of mews, purrs and growls which an observant owner will soon recognize. There are the standard everyday demands to be let out, to come in and to be fed; and there are other noises to announce the approach of a stranger, to warn of impending danger or perhaps to herald a storm. The sight of a bird flying overhead or even glimpsed through a window elicits a special sound. An excited miaow punctuates play; and the mother cat reserves an entire range of special talk for her kittens. The kittens, in turn, each give out a different distress cry which may be heard and acted upon by the perceptive owner.

Cats, of course, have their own language of love, such as the caterwauling stimulation of a group of males squaring up to one another around a young female in oestrus, and the excited yip of the successful suitor as he makes his preliminary advances to his intended mate. Both male and female croon gently to each other when mating is imminent; a sharp purring call follows; and the growl of the mated female, loud and alarming, is quite unmistakable.

Perhaps the most endearing feature of the cat's character is its ability to relax utterly and completely, creating a calm, peaceful atmosphere, an aura of serenity around itself, even in the most disorderly, tempestuous household. How soothing it is, after a busy day, to sit quietly with a purring, sleepy cat upon one's knees, letting the same soporific feeling spread through one's whole being. How easy it is to understand why, when the little foraging cat first crept into the warmth of Stone Age man's fire, it was not eaten but welcomed as a companion. And no wonder this furry creature, with its immaculate habits and totally independent nature, went on to win a measure of human love and devotion unequalled by any other domesticated animal.

Sometimes a cat's curiosity overcomes his hunting instinct.

Cat Behaviour

Angela Sayer

It is difficult to define intelligence, especially in an animal such as the cat. Most cat lovers, however, will insist that not only are cats intelligent, but that their own pet is certainly the most remarkable that ever lived.

Intelligence tests have been devised and used by researchers in animal behaviour. Subjects of most species have been used, but it was found that cats were extremely difficult to assess, for they were not unduly influenced by the action/reward processes that the scientists employed. The cat is less motivated by the basic drives such as hunger, thirst and fear than other animals, and this explains also why it is so difficult to train felines to perform tricks. Whereas a dog will beg, or perform other feats if rewarded with sugar or a biscuit, a cat would not regard a mere food morsel as sufficient recompense for demeaning itself.

If confined in a strange environment, the cat's instinct is to withdraw into itself. It would rather starve than eat, especially if the food is strange or presented in an unusual way. This is why the normal forms of intelligence testing for animals, fail with feline subjects.

In testing learning ability in the rat, for example, the creature is confined in apparatus known as a Skinner Box. There are various designs, but basically, the box is a large, smooth cube and one wall is fitted with a lever, perhaps a small light bulb, and a food dispenser. One wall of the box allows observation, but the subject is not aware of this. The operator watches the rat and when it approaches the lever, presses a button which flashes on the light bulb and simultaneously dispenses a tiny food pellet. By careful conditioning the operator reinforces the behaviour of the rat, rewarding 'correct' moves only, until the creature obtains its own food by pressing the lever a set number of times.

If a cat is placed in such a devise, it first explores the interior and tries to get out, pushing and scratching at the sides and scrabbling at the corners. It then sits down, exhibiting signs of stress. If food is dispensed, the cat may be startled, but will certainly not eat. It sits, hunched and dejected, until it is released. In other tests, puzzle boxes are used. These have levers and bolts inside, enabling the cat to let itself out if it can learn to manipulate them. Most cats get out fairly quickly, for in the initial escape attempt processes, the levers are pressed and the door gives a little. Once a cat has learned to escape from the box, it remembers the technique and if replaced, even after a few days, quickly remembers the sequence of movements necessary to open the door.

Cats learn tricks of their own, and many can open windows and doors and some even learn the special skills required to ease open the heavy door of the refrigerator. Door opening is usually possible only if the handle is of the latch type. The cat learns to jump up to the handle, grasp it, then with just the right amount of leverage, cause the door to swing open. This technique becomes so sophisticated in an agile cat that the whole sequence from being on one side of the door, to arriving safely on the other, happens in one fluid sequence of motion.

Most cat owners assert that their pets are possessed of extra senses. For example, cats seem to know exactly when their owners are about to arrive home, even if it is at an unusual time. If observed, they stretch, yawn and go to sit by the door, just prior to their arrival. Cats also know when the owners are going on holiday, and many simply disappear the day before the suitcases are brought down from store.

Many fascinating stories have been documented of cats returning to their old homes after removal to new houses, sometimes hundreds of miles away. It has been proved that they have covered great distances over strange, and sometimes, hostile terrain. While a built-in instinct for direction-finding can be deduced in the cat, a high degree of intelligence must

A Black Persian

also be present to enable a pampered pet to endure the hardships, to forage and to find shelter, all without being observed, on such a trek.

In hunting, cats have been seen to set traps for birds. This is rare, but has been proved several times by observation and by photographic evidence. The cat is seen to take a piece of bread or other scraps, and to place it in the garden near a shrub or bush. Concealed, the cat patiently waits until birds descend to feed, when he picks one off for his own dinner or sport. The patience shown by the cat in waiting for its prey to appear is quite remarkable. It will sit for hours if necessary, quite motionless apart from an occasional twitch of the whiskers, waiting by rabbit or mouse holes.

In the home, cats learn to live in harmony with their humans and soon learn what sort of behaviour is expected of them. To a certain degree, they stick to the rules, and when they do break them, they make sure that no-one sees. For example, cats not allowed to walk all over the tops of kitchen units spend their lives contentedly at floor level. When their owner comes home from shopping however, she often finds trails of damp paw prints tracing a network over the formica tops. No-one ever sees the cat stealing the gravy, the cream, the butter or the cheese. If the room is left unattended for a moment, then re-entered, the cat will still be in its basket, but, mysteriously, one of the jugs or dishes may be found to be empty.

Those people who detest cats, make derogatory remarks about their intelligence, supporting their arguments by referring to the cat's aversion to training, or coming when called. It is a matter for conjecture however, whether this shows a lack of intelligence. Could it not be that the cat is clever enough to know that only by ignoring such commands can it maintain its total independence and enigmatic air? The brain of the cat is highly evolved, similar in structure to that of man, and the areas involved in memory and learning ability are well defined.

The central nervous system

As in all mammals, the central nervous system, consisting of the brain and spinal cord, controls and co-ordinates the activities of the cat. All information received by the senses is constantly monitored and sorted for degrees of importance. Urgent signals are acted upon immediately, unimportant signals are discarded, while some information is passed to the areas of the brain concerned with memory, and stored away for future use. The brain and nervous system of the cat are designed to make it among the most perceptive and alert of all mammals. The complete system, developed through millions of years of evolution, has produced a highly efficient, powerfully made animal, built for survival.

The evolution of the cat's brain was slow, and even today shows characteristics found in very primitive brains. There are three distinct and clearly defined areas, the forebrain, the midbrain and the hindbrain, each of which has separate functions. In vertebrates, the forebrain is concerned mainly with the sense of smell. It is also the seat of the thalamus which deals with impulses sent by the spinal cord, and the hypothalamus which controls the processes of internal regulation. The midbrain consists largely of the optic lobes and deals with signals stimulated by sight. The hindbrain consists of the cerebellum, controlling balance, and the medulla, an enlargement of the end of the spinal cord, which controls respiration and circulation.

As brains evolved, new growths were built on the original core, each new brain structure evolving as an addition and modification of the older brain. In the cat's brain, the primitive core may still be found, plus the old brain centre, or limbic system. Overlying these structures can be seen the new brain very similar to that of man. All the sections of the brain are interdependent. In the centre, the old core performs the same functions as it did aeons ago, of regulating the endocrine glands, controlling the respiration and metabolism and maintaining homeostasis. Homeostasis is the key to life and means that processes such as temperature, blood pressure and heart beats are carefully controlled to work at steady rates, the balance being regulated by feedback mechanisms located in the hypothalamus.

The limbic system controls digestion, and even more important, it takes care of activities requiring sequential responses. These include such processes as hunting, eating, mating and escaping from danger. All these functions must be carried out in the correct sequence to be effective, and so this part of the brain network is vital for the survival of the cat.

Two large, symmetrical hemispheres at the top of the brain are made up of many nerve cells. The left hemisphere controls the functions of the right side of the body, while the right hemisphere controls those of the left side. Though a deep groove separates the two hemispheres, they are, in fact, connected by nerves and correlate incoming information.

In the cat, as in man, the most recently evolved brain area, the cerebral cortex, is deeply wrinkled or convoluted. This area resembles a giant, shelled walnut, and developed in this way to give a greater surface area to the brain, without the necessity of increasing the size of the skull. The front section of the cortex controls the legs and other extremities, while the main areas of the body are controlled by the central section. The rear portion of the cortex houses areas important to sight, and the processing of visual stimuli. Complex regions concerned with learning and memory are also present in the cortex. Because the cat's brain is so similar to that of man, the animal has been used extensively in scientific research. The results of experiments on cats have provided knowledge enabling the neurosurgeons of today to correct many serious, brain disorders in human beings.

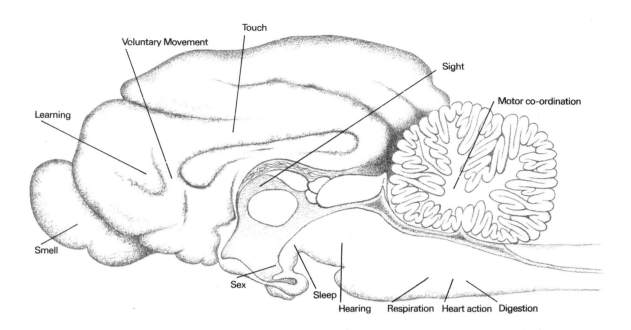

Touch
Voluntary Movement
Sight
Motor co-ordination
Learning
Smell
Sex
Sleep
Hearing
Respiration
Heart action
Digestion

The structure of the cat's brain is typically mammalian, and thus similar in many respects to the brain of man. This cross section shows which areas are responsible for vital functions.

Neurons and nerves

Neurons are the specialized cells which hold the keys of learning and memory, as well as performing all other mental functions. Each neuron has a nucleus, and the components found also in normal body, or somatic cells. The nucleus is contained within the bulging body of the neuron, from which project long, 'fingers' called dendrites. The dendrites act as receivers, picking up activity from neighbouring cells. The cell transmits its own activity to other neurons through a long fibre, the axon. Each cell is wired, similar to an electrical circuit, and the nerve impulses generally move in one direction. They travel from their reception by the dendrite through the body of the cell and then out along the axon to the dendrites of adjacent neurons. They are transported rapidly until they reach their destination, at a gland or muscle. Although neurons all have the same general features, they vary considerably in size and shape, depending on their position in the body.

Nerves consist of bundles of dendrites or axons from many neurons. Axons from hundreds of neurons may connect with the dendrites of each particular neuron, causing the wiring system to be extremely complex. The junction points, known as synapses, are like tiny fuseboxes, transmitting impulses through the neuronal network of the nerve. The transmissions are chemical in action and highly complicated in function. It is a knowledge of this chemistry that enables the use of anaesthetics and analgesics, which work by blocking the transmission of impulses at the synaptic junctions.

The peripheral nervous system

Nerves which lie outside the spinal cord are known as peripheral or somatic nerves and act upon the striped body muscles attached to the skeleton. These nerves consist of mixed afferent and efferent fibres. Afferent fibres convey incoming information to the spinal cord from the skin, pads, whiskers, muscles and joints, which is then transmitted to the brain. Return messages sent from the motor region of the brain to the spinal cord are then carried by the efferent fibres to muscles, causing them to react. Each area of the cat's body has its own, corresponding section of the spinal cord to act as a depot for receiving and giving its nerve messages.

Self-regulating activities such as circulation and digestion, which continue whether the animal is awake or asleep, are controlled by the autonomic nervous system. This has two clear divisions and the nerve fibres which form them are known as sympathetic and parasympathetic, being commonly antagonistic in their functions. Sympathetic fibres burst into action when the cat is emotionally aroused. They cause the heart rate to speed up, the arteries of the heart and muscles to dilate, and the arteries of the skin and internal organs to contract. These fibres also cause secretion of hormones into the blood stream, so that the animal is immediately prepared for action, be it fight or flight.

The parasympathetic system works differently, affecting only one organ at a time, and is employed in digestive functions and the conservation of the body's resources. Both systems often work together, or may function in sequence. An example of the latter effect is seen in the sex act of the male cat. First, the parasympathetic system causes excitement and the erection of the penis, while the sympathetic system is employed to allow ejaculation. The entire autonomic nervous system is highly developed in the cat for, as a solitary creature, it has to rely entirely on its own powers of sensitivity and co-ordination for survival. Because domestication has done little to modify the basic makeup of the cat feral and stray cats have been able to thrive in hostile conditions.

Mating behaviour

Although most cats breed in the spring, the species does not have set periods of oestrus, unlike bitches which come into heat every six months as a general rule. Some varieties of pedigree cat, in particular the Siamese, and other related breeds, would have three or four litters a year if allowed their freedom. The weather plays an important part in the sexual cycle of most female cats, if they live a normal life with the freedom of a garden. Cats kept indoors, in centrally heated accommodation and subjected to long hours of light conditions seem to breed at any season of the year. Feral and farm cats keep to a more usual pattern of reproduction, geared to the survival of the kittens, having one litter in late February and another in June. If the autumn is mild, yet another litter may be produced early in October.

After reaching sexual maturity, both male and female cats continue to breed throughout life. The prime years of fertility seem to be between two and seven years in the male cat and between two and eight years in the female. Very old queens still continue to give birth to kittens, but usually only once a year, and the litter consists of only one or two kittens. Old male cats, kept entire, continue to range looking for calling queens, but when past their prime, avoid fighting other males for the female's favours. Pedigree stud males fare better, possibly because they do not have to take part in fights, and also enjoy a better standard of living than free-ranging males.

Unless constant calling and the resultant weight loss is endangering the health of a young, pedigree queen, she should not be allowed to mate until about ten months of age. This means that she will be one year old by the time the kittens are born, and physically she should have attained maturity. Young queens must be nurtured during their first pregnancy, for the formation of the kitten in the uterus takes a heavy toll of their calcium reserves. This substance must be replaced by feeding a sensible diet or unusual behavioural effects may result. Queens seriously lacking in calcium at the time of confinement may attack the new-born kittens and even kill them. The lack of calcium has an effect on junctions in the brain. This prevents the transmission of the messages necessary for the body to release the hormones which start the flow of milk and stimulate the mothering instinct.

The long process of lactation also draws on the calcium reserves of the queen, which must be replenished in her diet. In the wild, cats get calcium by eating the whole of their natural prey. The calcium is present in the skeletons of small rodents and birds. Pet cats are often fed only on expensive muscle meat and this does not provide sufficient quantities of the important mineral. When a queen is allowed to breed too frequently, the calcium level in her body gradually drops if not replenished between litters. Eventually she may suffer from lactational tetany while feeding

a new litter, and will go rapidly into a state of shock, followed by death within hours.

Oestrus in the female cat is easy to recognize and consists of four stages. First there is the *pro-oestrus* in which the reproductive organs undergo changes in preparation for mating, fertilization and pregnancy. The queen is restless, extra affectionate when handled, but paces the house and often looks out of the window, gazing far into the distance. A very slight swelling of the vulva may be noticed by an observant owner at this time. About five days later *oestrus* begins and will last about seven days. The queen is very agitated and rolls about on the floor. She will cry and wail and try to get out of the house at every opportunity. As this period reaches its peak, her cries will become more urgent and take on a deeper note. Her rolling will become more violent and she will adopt the mating position if her back is touched. If mating does not take place, the third stage, *metoestrus* begins as the reproductive system relaxes gradually until *anoestrus*, the resting stage between cycles, is reached.

The male cat is not subject to periods of heat and so can mate at any time, having reached sexual maturity. He is attracted to the queen by her call and by her evocative scent. Calling queens do not emit an odour perceptible to human noses, but the subtle scent carries a considerable distance and is easily picked up by male cats in the neighbourhood. It is thought that the higher notes of her cry, inaudible to human ears, are also particularly attractive to the male cat, while her posturing excites him ready for mating.

When breeding pedigree cats as opposed to natural mating, the owner of the queen contacts the owner of the stud male at the first signs of oestrus. Arrangements are made to take the female to the stud on the second or third day of the heat period, or when the queen adopts the crouched, mating position when stroked. Male cats used for stud work are housed in large, airy sheds complete with spacious, wired runs. There is a small pen inside the shed, into which the queen is placed on arrival, in order to settle down. Cats do not take to each other at first sight, and it would be dangerous to allow the stud and queen access to each other at this stage. The female would resent the touch of the male, although in full breeding condition, and may attack him violently.

Within the pen, the queen relaxes and then starts to roll. She cries softly at first, then with increasing volume until the sound is almost a growl. The male cat watches intently, ears and whiskers alert, and makes crooning sounds to her. As her rolls and calls increase in intensity, he makes small movements towards her, until they are close together, only separated by the wire mesh. At this stage, the partition is removed and the cats are allowed to mate.

The queen adopts the mating position, head on her forepaws and her hindquarters raised with the tail held stiffly to one side. The male runs to her from one side and grasps the loose skin behind her neck in his

In mating, the tom will hold tightly onto the queen until he has finished.

jaws. He places one foreleg either side of her shoulders and treads at her haunches alternately with his hindlegs, encouraging her to raise her back even more. As soon as the queen is in the correct position, the male curves his back round her body and effects penetration, upon which the queen gives a loud, growling cry. At this stage an inexperienced male cat releases the queen, but the wiser, older tom holds tightly to her scruff until he has ejaculated. Then he releases the queen and leaps well away. The queen snarls, hisses and growls and turns rapidly to strike at the male, before rolling vigorously about on her back. After a moment or so, both cats sit quietly and wash and groom their genital areas. Very soon, both cats will be ready to mate again. The queen is kept with the male for about four days.

In the wild, several male cats are attracted to the queen by her scent and cries. She enjoys the attention and holds court. Much caterwauling is heard as the male cats decide their order of superiority, and silent, bitter battles are fought by the suitors. The queen appears to revel in the furore she has caused and eventually is mounted by the dominant male of the group. After mating, she soon rolls and calls again and may be mated by the same tom or by the next one in order of dominance. She will be mated many times during her oestrus period, and probably by several different males.

To the entire male cat, at liberty to come and go as he pleases, his home is merely a place to shelter and to acquire food. He is motivated mainly by his strong sexual urges most of the time, and spends his days in territorial marking, mating and fighting, punctuated with long periods of rest and recuperation. Tom cats fight very fiercely and their long canine teeth inflict deep wounds which heal on the skin surface trapping bacteria in the tissues below which soon form abcesses.

On meeting, two tom cats square up to each other, puffing out their already thickened jowls and hunching up the shoulder muscles. The fur along the spine and on the tail becomes erect, and walking stretched onto tip-toe, each cat tries to present the largest, most forbidding picture possible. If no female is present, the males may just sniff at each other and pass by, otherwise, they turn sideways on and perform a great threat display before attacking. The threat display consists of lip-smacking while emitting muffled growls, and the less experienced of the two may salivate excessively. Both males lunge at their opponent's throat region and bite hard. Locked together, the combatants roll about on the ground, screeching and raking each other with the long claws of the hind paws and tearing loose lumps of fur. When they break, one may attempt to run away and may well receive a deep bite at the root of the tail. Veterinary surgeons commonly treat full males for four abcesses around the tail and testes where the four canine teeth have punctured and almost met through the flesh. This bite is considered the *coup de grace* of the victorious male.

On subsequent meetings it is fairly usual for the dominant male to assert his position in the neighbourhood by merely biting other males on the neck, mounting them, letting go and walking, stiff-legged away. A submissive male that does not want to fight, possibly remembering a previous beating, either takes steps to avoid encounters with a dominant male, or on confrontation, crouches, mews and presents his scruff to the adversary. Cats rarely indulge in homosexual behaviour, and the action of mounting by a dominant male is merely to show his superiority. Males rarely fight with females, but female cats occasionally fight one another, usually through jealousy, over kittens or food.

Maternal behaviour

From the time of adolescence, the female cat is tuned to motherhood, and persistent in her desire to mate. She is a model mother, hiding her babies away from enemies and keeping them well-fed, warm, clean and contented from the moment of birth. She cares for them in a dedicated manner until they are independent, able to feed themselves and face the world alone. Male cats do not take any part in the rearing of kittens. Their role in life is solely that of fertilization. As female cats are spontaneous ovulators, they only shed ripe ova after mating. If allowed to continue having periods of oestrus without mating ever taking place, problems can arise such as eventual sterility, or periods of false pregnancy.

After mating, when conception has taken place and the tiny foetuses have implanted in the uterine wall, the hormones secreted by her glands give rise to certain patterns of behaviour in the queens. She is constantly alert to danger, eats well and very selectively, picking grass and herbs if allowed her freedom. She hunts with a sense of purpose, and eats her prey rather than using it as a plaything. She grooms herself even more meticulously than usual and tries to take her rest on a high shelf or concealed in a dark corner or box.

As the pregnancy reaches its end, her grooming sessions increase and she pays particular attention to her enlarging breasts. At this time she may be unable to groom her anal area, due to her bulky size, and a thoughtful owner will wipe the region for her, each day, using a damp tissue. The queen explores every possible kittening site, and should be provided with a large box with clean paper inside, that she can tear and shred into a nest.

When choosing a spot for giving birth to her litter, the queen does not always use good judgment, and kittens have been produced in the most unsuitable places—under floorboards, on top of high cupboards, even down rabbit-holes. It is a good plan to confine the cat to a suitable room when the kittens are due, and to make sure that the box provided is dark and warm inside. The room should be in a quiet part of the house and no small children or dogs should be allowed to bother the queen at this time.

When the birth is imminent, the queen paces restlessly, and if it is her first litter, she may sit and strain on her toilet tray, looking behind her occasionally with a puzzled expression. Eventually, with the right encouragement, she will go to her box and start second stage labour. Usually she will lie on her side and the contractions may be clearly seen as she pushes her hindlegs against the side of the box. When the head or rump of the kitten is presented, she may sit up and strain downwards until it is expelled. Kittens are presented head first or tail first, seemingly at random. Breech births rarely cause problems in the cat. Before the first kitten is expelled, an empty sac of fluid may be passed and causes concern to novice breeders. This is quite in order and prepares the way through the birth passage for the kitten. Often this sac is licked away in sections by the queen and so is not observed by the owner.

The membranes of the sac are licked from the newborn kitten by the mother's rough tongue, which also serves to encourage the tiny creature to take its first breath of air and to expand its lungs. The placenta emerges and is usually eaten by the queen, who also chews along the umbilical cord to a point about one inch from the kitten's body. The rest of the litter follow at irregular intervals and are usually dealt with in the same, business-like manner. When the last kitten is born the queen pays particular attention to her own toilet, and assiduously cleans her legs and flanks. Having thoroughly licked her litter dry, she gathers them all to her and, lying on one side and curling her body to encircle the kittens, encourages them to suckle. Purring, she relaxes and rests and will probably stay in the nest for at least twelve hours.

It seems that the instincts in the mother cat for hunting and eating prey are hormonally suppressed at the time of giving birth. This is probably to ensure that the kittens are not eaten, and also explains why cats which have just kittened will readily accept virtually any small animals for fostering. Even those which would be quickly dispatched at any other time are taken and treated as kittens while she is in this state. Baby rats, squirrels and hedgehogs as well as tiny breeds of pups, have all been fostered by cats. In the wild, the eating of the enriched placentas would provide enough nourishment for the queen to enable her to remain without further food for at least 24 hours. It is interesting to note that queens which do eat the placentas have a better milk supply than those which, possibly due to an unnatural environment, seem to be unsure of their role during the processes of birth.

It is rare for a queen to leave her new litter for any length of time, and she only goes away from the nest to relieve herself and to obtain food. The kittens only urinate and defecate when stimulated to do so by the licking of the queen, which she carries out each time they have nursed. The excreted matter is swallowed by the queen all the time the kittens are ingesting only milk. Thus the nest is kept spotlessly clean. At the age of three to four weeks when the kittens are just starting to eat solids, most queens exhibit an uncontrollable urge to move them to a new nest site. The mother may go to extreme lengths to satisfy this desire. Each kitten is grasped in turn, right round the neck in the queen's jaws, then by raising her head and flexing her strong neck muscles, she carries it between her straddled forelegs, clear of the ground. When grasped in this way, the kitten naturally goes completely limp and remains subdued until put down again. In a breeding establishment, or home, it is important to recognize this desire in mother cats and to allow a change of nest box and site at this time. A frustrated mother may damage the kittens by constantly endeavouring to move them and the stress she suffers may deplete her milk supply.

Towards weaning time, the kittens are taught to groom themselves by their mother. First, as she licks them, they lick her about the face and neck, then they lick their own paws and wipe them across their faces. A whole range of language is used by the queen and she plays games with the litter, helping to develop their reflex actions and teaching hunting techniques through play behaviour. The queen also takes the kittens on short excursions outside, but if any seem unsure, or mew in distress, she quickly lifts them and carries them back to the nest box. Now and again the queen chastises her kittens with well-directed slaps with her forepaws. If they become too boisterous in play she may pin them down firmly, again with her forepaws. Occasionally, her first lessons in weaning are given when they try to nurse, for instead of encouraging them to suckle as before, she grasps the youngsters in her paws and gently bites them, while raking at their bodies with her hindlegs.

The queen still grooms the kittens thoroughly, even when they are weaned and she is very protective towards them in the presence of strangers. Unusual noises will cause her to run around in an agitated manner and she may try to carry the now heavy kittens to a place of safety. If the queen is disturbed enough to growl in alarm, the kittens take this as an indication to run and hide. If touched at this time, the young animals explode into hissing, growling balls of fluffed-up fur, and will bite and scratch to avoid being handled. To wean the kittens finally, the queen brings them pieces of meat or encourages them to

follow her to the food bowl. When they attempt to nurse she sits down firmly and tucks all four feet under her body to prevent them reaching her teats. If the kittens persist and worry her, she will jump to some high vantage point out of their reach, but where she can still keep a protective eye upon them.

Should a litter die at birth, or suffer some accident or illness shortly after, the maternal behaviour is so strong in the cat that she will immediately start an oestral period, mate and conceive. Some bereaved queens have been known to try to mother other adult cats, trying to pull them by their scruffs into the nest box. Occasionally, such queens have attempted to mother small toys, and warm woollen objects such as socks and gloves. The hormone balance is, luckily, soon restored and the breeding cycle quickly resumes its natural balance.

Learning behaviour in the kitten

Blind and deaf, the newborn kitten moves, head waving from side to side, by crawling on its belly towards its mother's nipple. It is guided at this time only by a strongly developed sense of smell. Kittens weakened by the ordeal of birth are stimulated by firm strokes of the queen's rough tongue, which also cleans away the membranes adhering to the wet fur and promotes the circulation. Strong, determined, scrabbling movements are performed by the kittens as each stakes its claim on a particular nipple, for it has been noticed that kittens stick to a certain nipple during the weeks spent feeding from their dam. A treading action is performed by the kitten as it sucks, with one tiny paw placed on either side of the nipple. This action stimulates the milk flow, and even bottle fed orphan kittens perform this movement.

The unique smell imparted to the nestbox and material by parturition is important to the kittens for the first few days of life, bearing in mind that the only functioning sense they have is that of smell. Many owners of breeding queens probably cause untold psychological harm to their litters by taking care to remove every trace of soiled bedding from the nestbox straight after the birth, replacing it with a freshly washed, practically sterile blanket. The unique smells of the birth process are a comfort to the newborn kittens, and they require this scent for a feeling of security. The soiled areas are not dirty, for the secretions of birth are totally sterile. It is far better to leave the bedding as it is until the kittens have their eyes open, by which time they will not be unduly stressed by a change of environment.

At the time of birth the kitten has in its brain all the neurons that will be present through its life span. The cells of the brain are never renewed. Mammals start with millions of such cells which gradually decay, and this accounts for the gradual slowing of mental processes with old age. The kitten's brain is functional at birth, but then the more synaptic junctions which form during its first few weeks of

Queens occasionally transport their young kittens to new nest sites. Each kitten is grasped firmly around the neck in the mother's strong jaws. This action causes the kitten to relax and draw in its limbs in a characteristic pose.

life, the more intelligent will it be as an adult cat. It has been discovered that slight amounts of stress in these first critical weeeks help the development of the brain and so produce brighter cats. Experiments have been conducted where litters have been split, half being raised normally by being left in their dark, quiet nestbox until weaning time, while the other half were 'stressed'. The stressing process involved constant handling and examination of the kittens, allowing them to smell strange objects, and after the first week, allowing them to hear strange sounds. The results were quite conclusive in that the stressed kittens grew up to be nerveless, healthy, happy and intelligent cats, surpassing their siblings on all counts.

Already it had been noticed by developers of new colours and coat patterns in various breeds that the 'new' kittens seemed to grow up to be more intelligent and of better temperament than the 'normal' kittens in the same litters. It was put down to some form of hybrid vigour at first, but eventually it was realized that it was the constant handling from birth that achieved the effect. Obviously, precious and exciting kittens of new varieties were examined constantly from birth to make sure that their eyes were opening correctly and that their navels were healing satisfactorily, plus checking on their sex. All this proved stressful to the young creatures, but caused extra maturation of the brain at a critical stage in development.

During the first few days the kitten spends most of its time in one section of the nestbox, either suckling or sleeping. Depending upon the breed, its eyes open between two and ten days, and the box should be protected from strong light at this time. Very gradually the sense of hearing develops and the kitten crawls more strongly as it explores its limited environment. The kitten crawls by pushing itself along on its belly, the legs being too weak to support the body at this stage. The contact of the body with the ground leaves a scent trail which enables the kitten to retrace its path if necessary.

After the eyes open, signs of playful behaviour may be noticed and the kitten will begin to pat at its littermates. The eyes soon begin to focus and the sight gradually gets stronger as the kitten may be seen to look at near objects and watch the movements of its mother. At three weeks of age the kitten can stand up on its legs and take tottering steps. It will roll over and be capable of righting itself again. It will take playful bites at its siblings' paws and tails. Later, play becomes more vigorous and the kitten makes little excursions from the nestbox until loud or unexpected noises may cause it to dash back to safety. During its first journeys of exploration, the kitten will be seen to lick at most of the new surfaces it encounters, such as the floor and pieces of furniture. Other objects will be chewed or bitten as if to test whether or not they can be eaten. The nestbox, if made of cardboard, very soon bears the impressions of their tiny teeth.

At the age of five weeks the kitten's brain is almost mature and the synaptic junctions are formed and operational. The motor development which includes the co-ordination of the limbs and the development of the muscles takes much longer and care is necessary to protect the adventurous young animal from danger at this stage. The kitten should have freedom to exercise with its littermates and plenty of toys. Cardboard boxes with various holes cut in them, and some paper bags to get into are all appreciated. Ping-pong balls, feathers and matchboxes all make good toys. Various types of food should be offered to the kitten at this stage to prevent restricted feeding habits in later life, and it should be placed firmly, but gently, on its toilet tray after feeding or nursing.

In order to grow into a calm, sociable adult, the kitten must receive a lot of handling between the ages of four and eight weeks. This period is equivalent to the nest-vacating time in the wild, and is critical as it is then that the animal learns the difference between its friends and its enemies. At this time, very gentle grooming procedures should be carried out, brushing with a soft baby brush and careful wiping out of the earflaps. The kitten can be accustomed to having its mouth inspected and should be petted so that the procedure is enjoyed and not resented. After a while, the kitten will be seen to enjoy the session, lifting its tiny chin for the brush and waving its tail gently with pleasure.

It is also important at this stage for kittens to have contact with children and dogs. It is wise to accustom them to household noises, such as the vacuum cleaner, television, radio and washing machine. They should be allowed to meet visitors to the house, delivery men and so forth, and in this way grow up as extrovert, affectionate animals able to take life in their stride. Kittens raised in virtual isolation, such as in pens in large, quiet catteries, often remain very shy of human contact and may be difficult to handle at cat shows, or by the veterinary surgeon, even though they may be perfectly all right with their owners. Such cats are often impossible to cope with during boarding, and may also have breeding difficulties, resenting the approach of other cats.

One case is recorded of a tiny kitten, rejected by its mother at birth, and so hand-reared. The breeder was recovering from an illness and was pleased to have this demanding task to perform in the solitude of her bedroom. The kitten was a delight, very affectionate and fastidious in her habits. She thrived and the breeder was loath to part with her when she attained the age of thirteen weeks. Having been vaccinated without any trouble, the kitten went to her new home and soon settled in with her new mistress and two children. Eventually, at ten months of age, and having her second period of oestrus it was decided to send the now well-grown queen to stud. In the stud house, she was penned and became very agitated when she saw the male cat. She climbed the wire of the pen, clinging

Kitten showing aggression

Benign look

Defensive or aggresive, warning

Contented kitten

Nervous, inquisitive look

entative approach (slightly defensive)

Aggressive, preparing to attack

Kneading, showing contentment

on, terrified and wide-eyed, urinating. It was impossible to get hold of her as she bit and fought, obviously thinking that she was being attacked by the male. Later, when she had calmed down sufficiently to be basketed up, she was returned to her home until her next season. This time she was left until quite frantically on heat, then confined to the queen's pen in the stud house for three days to see and smell the stud cat without direct contact. It was to no avail, she was impossible to handle and would not mate. Eventually it was realized that the queen had never seen another cat, having been taken from her mother while still blind, reared in isolation and living confined in a normal house without any other pets. It was obvious that she did not recognize herself as a cat and would never mate, so reluctantly, she was speyed and lived out her long life as a part of a human family.

It is obvious that the treatment and handling of the young kitten have a bearing on the temperament and bearing of the adult cat. Just as important as the first three months of the animal's life are the subsequent months of the kitten's life until maturity at approximately nine months. At three months the kitten is independent but is still developing physically and mentally. At this age it may well be in a new home and isolated from other animals. All will be well if, at the critical time, it was exposed to other animals, and humans. Nevertheless, its environment should be as enriched as possible, and every opportunity to allow it to meet strangers and to have new experiences should be encouraged if it is to grow up into a well-balanced, likeable cat.

Territorial marking and defence

As we have seen, the typical territorial marking procedure carried out by the male cat is to spray droplets of strong-smelling urine as marker flags about the perimeters of his range. Sometimes, after marking in this way, the cat will back up to the marked object and rub his tail and hindquarters against it. At other times he may be seen to turn, and vigorously strop his claws on the marked area. Female cats, especially those whose hormone balance has been upset by doses of a contraceptive pill, are also seen to spray. They adopt the typical male position, tail raised and quivering, the spray being directed backwards in a short, sharp jet. While this spray does not have the noxious odour of the tom cat's mark, it is sticky and difficult to clean from household surfaces and wallpaper.

Even neutered cats occasionally spray and again, while there is no noticeable odour, it is annoying if performed in the house, leaving obstinate stains. Spraying, in neutered cats, is often triggered off by emotional upset. This may be due to the introduction into the household of a new kitten or other pet, or even the addition of a human baby. The cat feels that its position in the household is threatened and tries to assert himself in the only way he is able – by marking

everything as his own, personal property. As well as marking with spray, house cats may defecate and usually do this where it will cause the most concern. The spot picked is always very conspicuous, quite unlike the procedure normally employed in evacuating the bladder or bowel, when the cat hides away discreetly and afterwards carefully covers up all signs.

Cats also have other methods of identifying property. They have various scent glands on the head and body. Above the eyes, on either side of the forehead are found the temporal glands, while the lips have the perioral glands, and both types are used for marking. Other marking glands are found at the tail root. To employ these glands, the cat runs the areas vigorously against the chosen object. This may be inanimate, or the legs, hands, arms, shoulders or face of its owner or friend. The cat also marks other friendly cats and dogs, plus favourite objects in the home by this method. By rubbing the areas containing the glands against the chosen site, the cat deposits minute secretions on the area, thus marking it with its own, distinctive scent.

When rubbing with the forehead, the cat seems to obtain a pleasurable sensation and often purrs. When rubbing the lips and chin however, the animal becomes almost ecstatic, especially if another cat has previously marked the same spot. In this case it often drools, rubbing the lips firmly against the object and may even rear up in order to rub even harder. The tail gland is used as a sort of full-stop after the signature left by the temporal gland. It is easily observed while a cat is weaving around chair legs, or the legs of his owner preparing a meal. The animal winds itself around the legs, leaning inwards, allowing the forehead to rub the area first, followed by contact of the length of the body, and finally the tail is wiped along for almost its entire length.

Cats have a wide variety of facial expression and body postures which they use for communication with other cats and their human friends. By studying these expressions, we may perhaps understand our pets better and form more satisfactory relationships with them. In addition to its voice, the head, body, tail and eyes are all employed by the cat to express itself. The various permutations of expressions and body positions form an explicit sign language in the cat and occasionally, postures and voice are used in conjunction, or in sequence to convey messages.

A normal, non-aggressive cat may be in its own garden when it is threatened, perhaps by another strange cat or a dog. First the cat will stand stock still and look at the intruder, then its tail will start to slowly flick from side to side. Its whiskers and ears point stiffly forward as its senses attempt to identify the threat object. As the intruder approaches more closely the cat assumes a different stance. The tail is still lifted but the point is now turned downwards. The chin is tucked in and the ears flattened as the cat begins slowly to turn sideways on to the intruder. The hairs on the spine and along the tail begin to erect. This display will become increasingly marked if the intruder continues to approach, until the cat is in its fully offensive position. This stance is typical and menacing. The cat faces its enemy, but with the body turned sideways from the chest, presenting as large an area as possible. The hindlegs are tensed, ready to spring in flight or fight, the weight of the front portion of the body is taken on one foreleg while the other, claws unsheathed, is raised to strike. The chin is tucked in to protect the throat, the ears are flattened to the head and the lips are drawn back as the cat snarls fiercely.

If the intruder is repelled by this inspiring sight, and sensibly backs away, the cat will then come forward a few steps, probably performing some lip-smacking and drooling to accompany its deep growls, until the visitor turns tail and heads for home. The cat sniffs the invaded ground and may spray, defecate or scratch at the area before relaxing and resuming normal activities.

When a cat sees a friendly visitor approach, it acts in a totally different manner. The preliminary, inquisitive look is adopted, with ears and whiskers pointing forward for identification. When the scent has been received and recognized the cat raises his tail and, slightly stiff-legged, walks forward in greeting. If the visitor is feline, some mutual rubbing may occur followed by reciprocal grooming after a preliminary touch of noses, just to ensure that there has been no possible mistake in identity. Even when adult, friendly cats may then indulge in play pursuits, chasing one another in mock battle, often up into the branches of high trees, along fences and onto roof tops.

Facial expressions in the cat are very varied and fairly easy to understand by perceptive humans. The alert cat has a very direct gaze, with ears and whiskers pointing forward. If he is slightly nervous, the nostrils may twitch in an attempt to pick up more scent for identification purposes. A reassuring voice will calm him and he may mew, when it is safe to handle him.

Signs of extreme agitation in the cat are indicated by wide eyes, glancing rapidly from side to side, while the body is in a crouched attitude and the ears are held out to the side of the head. A cat in this state should be very gently coaxed before he is touched or he may bite in fear. When the eyes and ears resume their normal appearance, the cat has relaxed and is safe to touch. If, however, the ears are flattened even more and the eyes are narrowed to slits, the cat is not at all nervous but extremely angry and may well strike forward in attack. Sometimes, even a really angry cat can be coaxed into a more pleasant frame of mind by soft words, especially if the aggression is due to confinement in strange surroundings, such as a cat show or boarding cattery. A cat with ears laid flat to the head and lips drawn back, snarling, should not

be touched and must be left quietly to settle down in its own good time. Cats are strongly territorial in their habits, and are often prepared to defend their domain. This instinct should be recognized and allowances made for cats showing natural aggressive tendencies towards intruders.

The cat as a predator

Predatory behaviour can be observed in the young kitten from the age of about six weeks. The mother cat often brings small pieces of meat to the nest and makes a characteristic, chirruping call to attract her offsprings' attention. She pats and tosses the meat and encourages the kittens to pounce on it before eating. Occasionally one kitten will grab the scrap growling fiercely through the large mouthful of food, and striking out with tiny claws at its littermates if they approach too close. The kittens also practise hunting movements among themselves, crouching in ambush, then pouncing upon each other, making mock attacks and biting at the head and neck regions. By sitting quietly and gently waving her tail from side to side, the mother cat encourages hunting-practise play as the kittens pounce on the enticing appendage.

Even the most docile and gentle of pets will hunt, given the opportunity, unless a poor diet has caused extremes of emaciation or obesity. Properly nourished cats occasionally seek out prey for sport, and well-fed farm cats hunt better than those left entirely to their own devices. It is remarkable that even after centuries of domestication, the cat shows such skill in detecting, catching and killing other small animals and birds. It is important for owners not to endow their pets with human feelings and the cat should not be scolded for proudly bearing home its kill as a trophy for all to admire.

Cats prefer to hunt alone, although cases of co-ordinated expeditions between cats living together have been recorded. They prefer to hunt within the confines of their own territory although country cats often have favourite woods and coppices to visit, some distances from their homes. Having excellent vision in poor light conditions enables the cat to hunt successfully at twilight and as dawn breaks. Their acute hearing enables accurate locations of the prey. Whiskers, and eartufts also play a part in successful hunting, ensuring the cat's safe passage through dense, entangled undergrowth. The soft pads with retracted claws allow for speed of movement, and powerful hindlegs provide rapid propulsion for the attacking spring. The victim is grasped in the extended claws and held fast until dispatched with the clean neck bite so well-practised during the games of kittenhood.

Hunting birds on open land needs all the skill the cat can muster. It approaches close to the birds before flattening its body to the ground. Keeping motionless until the intended victims resume feeding, the cat glides forward with fluid, almost imperceptible movements. The ears, shoulderblades and hipbones

are kept quite level and ducked low. When within springing distance, the cat tenses its hindlegs and builds up momentum by swinging the hips and tail from side to side. The energy is suddenly released and the cat leaps forward pinning one of the birds with sharp extended claws. If the cat is reasonably sure that its victim cannot get away, it might indulge in what appears to humans as a deplorable habit of teasing the poor creature before killing it. Playing with prey enables the cat to practise its hunting and trapping techniques. The cat becomes highly aroused during such games and even after the wretched victim is dead, may still toss its body around, dive on it and continue to make rapid neck bites. The little body may be tapped under low furniture, then the cat will retreat, crouch, run and spring, hooking it out again with sweeping curved paws. Tossing the body high into the air is a favourite game, and the cat pretends not to notice where it lands, and walks around in a nonchalant fashion. Then, as though noticing the dead creature for the first time, performs all the crouching and leaping motions again. If the cat decides to devour its prey, the entrails are eaten first, then it may or may not eat the rest of the body. Nursing queens often eat every scrap of a mouse or a bird including the fur or feathers, and the entire skeleton. The less digestible portions may be regurgitated later with no apparent ill effects. A cat will eat the entire carcase of a wild rabbit, weighing almost as much as the cat itself. It will then rest and fast for two or three days before hunting again. Wild cats probably eat only occasionally, gorging themselves, then resting in this way. Cats eating fresh prey seldom need to drink because of the high fluid content of fresh meat, whereas pet cats fed unnaturally, must be allowed access to clean water at all times. Eating fresh prey is also beneficial to the cat's teeth, gums and jaws, and this should be borne in mind when feeding the pet animal.

Hunting and killing are inborn traits in the cat and provide exercise, both physical and mental, as well as food. Flat-dwelling cats can be compensated to a large extent for the loss of their sport. Intelligent, caring owners can devise many interesting and stimulating games for their cats. Pulling toy mice around on strings, playing games with bunches of feathers, scraps of fur or even paper balls can prove exciting for the cats so long as the owner enters into the proceedings in the right spirit. When playing with a cat-nip mouse, one must think, and make the toy act like a real mouse. Subtle jerks of the string make it appear to scurry forward with hesitant movements. It can be tugged so that the toy appears to try to hide behind the leg of a table or chair. All this serves to excite and stimulate the cat into indulging in a close simulation of a serious hunt.

The sophistication of the hunting technique in the domestic cat accounts for its remarkable powers of survival if suddenly left to its own devices. Cats have gone missing when their owners have moved house, and have eventually arrived, possibly after many months absence, back at the old home. Sometimes the animal has had to travel many miles over rough and hazardous terrain, but in most cases completes its journey healthy and well-nourished, if a trifle foot-sore. While it is likely that such travelling cats have managed to scavenge some food *en route*, it is obvious that they have also had to hunt in order to stay so fit and well. Even cats which have led sheltered, indoor lives seem able to revert to nature when necessary. They appear a little clumsy in their first attempts at hunting, but having overcome their initial over-enthusiastic rushes, settle down to perfect a workable plan of attack. It is obvious that hunting and killing are inborn traits in the cat and trying to repress them can only destroy the very essence of the spirit of the creature.

Sleeping and dreaming
Sleep in the cat has been studied in great depth during research into the sleep patterns of humans. It was discovered quite early on that cats have two distinct

types of sleep. During the odd catnaps taken throughout the day, the sleep is of the light variety and the blood pressure remains the same as during the waking state. The temperature drops very slightly and the muscles are in a slightly tensed condition. Electroencephalograph recordings, known as EEGs, taken of cats in this light sleep, show characteristic, slow wave patterns. In deep or paradoxical sleep the temperature rises and the blood pressure falls, the muscles relax and EEG recordings taken at this time show short, sharp patterns. The hearing of the cat becomes extra acute during paradoxical sleep and acts as a defence mechanism, for any sharp or sudden noise will arouse the animal instantly.

Cats seem able to sleep at any time of the day or night, and in any temperature. They obviously prefer to curl up in a warm, draught-proof and dry spot, and are adept at seeking out such places. The softness or hardness of the sleeping area does not seem to bother cats very much, and they appear able to relax completely even on unyielding surfaces such as wiremesh, rough brick walling or coals in a bunker. They may be observed, sound asleep, on corrugated roof sheets, wedged into tree boles or on precariously high ledges.

A favourite attitude in the home is to sleep with the head hanging down over the side of a chair. It is not known just how much sleep an adult cat requires each day. Some cats seem to virtually sleep their lives away, while others are much more active and seemingly only take the occasional catnap. In settling down to sleep cats vary in the postures they adopt. Some stretch out on their stomachs while others curl up on their sides. If the temperature is low, the cat will curl into a tight ball, head tucked under the tail and all four paws turned in towards the body. Some cats place their forepaws over their eyes as if to shield them from the light. Small kittens require a great deal of sleep and simply stop in the middle of a game and go to sleep wherever they happen to be. If the weather is cold, kittens heap themselves into a pyramid, each trying to scrabble into the centre of the pile in order to keep warm.

During the periods of paradoxical sleep, cats dream. What it is that they dream about, we have no means of knowing. It is thought that the experiences of the day are being sifted and important items learned are stored away in the long-term memory bank. While dreaming, the cat sometimes purrs and mutters. The legs may stir and twitch as though running and the paws flutter. Occasionally, sucking motions are performed, and the tail occasionally swishes. A third of the cat's sleeping time is made up of paradoxical sleep and it is essential that they have peace and quiet in order to enter this deep phase. It is known that these periods of deep sleep are as vital to the well-being of the cat as they are to the human being. In experiments, cats were deprived of deep sleep for several weeks, and it was recorded that the heart rate speeded up. After the experimental period was over and the cats could sleep as and when they wished, they spent very long periods in deep sleep as though trying to catch up on the backlog. Only after some time, when the normal pattern of alternating sessions of light and deep sleep had been regained, did the heart rate of the cats return to normal.

The cat's rough tongue is used as brush, comb and sponge for cleaning and grooming its coat. To wash its face the cat licks each forepaw in turn before passing around the eye, over and behind the ear and along the jaw.

New-born kittens spend most of their first week of life in paradoxical sleep. From one week to four weeks they have increasing periods of wakefulness, going directly back into deep sleep without the usual light sleep interim phase. Only at four weeks does a kitten start experiencing light sleep periods, and it is interesting to note that this coincides with the completion of the wiring system of synaptic junctions within its tiny brain.

Washing

On awakening, the cat stretches its entire body length in a sinuous flow of movement, flexing each muscle and claw. It usually yawns widely, then is instantly alert and ready for any eventuality. If it has been sleeping in sunlight or under a lamp, the animal may well start its complicated washing routine for it appears that the action of light and warmth on the coat of the cat stimulates the washing reflex action.

Tongue and paws are employed by the cat in washing itself. The tongue is well designed for the purpose being covered with tiny projections called papillae, causing it to have a roughened, comb-like action when used to clean the fur. After waking and stretching, or feeding, the cat sits up and flicks its tongue all around its mouth and lips. Licking its favourite paw until it is quite damp, the cat passes this over its face and head, into and behind the ears, across the eyes and down the nose. Then the other paw is licked well and used in the same fashion on the opposite side of the head and face. Each shoulder and foreleg is then licked in turn, followed by the flanks, the genital area, the hindlegs and finally the entire length of the tail.

If any tangles are encountered in the coat during washing, these are teased out by the cat's sharp teeth as are any rough patches of skin, burrs or matted hair between the toes. Some cats wash a great deal, others only when really grubby. Most cats lick and groom themselves after being touched by strangers as if to remove the alien scent from the coat. Cats in the same household often indulge in sessions of mutual grooming. They seem to really enjoy this and often wash each other's faces after a meal, before settling down to sleep together.

Mother cats spend a long time in washing their offspring. Having cleaned them thoroughly at birth and stimulated excretion from their bowels and bladders during their first four weeks in the nest, she continues to wash them meticulously until they go off to new homes. Sometimes she licks the kittens so hard that they are lifted off the ground. Kittens start their own washing routines even if rather ineffectually, at about three weeks of age. Orphan kittens, hand-reared by humans, must have this constant washing simulated or they cannot function properly and do not thrive. The human foster-mother uses cotton-wool slightly damped in hot water to take the place of the mother cat's tongue and finishes off with a small square of terry-towelling. After each feed the orphan is washed carefully around the face and mouth, and it is stimulated to evacuate its bladder and bowel into the damp cotton-wool. A firm, gentle rub with the towelling then stimulates the circulation and promotes feelings of well-being. The tiny kitten is then put in a warm box to sleep.

Sometimes cats become excessively soiled or contaminated with toxic substances such as oil and grease. These cats benefit from being bathed. There is an old saying that bathing a cat means that it will never again wash itself, but this is a fallacy. It is quite simple to bath a cat especially if one has a double sink. If not, two deep bowls will do instead, one in which to sit the cat, and one holding clean, warm water. The cat is thoroughly soaked first of all, with the comfortably warm water. This is harder to accomplish than it sounds, for the coat naturally repels water. Then the shampoo, which must be specially formulated for cats, is worked well in and finally rinsed away thoroughly. The cat shakes itself if allowed to do so, which makes quite a mess, therefore it is wise to quickly enfold it in a thick towel and rub the coat dry without delay.

After bathing, cats take a while to dry out completely and must not be allowed outside or to become chilled. Rubbing with a towel does the job, but takes some time. A few cats will tolerate the use of a hair dryer, but these animals are the exception rather than the rule. As soon as he is released from the towel, the cat will start to meticulously lick each hair back into place, hence the necessity for thorough rinsing away of the shampoo. When virtually dry the coat can be carefully brushed and combed. The coat will seem extra soft for a few days after the bathing session, so for show preparation, the procedure should be carried out about a week before the important date.

A cat that is used to having the occasional bath, is easy to treat, if it is unfortunate enough to contract one of the skin diseases. Various preparations can be added to the bath solution depending on the condition apparent in the animal. Infestation with parasites, such as lice or fleas, are easily treated with an insecticidal bath. Not only are the pests killed, but the skin is soothed and the fur is treated making it safe from reinfestation for about three weeks. When using such preparations however, it is essential that an Elizabethan collar is fitted round the cat's neck until he is thoroughly dry so that he cannot lick, and ingest, the preparations which may prove toxic if taken internally.

Entire male cats have very active sebaceous glands in the tail, running along the surface for about three inches from the root. A greasy liquid is exuded from tiny pores in the skin over this area and, on contact with the air, this oxidises and form spots rather like blackheads. If not removed, this grease forms a crust under which bacteria soon multiplies and forms an abcess. This condition is commonly known as 'stud tail' and the area should be regularly washed to avoid trouble.

Sick cats lose the inclination to wash themselves, and in the upper respiratory illnesses, become moribund as well as exceedingly soiled. They must be made to feel comfortable, for cats are normally fastidious creatures, and in such cases must be cleaned each day. The caked mucous membranes are gently sponged, and if ulcerated, a bland cream applied to soothe and heal. The face, bib and paws will also be stained with dried mucous and spilt food from forced feeding. These areas are also sponged clean with a detergent solution, rinsed and dried carefully. Grooming powder should be rubbed well in once the hair is dry and left to absorb every bit of grease and dirt. A baby's bib should be tied carefully around the cat before feeding. The sick animal is usually incontinent, and so the rear end must be looked after much as one would care for a small baby. Human babies' disposable nappies are invaluable for keeping the area clean and fresh. When the animal is well on the road to recovery a really gentle bath in handhot water is possible, as long as the cat can be completely dried without chilling, in a very short space of time. Once cleaned up, most cats make a determined effort to regain full health.

Unusual behaviour

To be able to discuss unusual behaviour in an animal such as the enigmatic cat, it is necessary first to decide just what is constituted by usual behaviour. We generally accept usual behaviour in the domestic cat as that which we have come to expect, after adaptation to life in the home and a peaceful co-existence with humans. What must be remembered about the cat is that even though it lives in harmony with humans, it still retains a high degree of the independence of its wild cousins. In the wild, the cat hunts in order to survive; its sexual drives are strong to ensure the survival of its species; it has highly developed powers of perception and reflex action for self-preservation, and it is basically a solitary animal.

When we take a cat into our homes we remove the need for hunting by providing adequate food. We neuter the animal to take away its need and desire to reproduce, or, alternatively, we may breed litters in far from natural conditions. We also protect the cat from hazards, extremes of temperature and, in fact, anything that might harm or frighten it. It is hardly surprising, therefore, that occasionally cats show strange or abnormal behaviour patterns.

The brain in all animals needs proper nourishment in order to function properly, and deficiencies in certain vitamins and minerals can cause the appearance of nervous symptoms. One dramatic instance of the effect of diet on the brain was given publicity in recent years. A certain dog meat was manufactured, and the substance known as benzoic acid was added as a preservative in order to give the product a long shelf-life. Benzoic acid, even in large doeses, does not have any adverse effects on dogs. Unfortunately, one large establishment housing both dogs and cats bought a quantity of the attractive meat and fed to all the animals on the premises. Very soon a condition resembling epilepsy was observed in many of the cats. They became unmanageable, wild, hysterical and seemed afraid of the light. Veterinary treatment was attempted, but the cats went into convulsions, some developed severe muscular spasms and appeared unable to see. Most of the unfortunate creatures died, some had to be humanely destroyed, while only a very few eventually recovered after extensive treatment. Although quite safe for ingestion by dogs, it was thus determined that benzoic acid had caused these devastating effects on the nervous systems of the cats.

Any form of shock or trauma can also cause behaviour disorders. Gunfire and shelling affects the cats of countries at war. They may be observed crawling into dark corners to die or be so disturbed that they have to be destroyed. Very rough handling or unskilled treatment can also cause disturbed behaviour in the cat, resulting in an unbalanced and unpredictable animal. Severe shock can result in reactions which bring about a vasovagal attack in the animal, followed by collapse and death. This occurs mainly in cats which have been greatly humanized and is a direct result of the over-stimulation of the nervous system. It seems ironical that too much care and affection can cause a creature to be so sensitive' that restraint or confinement by force can distress it so severely as to bring about reactions which cause its death.

A cat may suffer severe shock after a road accident, after fighting with another cat, or being attacked by a dog. The animal apears listless and depressed. It will not eat or drink, its pulse rate is high and its pads perspire. It tries to hide its head, its pupil dilate, it may shiver, and in some cases it will be too hypersensitive to be touched. In the last instance it is dangerous to try to pick the cat up for it will react violently and may bite and scratch severely. Any cat in shock must be covered by a thick towel, rolled over and put into a large carrier. This is then placed in a very quiet, dark place until the cat has calmed down sufficiently to be examined by the veterinary surgeon. Occasionally, tranquilizers are required to treat the distressed creature, but the best cure is quiet, dark and kindness. Some cats develop phobias following severe cases of shock, from which they never fully recover.

Appropriately, if very frightened, cats are known to occasionally assume a state known as catatonic. This is also called 'playing possum', and the cat looks as though it has dropped down dead. This effect is thought to inhibit the chase response in some larger predators, and so acts as a protective mechanism when the cat is the hunted animal. If this state occurs in the home, following a shock, the usual treatment should be given by providing complete rest in a dark, quiet place.

It is comparatively rare for a pet cat to become aggressive unless it is reacting, in fear, to being cornered or tormented. Unkind handling as a kitten or young cat may have formed unpleasant associations for the cat, or it may be aware of some strange smell or high pitched sound which it associates with danger. A cat may react to a dangerous situation, either when being threatened by a dog, or the sound of a household appliance, such as a vacuum cleaner. Then it may severely bite its owner if touched at this time. The cat thinks that it is being attacked by the object that is causing its fear. This behaviour is quite usual and forms part of the cat's complex defence mechanism.

A great deal of unusual behaviour in our cats is a side effect of disease, or can be caused through treatment with certain drugs which affect some of the vital brain areas. Behaviour patterns may be only temporarily upset, in which case they can be treated with care and good diet. In some cases the damage may be permanent and result in a complete personality change in the animal. The irresponsible use of experimental drugs has been known to have far-reaching effects on the physiology, as well as the psychology of cats, and often one has a bearing on the other. An example is brain damage caused by antibiotics which, in turn, cause deafness. Deaf cats are very vulnerable to road accidents, and, in their silent world, are often unaware of impending danger. Many deaf cats are fortunate in having intact that part of the hearing mechanism which reacts to vibrations. If this is so, it is possible to communicate with such animals by teaching them to associate those vibrations caused by banging certain household objects, such as their food

When cornered by a strange dog, the cat adopts a typical defensive sideways position, with body hairs erect and back arched.

bowls, with calls for meals, and so on.

As we have seen earlier, the introduction of a new kitten, a puppy or even a new baby into the home can disturb a cat. Cats are also upset by being moved to new homes. When the animal has its routine disturbed, its behaviour may change radically, and usually for the worse. Anti-social ways of showing its displeasure are quite usual and include the breakdown of normal hygiene habits. The upset cat may urinate in strange places.

Scolding makes matters worse, but with lots of extra care and affection, difficult to give with the cat in such an unlovable state of mind, he should eventually resume his previous good manners. Having their home territory violated by strangers causes other perverse behaviour, such as the deliberate breaking of small ornaments and fierce stropping of soft furnishings and wallpaper. Some cats refuse to eat for days, while others indulge in self-mutilation, licking furiously at tail, paws and flanks until the areas are raw and bleeding. Others sit and pull out all the fur on their chests and flanks and some may chew bad wounds in their paws, knuckles or tail tips.

Cats which are extremely bored, or very badly reared, may indulge in excessive grooming. Most of these cats have been confined for long periods in bad kennels with nothing at all to occupy their minds, in fact, a total lack of stimulus. Such cats lick and groom their bodies until whole areas are sore and bleeding. If they become tired of licking, they may start to suck at their own forepaws, tailtip or rear nipples. While indulging in this habit they knead with the forepaws and purr, regressing mentally to early kittenhood.

95

Related to self-sucking is the annoying habit of wool-eating, which is found mainly in some strains of Siamese. This is thought to be an inherited trait, for it is known to run in certain feline families. It is virtually impossible to live with a wool-eating cat in a normal household. As soon as it gets into a relaxed state, its eyes glaze, its paws start kneading and it will lick at the nearest woollen object. After licking at it, the cat then starts to tug at the wool with its teeth, sucking and chewing simultaneously. Some such cats only go this far, while others continue to chew at the wool, ingesting quite large quantities. Such afflicted cats also chew on other fabrics, but most seem to prefer good, pure wool. These cats can do extensive damage in the home.

Wool-eating cats also damage themselves, for the ingested wool often becomes impacted in the stomach or intestines. The problem is even worse when the material is wool mixed with one of the man-made fibres, for a ball of such matter lodged inside the cat can prove fatal. Various cures and remedies have been tried for wool-eating. Courses of minerals and vitamins have been given, but it seems that total isolation from temptation is the only way to correct the cat, and in some rare cases the habit has been cured.

Sexual disorders sometimes exhibit themselves in pet cats. A young male may become difficult to handle and rather aggressive if kept entire and confined to the home. A marked improvement for the better is often observed after castration. Female cats, not allowed to mate, have frequent periods of oestrus and often become dirty in their habits. Cats not to be used for breeding should be neutered at about six months of age, when they usually settle down.

Most cats dislike water but a very few are intrigued by it. These cats like to play with dripping taps and to roll in the dampness left in the bath. Some even like to swim. Most cats will catch fish if they are given the opportunity, hooking them out of the shallows of a fishpond with hooked claws. Allied to this fondness for water is a fascination for ice and snow. Cats bound about in such conditions, pushing their noses into the snow and rolling. Other cats seem to get the same satisfaction from rolling on cool concrete slabbing, pushing their backs against the cold paved surface, then sitting up to wash and groom.

Cats have many small quirks of behaviour. A cat given food not quite to its liking may perform covering-up movements as though hiding its excreta. A cat shut in a room may paw monotonously against the window pane, as though, with persistent effort, it may manage to work a way through. A cat that has been scolded will sit with its back to its owner, sulking, and totally ignoring all friendly overtures, even the offering of a favourite food. On the whole, considering the unnatural way in which we expect it to live, the domestic cat is a very well-adjusted creature and should be allowed the occasional lapses in good behaviour.

The behaviour of the old cat

Old age is said to commence in the cat at nine years. The animal then requires more care to ensure its well-being and comfort. A cosy, comfortable and draught-proof bed is essential, for the old cat will spend more time resting and sleeping. Varied food of good quality must be offered and a daily grooming session should be the rule. Care must be taken not to overfeed, for obesity can cut short the life of the cat as well as of a human. The older cat enjoys his food, but will take less exercise than in previous years, so there is a risk of adding surplus weight. It should be examined each year by the veterinary surgeon, with special attention to teeth and gums which may quickly deteriorate, or become coated with tartar. Any unusual behaviour should be checked out for it could point to disease. Old cats suffer from complaints such as kidney disease, arthritis and incontinence.

If the old cat's teeth deteriorate, soft food can be given, and if the kidneys begin to fail a low protein diet can be fed with pasta, rice and cheese replacing the red meat of earlier days. Plenty of fresh, clean drinking water must always be readily available to all cats, and is especially important to the old cat.

As ageing progresses, so a certain amount of degeneration of the tissues is inevitable. While these effects cannot be prevented entirely, they can be arrested by correct care. The regular visits to the veterinary surgeon ensure that the animal's life is prolonged, whenever possible. Chronic illness in the old cat can produce disturbed behaviour patterns. A previously house-clean animal might start to have little 'accidents' on the chairs and carpets. Sometimes the trouble can be remedied by treatment, but if due to general deterioration, it is kinder to confine the cat to an area of the house where the small lapses will not cause problems. It is pointless to scold or chastise the cat, and cruel to ban him from the house. If the deterioration continues, euthanasia is the only gentle solution.

It is not realized that the old cat needs a great deal of love and affection. While most people spend a great deal of time playing with and petting a kitten, few seem to bother with the old cat apart from feeding him regularly. Although the animal is less energetic and so does not make his presence so obvious, its need for affection and care does not diminish. Many owners introduce a new kitten into the home as their pet cat approaches old age. If the old cat is the only one in the household, this can be very unkind. If there are already several cats in the home, the introduction of a new kitten does not present problems.

The company of an ageing cat in good health is soothing, and very welcome at the end of a busy day. To play with an old cat is as rewarding as playing with a kitten, for his reactions are as sharp but his movements more subtle. The old cat will chase string and feathers but there is one golden rule in playing games with him. He must never be made to look foolish.

Longhairs and Shorthairs

Angela Sayer

Right
A Cream Longhaired kitten. Breeders have problems in breeding this variety true because of persistent tabby markings. These often show in the kittens but should disappear as they grow older. The eyes should be a beautiful brownish copper. This kitten still has the blue eyes of all kittens.

Pedigree cats can be divided into two basic types, defined by bone structure and overall conformation. The first group is close-coupled and stocky, round of head and eye, with small ears and short legs and tail. The second group is much lighter in build, long and lithe with slender bones, longer head, neck and tail and large pricked ears; most varieties in this latter group stand tall, their hind legs being longer than the forelegs. The first group, with which this chapter deals, is further categorized, according to coat length, into Longhaired (or Persian) cats and Shorthaired cats variously known as British Shorthaired, American Shorthaired, European Shorthaired and so on, depending on their country of origin.

The Persians

Longhaired cats, popular throughout the world, were first recorded in Europe at the end of the sixteenth century, when they were known as Angora cats, having been brought from Angora (now Ankara) in Turkey. Then, as further stock was imported from Persia (modern Iran) the name was changed to Persian Cat. It is from these original Angoras and Persians, as a result of careful and selective breeding, that the many beautiful Longhaired varieties of today have emerged.

These cats are known by different descriptive names to distinguish between the varieties, and slight variations in type are often apparent between them. All Persian cats, however, must have long, flowing silky coats and a full 'ruff' or frill around the neck which can be brushed up from the body to form a soft frame around the broad head. The standard of show points for perfection requires almost all Persians to have small, tufted ears, set well apart, and large, wide-awake eyes, plus a very short nose; but as will be seen the standard is somewhat modified in the breeds regarded as being only semi-Longhaired, for example, the Birman and the Turkish cats.

Most Longhaired cats are ideal for people who wish to own only one really decorative cat which is not too demanding or mischievous, yet which is affectionate and playful. All breeds may be kept quite successfully confined indoors if a toilet tray, a scratching post and some pot-grown grass for healthful nibbling are provided to compensate for lack of garden amenities. Persians are normally very healthy and hardy and need little special care except for grooming; but for this reason alone, folks with little spare time or patience should not take on any Longhaired breed, for the coats really do need constant attention with thorough brushing and combing every single day. The result of this daily titivation, combined with good feeding, will be a cat with bright eyes and a softly flowing coat. Careful handling from early kittenhood, will help to ensure an even temperament and affectionate nature, and the daily grooming must be carried out gently and firmly so that it is never resented by the kitten.

The Self Longhairs

For convenience in showing, Persians are split into 'self' varieties—in which the cats are coloured uniformly—and 'other colours' which include the various tabbies, cats with the silver gene present, and cats with particoloured coats. The Self Longhaired group comprises Black, Blue, Cream, White and Red Persians.

Superior type in this group is shown by the most popular of all Longhaired breeds, the Blue Persian, which may have a coat of any shade of blue provided that the cat is quite uniformly coloured and that the colour is sound right down to the roots. Most fanciers of this variety prefer the paler coloured cats, and understandably so, for a pale blue, almost lavender toned Persian of exceptional type, prepared expertly for the show bench, is a sight of breathtaking beauty.

The Black Persian is also approaching perfection in type, and is most striking with its deep orange or copper eyes glowing from a coal-black face. Damp weather and a surfeit of sunlight can have an oxidizing effect on the coat of this variety, causing a rusty appearance which sometimes detracts from its full beauty. Kittens often have disappointingly shaded coats, although this effect clears as the new coat comes through. It is easy to understand why the raven-coated Black with its expressive face was once associated with witchcraft, demons and pagan rites.

The Cream, another variety in which type is outstandingly good, is nevertheless difficult to breed to perfection. The problems are encountered in trying to achieve coat colour sound to the roots, and uniform over the entire body. A pale cream shade is desired without any hint of tabby or bars. These blotched markings are very often seen in kittens which later grow into superior, clear-coated adults. White hairs, especially on the tail tip, are taboo. A good specimen of this breed with its burnished copper eyes can be a show-stopper, and a Cream Persian may often take the coveted Best in Show award in top class competitions.

White Persians may be Blue-eyed, Orange-eyed or even Odd-eyed, in which, as the name suggests, one eye is blue and one orange. Originally, all were of the Blue-eyed variety and many were found to be deaf, due to a malformation of parts of the inner ear, genetically linked with the eye colour. In attempts to breed out this distressing condition, outcrosses were made, to other Self varieties and the Orange-eyed White was produced, happily possessed of perfect hearing. Another result of this cross-mating was the appearance of the Odd-eyed White, which so delighted breeders, that this, too, was developed as a separate variety. In caring for the White Persian, daily grooming to ensure scrupulous cleanliness is even more vital, as soiled areas quickly become stained yellow and detract from the overall sparkling appearance.

The Red Persian is rare, and of less good type than the other Self varieties, possibly because judicious breeding to Blue and Black (which necessitates long-term planning in order to be successful) has been avoided in the past. It is very difficult to breed a cat free from tabby markings, and it is unfortunate that this most striking, copper-eyed variety so seldom graces the show bench today.

Tabby and silver genes

The Red Tabby Persian differs from the Self in having the classic marbled tabby pattern clearly etched in a deep, copper-toned red on a paler base coat, and eyes of deep orange. The white markings so often seen on non-pedigree counterpart of this variety are a very serious fault, and kittens showing any such markings are neutered and sold only as pets. Persian Tabbies may also be had in Brown or Silver, and the desired pattern is the same as for the Red. The Brown Tabby is perhaps the most natural-looking of all the Longhaired breeds, the classic pattern being densely defined in black on a rich tawny base, and the eye colour being hazel or copper. The Silver Tabby Persian is rare, but very beautiful with the black marbling on a clear silver ground, and green or hazel eye colour. One of the most difficult of the Longhairs to breed to perfection, type, in this, as well as the other Tabbies, is far less extreme than in the better Self varieties.

Another Persian achieved by the introduction of the silver gene responsible for the Silver Tabby, is one of the most exquisitely beautiful of all cats—the Chinchilla. In great demand as a model for films and advertising, this charming cat has a temperament well suited to such a glamorous career. Basically pure silver-white, each hair, on a good specimen, is tipped with black, producing an exotic, sparkling, ethereal look. The lustrous eyes, emerald or sea-green in colour, are outlined in black, giving them an unparalleled depth of expression. Although the cat is slightly lighter in build than other Persians, it is strong and firmly muscular without ever appearing

98

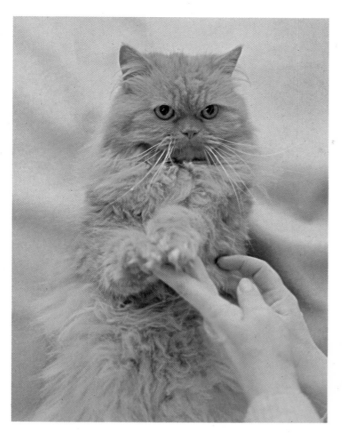

Left
The Longhaired Orange-eyed White. This cat is of excellent type with widely spaced ears well set on the head. *The Blue-eyed Longhaired White* far right, is the original and much older breed, but as blue-eyed cats are very often deaf, breeders introduced crosses with other self coloured breeds and produced the spectacular Orange-eyed cat.

Above
A beautiful *Red Persian.* This is a rare breed and they are very difficult to produce to standard. Many of the kittens retain their tabby markings or are rather pale in colour like the 'moggy' ginger and marmalade cats.

Right
The Brown Longhaired tabby is perhaps the most natural looking of all the more highly bred cats. The eyes should be hazel or copper in colour and the classic markings clearly defined in black.

page 103
A champion *Chinchilla* and her four-week-old kitten. Chinchillas are slightly smaller than other Persians although they are strong and healthy cats and have very gentle and affectionate natures.

coarse, and overall type is extremely good. Very heavily ticked Chinchillas are recognized as a separate breed in some countries, and known as the Shaded Silver Persian.

The unique colouring of the Smoke Persian, with a body of jet black shading down to pure silver at the roots and on the sides and flanks, is also due to the presence of the unusual silver gene. The mask and feet are densely black, while the frill and ear tufts are silver. With the usual massive Longhaired build and enormous orange or copper eyes, the Smoke is a very impressive creature. The Blue Smoke cat is also recognized in many countries but is not quite so striking in appearance, as the dilute blue colour replaces the black of the normal Smoke, and also tends to diffuse into the base colour.

Females to the fore

Tortoiseshell, Tortoiseshell-and-White and Blue-Cream Persians are almost without exception female only. This is because the Red colour (or yellow, as it is known by geneticists) is due to a semi-sex-linked genetic factor. The tortoiseshell is the female counterpart of the Red Self male, an appealingly patchworked creature of red, cream and black in well-defined areas

Left
A Blue-Cream Longhaired cat with excellent inter-mingled pastel shading. These Persian cats are invariably female and are the result of cross breeding between Blues and Creams. Breeders have worked out a breeding pattern so that the colours of the kittens are predictable. They are striking cats with deep orange eyes glowing against the misty effect of the coat.

Below
Another variety which is only female is the Tortoiseshell-and-White. These are dilute Tortie and White Persians where the black becomes blue and the red is paler. The white patches should be clear but not predominant.

over the head, legs, body and tail. The most attractive specimens also have a prominent red or cream blaze running down the mask between the deep orange or copper eyes. The Tortie-and-White is very similar, except that white patches must be present though not predominant in addition to the red, cream and black. As there are no fertile Tortoiseshell males, the lovely females are best bred to self-coloured cats, and give birth to fascinating mixed litters. If a Black stud is used, the resulting litter may have either Black or Red male kittens, or some of each, while the females will be Black or Tortoiseshell like the mother. If a Red Self male is used, the male offspring can again be Red or Black and there could be some Red females in addition to Black and Tortoiseshell kittens of the same sex.

Tortie-and-White females are usually mated to Bicoloured males to help control the amount of white produced in the kittens; and the colour of the kittens will depend upon the choice of male in the same way as in the case of the Tortoiseshell, except that each will have the desired white markings in addition to the three basic Tortoiseshell colours.

The Blue-Cream Persian is among the top few breeds for excellence of type and is the female counterpart of the Cream variety. Blue-Cream females mated to Cream males produce both Blue and Cream male kittens and Blue, Cream or Blue-Cream female kittens in the same litter. Mated to a Blue male, the same offspring may be expected, with the exception of the Cream females. One of the most aesthetically appealing of all Persians, the softly intermingled pastel blue and pinkish-cream of the coat gives a misty, flowing look, and the contrast provided by the deep copper or orange eyes is quite startling.

The Bicoloured Longhair is, as the name implies, a cat of two colours—either Red-and-White, Black-and-White, Blue-and-White or Cream-and-White. The colours must be present in equal amounts and for perfection the chin, neck, shoulders, forelegs and feet should be pure white. In addition, a neat white blaze should bisect the face. The most common of the Bicolours is the Black-and-White variety, often affectionately referred to as the 'Magpie'. The eye colour in this variety is required to be either copper or deep orange, and green or yellow eyes are considered to be show faults. The coat must have clearly coloured areas on the white, and these must not contain any white hairs, spots or patches.

The eastern influence

In recent years, the Himalayan factor has been introduced into the Persian breed. This is the genetic factor responsible for the exotic colouring of Siamese cats. It ensures that the cat's coat colour is restricted to the extremities of the body, namely the mask, ears, tail and paws, and that blue eye colour is also produced. A few very dedicated breeders, using selective breeding methods and carefully planned family trees,

Above left
A Turkish or Van kitten with excellent bright orange markings. These cats have very soft silky coats which are a dense chalky-white in colour.

Left
A Bi-coloured Longhair cat well marked with even patches of cream and white.

Above
A Blue Smoke Persian. These cats can be very striking indeed, particularly the Black Smoke when the contrast between the coat colours is greater. The under coat is silver, shading to the over coat of jet black or blue at the tip. The mask and feet are of solid black or blue while the ruff and ear tufts are of silver.

priest had a white cat as his oracle, and together they sat before the golden statue of the sapphire-eyed goddess Tsun-Kyan-Kse in the temple of Lao-Tsun, sharing their meditations. Raiders killed the priest one day, and the faithful cat Sinh laid its head against the silver hair of its murdered master, all four paws placed upon the body. A miracle occurred – the white fur turned as golden as the light radiating from the goddess, the yellow eyes took on her sapphire hue, while the ears, nose, legs and tail became as brown as the earth. Only the paws, still in contact with the dead priest, remained white, denoting his purity. Refusing all nourishment, Sinh remained to guard the body for seven days, then died, taking the perfect soul of its master into heaven. From that day the appearance of all the temple cats changed in the same miraculous manner. Since that day, whenever a sacred temple cat dies, it is said that the soul of a priest ascends with it to heaven.

Recent additions

A semi-Longhaired cat, really deserving a category of its own, is the Turkish or Van Cat. This gained a reputation for being very fond of swimming when first brought out of Turkey by an intrepid English lady in 1955. It is not really true, however, to say that this breed seeks out water in order to swim. Like most cats, it is a good swimmer, but is rather less averse than other breeds to water. The Turkish cat does not have the extreme type of the more usual Persians. Its chalk-white coat is of medium length, the silky hair patched with deep, bright auburn markings on the head, plus a bushy auburn tail. With large, round amber eyes and delicately pink nose leather and pads, it is most unusual in appearance and quite delightful to own.

During the initial matings necessary for producing the Colourpoint Persians, the chocolate gene, only previously found as a dilution of Seal Point in Siamese cats, was introduced into some Longhaired lines and caused two very rare and beautiful new Self-coloured varieties to emerge. Where the chocolate gene was present in both sire and dam, Longhaired kittens were born of a uniform milk-chocolate shade all over, and when both parents carried the blue factor in addition to the chocolate, some delicately pale lilac kittens also appeared in those litters. Having lustrous orange eyes, the two new varieties were thought to be most attractive by several fanciers, and breeding programmes were drawn up to develop them into well-typed Persian varieties.

Many more new varieties are genetically possible in the Persian ranks and some, owing their origins to the elusive silver gene, are occasionally seen at the larger cat shows at various stages of development. Included in these 'Any Other Colour' classes are such cats as the Blue Chinchilla and the Cameo. Both are very similar to the Chinchilla, with changes in basic coat colour and ticking. The Blue Chinchilla looks

have now produced a whole range of fascinating 'pointed' Persians, known in some countries as Colourpoint Persians and in others as the Himalayan. These cats are not simply Longhaired Siamese but true Persian cats in type, conformation and coat length. The distinctive colouring is, however, restricted to the points alone, and the eyes are always blue. So far they exist as Seal, Blue, Chocolate, Lilac, Red and Tortie Points, and it is quite feasible that any and all 'Siamese' colours will eventually appear – Cream, Chocolate-Cream, Blue-Cream, Lilac-Cream, and Tabby in Seal, Blue, Chocolate and Lilac. What has proved so hard to achieve in this variety is the deep blue eye colour. Many examples have pale, watery-blue eyes, causing breeders to intensify their efforts to increase the density of the blue colouration so that it approaches that of the standard Siamese.

The Birman or Sacred Cat of Burma may at first glance look very like the Colourpoint. But although the same genetic Himalayan factor is responsible for the restriction of the colouring to the points, this ancient breed does differ considerably in appearance. The Birman is bred only in Seal-pointed or Blue-pointed forms, and the body is longer than that of other Persian cats, as is the length of nose and tail. The most distinctive feature of the Birman however, is the presence of flawless white 'gloves' on all four paws, extending on each hind leg to a point, rather like a gauntlet.

Legend has it that hundreds of years ago, a Kittah

extremely exotic, being heavily ticked with steel blue against a pale blue base. The Cameo Persian Cats have the red gene present, and three varieties are presently being developed, each of which can also be dilute (cream rather than red), giving six alternative shades. The palest of the group is the Shell Cameo, which has a pure white undercoat and palest apricot-pink ticking. The Shaded Cameo is considerably darker than the Shell, with quite intense red or cream shading gradually to white on chin, chest and belly. Even deeper toned is the Smoke Cameo with its white undercoat shading to a deep red-beige, and with deep red points and mask enhanced by the white ruff and ear tips. The Shell and Shaded Cameos have beautiful rose-pink eye-liner and nose leather, and their eye colour may be deep orange or copper, while those of the Smoke Cameo may be either copper or gold. The many problems besetting the pioneer breeders of these unusual cats have been largely surmounted, and a fine nucleus of unrelated breeding stock has been established, ensuring that the Cameo Persian is here to stay.

The Shorthairs

Many of the shorthaired varieties are merely short-coated versions of their Persian cousins and all conform to a basic standard of points of perfection. British cats must have a sturdy body, medium in length and with a broad chest. The legs are shortish and the paws, round and neat, while the tail is short and fairly thick. The large round head is topped with small ears, having plenty of width between, the eyes

are full and round, and the nose short. The short close coat must never feel harsh or be open, but feel firm to the touch, with a pleasant texture. It is easy to keep in immaculate condition, only requiring once-weekly brushing and combing, although a thorough hand-grooming should be carried out each day as this keeps the muscles toned up, removes all dead hair and imparts a healthy sheen to the animal.

To the layman, some shorthaired breeds may seem to be no more than particularly striking examples of ordinary house pets; but the pedigree shorthairs are of sound background and have inbred health, stamina and excellent temperaments (making them ideal for showing). As pets, they are intelligent, charming and extremely affectionate. Less mischievous than their Oriental cousins, the shorthaired breeds are graceful and active, fond of outdoor exercise, and are best kept in homes where they may have the run of the garden.

It is believed that the forebears of the British Shorthair came by ship from both the east and the north. The Phoenicians and the Romans probably introduced tabby-type cats, whereas the cats brought in by the Vikings evidently had thicker, double coats. Long before the Viking era, in fact, blue shorthaired cats are reported to have been kept in Scandinavia. It was from these early arrivals that the lovely and varied breeds of British Shorthair have gradually been developed over the centuries.

Aristocrats of the show bench

Most popular of all the British cats is the Blue, often described as the aristocrat of the Shorthairs. The well-knit powerful body is covered by a lovely thick, close-lying coat of light to medium blue, which is admirably set off by large, lustrous copper or orange eyes. The coat must be sound without any tabby markings or bars and no odd white hairs. Originally, this breed was a dark slate-blue, and much injudicious cross-breeding was carried out with Russian and Siamese cats, and also with Blue Persians. Recently, however, the breed has been more carefully nurtured and the general standard at shows is very high.

Although the world is full of handsome Black Shorthaired cats it seems, it is no easy task to breed and rear a near perfect pedigree specimen to its exacting standard of points, and the most difficult problem to be overcome is the elimination of white hairs. The kittens are often brownish-black, and this effect is also often seen in adults who have been exposed to very damp conditions, or too much sunlight. The eye colour required in this variety is copper or deepest orange, any trace of green in the eye being a serious fault. A really good Black can be buffed-up with a chamois leather until it gleams like polished ebony, and with its glowing eyes defies anyone to doubt its ancestry.

Shorthaired Whites, like White Persians, come in three types—Orange-eyed, Blue-eyed and Odd-eyed.

Left
Seal and Blue Point Birman kittens. Notice the attractive white gauntlets on the back legs.

Right
A Shaded Cameo cat. The Cameo Persians are similar to the Chinchillas in that each hair is tipped with a darker colour than that of the under coat. The Shaded Cameo has quite intense red or cream shading, with deep orange eyes. Cameos were bred originally from Chinchillas but with the introduction of the red factor. Breeders are now using a Blue-Cream female and a Smoke male to avoid the Chinchilla's green eyes.

Left
A Shorthaired Red Tabby with a rich russet-coloured coat.

Below
A Shorthaired Cream kitten with faint tabby markings on the face and body. These will go as the kitten grows older.

The same problems with deafness have been encountered in the Blue-eyed variety. It is thought that a Blue-eyed White Shorthair born with black smudges on the crown of the head will have perfect hearing, although the smudges fade and completely disappear as the kitten grows. The White varieties are all very sweet and docile and make delightful affectionate pets. They need little grooming, just a weekly brush and comb through to remove dead hairs, but the tail ends must be watched, for if soiled and neglected, an unpleasant yellow staining appears which is difficult to remove.

One of the oldest established British breeds is the Cream, yet it is quite rare, even at the largest cat shows, possibly because the standard, which calls for a rich cream colour, with no bars or tabby marks, is very exacting and difficult to reproduce. A good specimen,

with its copper or hazel eye colour and typical massive build is a most arresting sight; but despite the efforts of a small band of dedicated breeders, really good kittens are in very short supply the world over.

The female equivalent of the Cream is the Blue-Cream, a very useful cat to have as a breeding queen, for, depending upon her chosen mate, she may have Blue, Cream, and Blue-Cream kittens. This cat is most attractive, the palest blue and pinkish-cream hairs softly intermingling to give an almost shot-silk look, especially in a good clear light. The soft, fine-textured coat is easy to keep in immaculate condition with the minimum of grooming, but the loose dead hair should be combed out weekly to prevent them being swallowed by the cat and producing a hairball. The Blue-Cream, whose eyes may be copper, orange or yellow,

Far left
The British Blue is one of the most popular of the Shorthaired cats and they breed very well to type.

Below
An Odd-eyed White.

makes a charming house pet, tending to devote its affection to a particular member of the family, and is very intelligent, often scooping up its food with a dainty paw and preferring to drink from a dripping tap rather than from a water bowl.

Tabbies

Blotched, striped and spotted cats have been depicted in scrolls and ancient records, and the majority of mongrel and wild cats are marked with some form of tabby pattern. Selective breeding has ensured, however, that pedigree Tabbies are quite distinct from their cousins of unknown ancestry. Three colours are recognized in tabby-patterned cats, and a very exact and classic marbled design is essential in show and breeding stock, whatever the coat colour. The classic tabby pattern has marks resembling a butterfly on the shoulders and swirls of oyster patterns on the flanks. A large letter 'M' marks the forehead, and the neck has two necklaces or mayoral chains encircling it. Rings on legs and tail must be evenly distributed and clearly defined, and there must be no trace of white hairs in any of the three varieties, a white tip to the tail being a particular fault.

Perhaps the best of the Tabbies, for type, is the Silver, a truly exquisite creature with jet-black markings showing clearly against the pure silver ground colour and offset by clear, distinctly green eyes. Showy, yet shy and gentle, the Silver Tabby Shorthair has recently become very popular throughout the world, and classes at most shows are well filled with worthy examples of the variety.

The Brown Tabby, with its pansy-like expression, is, perhaps the most 'ordinary' of the pedigree breeds, for the really russet-brown coat colour of pre-war days is hard to achieve and rarely seen today. The standard calls for dense black markings in the classic pattern on a rich sable or brown base, and the eye colour may be either orange, hazel, deep yellow or green. The worst fault seen in this breed is a white

Below
A Shorthaired Brown Tabby with excellent markings.

chin, the ideal being cream or light brown. Only careful selection of breeding stock can eradicate this shortcoming.

A Red Tabby cat of good type and colour is rare, but well worth seeking out if one requires a sure-fire show winner. While its mongrel counterparts are sandy or marmalade, the pedigree Red Tabby has a coat with the ground colour of a deep even orange-red, with densely etched classic markings in a much darker tone. The eyes are deep orange or hazel.

The widely held belief that all Red cats are male and that any female that does turn up is worth a small fortune is, unfortunately, not true. Red male cats can be produced from Tortoiseshell or Red mothers, mated to any coloured stud male, but only if the Tortoiseshell or Red mother is mated to a Red male will a Red female kitten be born, due to the sex-linkage of the genetic factor involved. Red Tabby females mated to Red Tabby males will, however, give birth only to Red Tabby kittens, of both sexes.

Coats of many colours

The Tortoiseshell Shorthair is among the oldest known of all varieties, being depicted in paintings centuries old. The fine, glossy coat of this all-female variety makes it easy to prepare for showing with the minimum of grooming, and its delightful nature makes it a perfect house pet. The variety must be evenly patched in black, red and cream and must not have any white hairs, or tabby or brindled markings. It is important that the legs, face and tail are as evenly patched as the body, and a red blaze, bisecting the face, is desirable. The large, expressive eyes may be orange, copper or hazel.

Once known as the Spanish cat, and called the Calico Cat in the United States, the Tortoiseshell-and-White Shorthair is another all-female variety which is difficult to breed to standard, most kittens having too much white and lacking coloured patches on their legs. Recently, Black-and-White and Red-and-White Bicolour males have been used in breeding, with greatly improved results. The few males of the variety which are born from time to time all proved to be sterile.

Bicolour cats were originally expected to be marked as precisely as Dutch rabbits, but it was soon apparent that this standard was too exacting, with an excessive number of good cats having to be discarded for breeding purposes because they did not quite conform. The standard was then amended and now demands that

Below
A Silver Spotted kitten and a Silver Tabby. Tabby and Spotted kittens can appear in the same litter and it is important that the markings of the Spotted cat do not merge into one another. They should contrast well with the background.

the patching is clear and evenly distributed, with not more than two-thirds of the coat being coloured and not more than half of the coat being white. Bicolours may be bred in any colour plus white, and a white blaze down the mask is highly desirable. The white areas must be free from coloured patches and the coloured areas free from white hairs, exactly as in the equivalent Persian variety. The eyes should be deep copper or orange.

Spots and stumps

Although spotted cats have been recorded throughout history, even in the Dead Sea Scrolls, it was not until 1966 that they were officially given recognition in Great Britain as a *bona-fide* breed. Type is as for all the shorthairs, with a poweful, well-knit body, shortish, thick tail, broad, full-cheeked head and a short, fine and close-lying coat. The spots may be either round, star-shaped or triangular, and the spotted pattern carries more points in judging than type. Tabby pencil markings are faults.

Spotted cats may be Silver, Brown, Blue, Red, Cream, or any other definite colour and the eye colour must correspond to the standard required by their Tabby equivalents. The Silver Spotted, looking like a miniature snow leopard is not only the most spectacular of all the spotted varieties but arguably the most exotic of all shorthaired breeds.

Last, but by no means least of the recognized breeds, is the mysterious Manx, the tailless cat first found on the Isle of Man and purported to have been washed ashore from a Spanish ship wrecked there in 1588. Manx cats are not prolific breeders, due to the factor which makes them tailless and which also sometimes adversely affects the unborn kittens, causing them to be resorbed by the mother, and thus be stillborn.

These cats are most amusing pets to own and develop their own unique characters in human company. They may be of any recognized cat colour or pattern with the matching eye colour and can be either Rumpy – the completely tailless type–or Stumpy, with a tiny tail. Sometimes, even when two Rumpy Manx are mated together, the kittens born have normal tails! Having much longer legs at the hind end gives the Manx cat a characteristic, rabbit-like gait. Furthermore, because the unique, double coat is soft and open like that of a rabbit, it is not surprising that the breed was once thought to be the result of a cross between a cat and a rabbit.

Left
A red and white Manx cat with her tabby kitten. Notice this kitten does in fact have a tail although it is still a Manx. The father of this kitten was also a tail-less cat so the kitten is a throw-back.

Siamese and other Foreign Breeds

Mary Dunnill

Following page left
A beautiful Lilac Point Siamese admiring herself in a mirror. The character of a Lilac Point is calmer and gentler than that of other Siamese. Their temperament seems to be in keeping with their delicate shading. In America this cat is known as the Frost Point.

Following page below
A Lilac Point Siamese and a Blue Point Siamese. These cats dislike the cold and appreciate a well made basket with a comfortable warm blanket. They always look a little exotic out of doors and are rarely able to find any camouflage when they hunt birds and mice.

Two medals have recently come into my hands, one won by Lady Vyvyan for Best Two Kittens in Class 20 at the 20th Cat Show held at the Crystal Palace in 1888, the other by Miss Forestier-Walker for Best Cat in Classes 7–15 at the 25th Annual Cat Show at the Crystal Palace in 1893. These two ladies were among the original importers of Siamese cats; they brought a Siamese male and female and a pair of kittens home to England in 1886 from the Far East and no doubt these medals were won by progeny of these cats.

It is generally accepted that the Siamese cat is of Eastern origin and is often referred to as an Oriental, together with the Abyssinian and the Burmese. Today Oriental is being used as an umbrella-name, covering Foreign Shorthaired cats and all the new varieties derived from the Siamese; but since the name has not yet been given official blessing, we have Foreign White, Foreign Lilac, Foreign Black and so on. Numerically however, the Siamese cats and the Burmese cats are still the most important of the Orientals.

The Siamese
Early records of Siamese in England refer to two types, the Royal Cat of Siam whose body is 'of a dun colour, nose, part of the face, ears, feet and tail of a very dark chocolate brown, nearly black, eyes of a beautiful blue by day and of a red colour at night'. The other type, the chocolate, is 'of a very rich chocolate or seal, with darker face, ears and tail; the legs are a shade darker, which intensifies towards the feet. The eyes of a rich amber colour'. It could be that these chocolates were, in fact, Burmese/Siamese hybrids but at that time the Burmese, as a breed, had not been named as such. Harrison Weir comments that the grey or fawn colour, with black and well-marked muzzle, ears and legs, is the typical variety, the markings being the same as those of Himalayan rabbits. It is this coat pattern that is the characteristic feature of the Siamese cat, whatever the variety.

Whether Seal Point, Blue Point, Tabby Point, etc., the colour is always restricted to the points.

Many of the early cats had a kink in the tail, sometimes almost a hook. There were bob-tails, too, and one very famous stud cat had a short, stumpy tail. Today we look for a long whip-like tail and only a small, almost imperceptible kink at the end of the tail is permissible. However, there are many people who regard the kink and the crossed-eye as characteristics of the Siamese and deplore the endeavours to breed them out.

The appearance of the Siamese cat has changed in the ninety-odd years since the first two, Pho and Mia, arrived in England. Pictures of the early cats show a rather round head, with smallish ears. The present day Siamese cat has a long wedge-shaped head, long, lean body, long legs and a long tail. It is an elegant, beautiful creature, graceful in movement, with vivid blue, almond-shaped eyes. The unusual coat pattern and inscrutable expression makes this a 'cat with a difference'.

The Seal Point, with points of dark brown and a cream body colour, is the best known and most popular variety. For many years Blue Point were regarded as freaks or sports, but 'very lovely animals with the palest of cream coats and lavender blue points. Sometimes the points are of a stone grey colour, which detracts from their beauty'. One wonders if the so-called lavender blue could have been what today is the Lilac Point. The Chocolate Point has points of milk-chocolate colour whereas the Seal Point's colour is plain chocolate. There are now Red Points, Cream Points, Tabby Points in all colours (Seal, Blue, Chocolate, Lilac and Red), and Tortoiseshell Points all officially recognized as varieties of Siamese. Smoke Siamese and the Pastel Tabby Points have not yet received an official blessing.

Siamese kittens are born white, and there is the story of a novice breeder who put down a litter of

Right
A young Tortie Point Siamese cat. These are sometimes laughed at for their strange markings, but they have very sweet temperaments and are particularly useful to the serious Siamese breeder as they have evenly patched points and are usually of beautiful type. Mated to a basic colour they can produce all the various points.

Below right
A beautiful Tabby Point Siamese. These cats are 'show stoppers' with their well ringed tails with solid black tips and black stockings up the backs of their hind legs.

kittens, thinking her queen had mismated, when no characteristic coat pattern was seen. The first sign of colour is a faint pencil line on the edge of the ears. The dark brown of the Seal Points is relatively quick to show, though sometimes the Seals have a blueish tinge. It is difficult to distinguish between Chocolate, Lilac and Blue in a mixed litter. Sometimes the colour of the nose leather or paw pads will help one to decide, but this is not infallible. Ideally, whatever the colour, all the points should match. It is particularly difficult to achieve this with the Red Points and the Chocolate Points. All Siamese cats should have blue eyes, though the exact shade of blue can vary with the various points' colours.

Seal Points, Blue Points, Chocolate Points and Lilac Points are all classified as the same breed, with separate subdivisions according to colour. The Tabby Points ('their mother a wandering Siamese, their father a travelling man') and the Tortie Points are classified in a separate breed. They, too, come in all the afore-mentioned colours and with the introduction of orange a considerable number of variations are added to the breed. Recently, Silver (Chinchilla) has been introduced, giving us Smokes and Pastels in all colours.

Siamese cats are prolific breeders and are good mothers. An average litter is five kittens, but there are instances of ten or even twelve kittens being reared, with assistance perhaps from a foster-mother or nurse cat. One of my own queens, with her first litter, reared eight kittens, feeding them in two sittings, four at a time. For the most part, the male takes little or no part in the rearing of kittens, but an interesting story is recorded in an American cat magazine of a Siamese Champion who was devoted to a certain queen—Champion Miskin. When the latter was nearly due to kitten he started to make a bed by deliberately plucking himself, pulling large tufts of hair from his tail and haunches. He placed these tufts with great care on a large round cushion, beginning with a circular outer rim, gradually working towards the centre until a luxurious nest had been completed. He would then grab his mate by the neck and place her on the bed, talking to her for hours. When the kittens arrived he showed evident signs of pleasure, placing them on his cushion and waiting for more to arrive.

Breeding should not be undertaken unless one has the proper facilities—plenty of space, time and patience. The voice of a Siamese queen in season is unbelievably raucous and can be very nerve-racking. An entire male needs to be confined in his own stud quarters. He should not be allowed to roam in search of wives, but should not be so isolated as to become lonely.

The Siamese cat is highly intelligent and easily trained. It is very demanding of love and attention, likes to converse, and makes a wonderful companion; and since it is not happy left alone, the best notion is

to have a pair, or even more! But one cannot generalize about the Siamese. Each is an individual, telling you how he wishes to be treated, demanding to be loved, petted and played with, expecting you to understand what he says, and giving you, in return, his deep devotion.

The American-bred Burmese

The Burmese cat is, in most respects, like the Siamese. In America, as recently as 1949, Doris Bryant wrote that 'very dark Siamese are sometimes called Chocolate Siamese and sometimes they are called Burmese'. It is probable that the 'other type (of Siamese), the Chocolate, of a very rich chocolate or seal, with darker face, ears, tail and legs; eyes of a rich amber colour', imported into England with the first 'dun-coloured Siamese', were in fact hybrids from crosses between Siamese and an un-named dark-coated cat. In many of the early books about cats the name Burmese was applied to the cat we now call Birman, or the Sacred Cat of Burma, but this breed is very different from our present-day Burmese cat. In 1927, Mrs French's Granny Grumps, herself all-brown, was mated to a Seal Point and produced a hybrid, Timkey

Browne, who himself sired a litter of brown kittens which were exhibited at the Siamese Cat Club's 5th Show. 'We were rather struck by Mrs French's brown kittens and think this variety well worth developing. They are quite different from the chocolates, their colour being much that of a Havana cigar, with darker points. If the colour can be fixed and better eye colour obtained, we have here a very pretty and uncommon-looking cat.' (Cat Gossip, 1928.)

The Burmese breed as we know it today was made in U.S.A. In 1930 Dr Joseph C. Thompson took a brown cat named Wong Mau from Burma to America. She herself was a hybrid from Siamese and a dark-coated breed named Burmese. Mated to a Siamese, she produced hybrids and Siamese. When the Burmese/Siamese. hybrids were mated together, the darker coated Burmese were produced. These bred true, and in 1936 the Burmese was officially recognized in the United States of America as a new show breed. However, official recognition was withdrawn in 1947 in an attempt to control the breeding and to stop hybrids being exhibited and sold as pure-bred Burmese. Full status for the Brown Burmese was restored in 1953, due to the work of the Burmese Cat Society of America.

Below
A Brown Burmese basking in the sunshine. Cats have an uncanny ability to find the warmest spot in which to sit. This cat has the typical coat of the Burmese with a high glossy sheen on it.

*Right
A Cream Burmese and
below a Blue Burmese.
Burmese are great
individualists and it is
impossible to generalize
about their characters.
Every Burmese will have
its own definite
personality and will make
a wonderful companion,
and indeed demand to be
taken as a serious
member of the family.*

into England from the West Coast of America by Mrs Lilian France in 1949. These were Champion Laos Cheli Wat and Chindwin's Minou Twm, both females, and a male, Casa Gatos da Foong. Another male, Casa Gatos Darkee arrived in 1953. These early Burmese, like the first Siamese to come to England, did not take kindly to the climate and were chesty and delicate. I well remember seeing one of the first Burmese kittens bred by Mrs France and owned by Miss Lant of Loughborough, who gave me my first Siamese kitten. The little Burmese was a pathetic mite, wheezy and full of snuffles; I much preferred my Siamese kitten Beaumanor Becky. However, as the cats became acclimatized, their stamina improved and today, generally speaking, Burmese cats are tough and very healthy. Mrs France passed this stock to Mr and Mrs V. Watson, who imported another un-related male, Darshan Khudiran, from the East Coast of America in 1957.

The Brown Burmese has a rich, dark seal-brown body colour, shading to a slightly lighter colour on the chest and belly; no decided contrast of points and body colour should be evident. Young adults and older kittens may be slightly lighter and show greater contrast; young kittens generally are lighter and may show ghost tabby markings which will disappear later. White hairs (indicating white-spotting) are undesirable, and a white patch, as with white toes in Siamese, is not permissible. The general type is similar to the Siamese cat, the body being medium sized, not so long as a Siamese but not cobby, svelte, with a slender neck, slim legs and oval paws; the hind legs should be slightly longer than the front, giving a slight tilt from the horizontal to the back level. The tail is long but should not be whip-like. The face is wedge-shaped but shorter, blunter and wider at the jaw than Siamese. The skull should be rounded and the profile shows a break at the top of the nose. The chin should be firm and a jaw pinch is a fault. The ears should be large, continuing the line of the wedge-shaped face, wide at the base and slightly rounded at the tip. The eyes should be a golden yellow, wide apart and almond-shaped. Green or blue-green eyes are a fault. The coat should be short, fine-textured and close-lying, with a high glossy sheen.

The Blue Burmese was the first unexpected colour to arrive. In 1955, Chinki Golden Gay (Chinki is Mrs France's prefix) was mated back to her father, Casa Gatos Darkee, and produced a litter of four kittens, one of which was much lighter than the other three. As this kitten grew, her coat colour became a bluish grey. She was registered as Sealcoat Blue Surprise. By 1960 breeders had succeeded in establishing three generations of blue-to-blue matings, and sought official recognition from the Governing Council of the Cat Fancy, this being granted in June 1960. Since then many colour variations have been added to the Brown

and Blue varieties. There are now Cream, Blue-Cream, Red, Tortie, Chocolate (Champagne in America) and Lilac (Platinum) Burmese.

At the National Cat Club Show at Olympia, in 1974, at which I was show manager for the Shorthair section, there were no less than ninety kittens entered in the Any Colour Burmese Kitten Class offered by the Burmese Cat Club. This club, very properly, will not allow Burmese kittens to be entered in shows under the age of three calendar months, not even in litters. The club caters for all the colours of Burmese, and from small beginnings in 1954 is now second in numbers to the Siamese Cat Club, and very strong in unity of purpose.

The Burmese cat is affectionate and demonstrative, loving human companionship. It is high-spirited and quite irrepressible. I know one wicked little female that can squeeze through the letter-box to get out. She will then rush to the top of a tall pine tree and cry to be rescued. She has never learned how to clamber down and enjoys the trouble she causes.

The Havana
The Havana is also an all-brown Shorthaired cat of Foreign type, basically a self-brown Siamese with no visible signs whatsoever of the Siamese coat pattern. Brown cats are mentioned in the early literature, 'Mrs Herbert Young's chocolate Fatima, imported, won First Prize, Pulborough 1888, supposed to be the only Chocolate Siamese in Europe'. Major Woodiwiss

registered Wendie and Wander in 1921, Wendie a pointed Siamese, Wander a Chocolate Siamese. Their dam was Winkie and the sire, Chocolate Cream; both these cats had identical ancestors—imported cats, 'particulars unknown'. Wander won a First Prize at Croydon Show in 1923. Sister Stockley's Adastra won First Prize in the Chocolate Class at the Siamese Cat Club Show in 1925. Mrs French's afore-mentioned Timkey Browne was born on 16 August, 1927 and registered with his litter sisters, Dido and Cora Capps, as Seal Point Siamese. Their dam was Granny Grumps, an imported all-brown cat, their sire Champion Bonzo. Timkey Browne was different – born the colour of café-au-lait, not white. In 1928, he won a special prize for best body colour in the same class as his litter sister Dido, who became a famous Champion Seal Point; and he sired the litter of brown kittens shown at the Siamese Cat Club's 5th Show, whose colour was described as being much that of a Havana cigar, with darker points. The late Mrs Kent once told me that Mrs French 'knew an awful lot, all about the Selfs all these newcomers think they have invented. They were there but not recognized or admitted to shows'. It is reasonable to think that many of these brown cats were what today would be termed Siamese/Burmese hybrids.

The Havana, as we know it nowadays, is a manufactured breed, the end result of a planned programme for the breeding of a self-brown cat of Foreign type. In the 1950s, five lines were started. Miss Von Ullman

Left
The Havana, a manufactured breed which is basically a self-coloured Brown Siamese but with no sign of the Siamese coat pattern. They have green eyes as opposed to the yellow eyes of the Burmese and the face shape is similar to that of a Siamese rather than to the more wedged shape face of the Burmese.

Right
A Foreign White kitten. This is the one self-colour cat of Siamese type which has proved difficult to breed true.

(Roofspringer) mated a black cat to her Chocolate Point stud Siamese, Mrs Hargreaves (Laurentide) crossed a Russian Blue hybrid, Laurentide Aretoo Pearl with Mrs Fisher's Chocolate Point, Briarry Saccharin. Mrs Fisher (Praha) had Laurentide Arduo Prizm, a black/Russian hybrid and mated her to a Chocolate Point. Mrs Monro-Smith (Elmtower) mated a black queen from a mongrel mating of her Chocolate Point back to her Siamese grandfather. Mrs Judd started an outcross line, with her prefix Crossways. Mrs Dora Clarke mated a Seal Point queen, Our Miss Smith, to Elmtower Bronze Idol and produced Craigiehilloch Bronze Leaf and Craigiehilloch Bronze Wing. The 1960s saw several more breeders and new prefixes – Mrs Warren (Senlac), Mr Scott (Bluetower), Mrs Dunnill (Sumfun), Mrs Kirby (Crumberhill) and Mrs Stewart (Sweethope). The 1970s have brought many new enthusiasts to the breed and many new prefixes appear among the prize winners on the show bench – Dandycat Brown Bear, Florentine M'Bele, Kalaya Butterscotch, Samsara Saburi, Scintilla Copper Beech, Siavana Feu Follette and Solitaire Maneki Neko, to name just a few.

The breed was granted official recognition in 1958 under the name Chestnut Brown (Foreign). This name certainly describes the coat colour aimed at by all breeders of this cat, a warm ruddy brown like a ripe conker, but it was clumsy and we were all pleased when, in 1971, the official name was changed to Havana. This cat should have a long, well-proportioned head narrowing to a fine muzzle, the ears large, wide at the base, with good width between. The eyes are green. The body should be long and lithe, legs slim, paws oval. The tail is long and whip-like, with no kink. The coat may be any shade of rich chestnut brown, short, glossy, even and sound throughout. Any tendency to black is penalized. Nose leather matches the coat colour but the paw pads should be pink.

The Havana is very intelligent, full of character, with a charming nature. His voice is quiet and he is a happy, healthy and playful cat, a wonderful companion and a joy to watch. I have been very fond of all the Havanas I have known.

Below
A famous family bred to create the Egyptian Mau already recognized in the USA. A female Havana carrying the Blue and Siamese factors was mated to a Chocolate Tabby Point carrying the Blue factor. They produced two foreign Lilacs, one Havana (later to be a champion), one Lilac Havana and one Chocolate Point Siamese, as well as the new Bronze and Lilac Egyptian Mau kittens.

Right
The Korat cat has a blue-grey coat with green eyes.

Recent introductions

The most recent Foreign Shorthairs to be elevated from the Any Other Variety category are the Foreign Lilacs and the Foreign Whites. The Foreign Lilac is genetically similar to the Siamese Lilac Point. Both parents must have the two genes, chocolate and blue, but they lack the gene restricting the colour to the points. Self Lilacs were produced by the Laurentide line in the 1950s, but, as I remember them, they were much paler and pinker in coat colour. Type is today much better and the Foreign Lilac, with sparkling green eyes, is a most attractive addition to the Show Bench.

The Foreign White is also a manufactured breed, a coloured cat of Siamese type, wearing a white over-coat. The breed has been built up by very careful matings with first-class Siamese for several generations. It began in 1962 when Miss Elizabeth Flack in Ireland, Miss Patricia Turner and Mr Brian Stirling-Webb decided to develop the idea of a blue-eyed white cat of Foreign type. Mr Stirling-Webb had crossed a non-pedigree white cat with his Seal-pointed

stud in his Rex breeding programme, and I suggested that he used this white hybrid to establish a white breed similar to the Havana. Miss Turner had a similar idea after studying some over-exposed photographs of her Lilac Point queen which made it look like a pure white Siamese. Miss Flack's Seal Point queen had mismated and produced three white kittens, one a blue-eyed female, and she decided to breed from her; so El Maharanee Saengdao became the foundation queen of the Irish line. Mr Stirling-Webb promised me the first blue-eyed female white that he bred, but I had to wait until 1966 for Briarry Venus Improved, for until then all the blue-eyed white cats had been males.

By 1965 eight breeders were actively involved in carefully formulated breeding programmes, and a provisional standard of points was drawn up. Very careful records were kept and only the very best white offspring used for breeding; the inevitable non-white kittens were neutered. Deafness, head smudges, long coarse coats, poor eye colour and odd eyes were some of the problems and defects that were encountered. The Foreign White today has achieved a high degree of perfection, but there are still stumbling blocks to be overcome. Breeding stock is carefully graded, and test matings establish the colours that the cats carry under their white overcoats. The lines that are red or tortie underneath are classed in a separate category and must only be bred under controlled conditions. They are not approved for white to white matings. They may be upgraded if the red complex can be bred out, but this can be a very lengthy process. A very careful breeding policy is laid down and the goal of establishing a fertile, pure breeding white cat free from inherited defects is still in the future. Meanwhile, more and more of these beautiful cats are seen and greatly admired.

Still to be officially recognized are the Foreign Blacks, Foreign Blues, Foreign Tabbies and Egyptian Mau. They are essentially the same in type and are derived from crosses with Siamese. All are very attractive, elegant cats and can be seen at most shows, either on exhibition or competing in the Any Other Variety classes.

The Foreign White, Foreign Lilac and other self-coloured cats that are derived from the Siamese are very similar to them in temperament, but perhaps a little quieter and less demanding. They are very intelligent, amiable, well aware of their beauty and elegance, and always ready to be admired.

The Korat is a silver-blue cat with green-gold eyes. Its origin is believed to be the Malay Self-Blue and is thought by some to have had a hand in the making of the Blue Point Siamese. A pair of Korats were imported into America in 1959, direct from Thailand, followed by others. A band of enthusiasts formed the Korat Cat Fanciers' Association in 1965 to look after the interests of the breed, and very strict conditions of ownership are enforced. Breeding is closely guarded

and is documented in detail. The breed is officially recognized in America, and is permitted to compete for show honours and championships there.

A small number of Korats have been brought to England from America but they have not yet received official blessing and a breed number.

The attractive Abyssinian

The Abyssinian is one of the oldest breeds of cats. It looks very much like the cats portrayed in ancient Egyptian wall paintings, but whether it actually originated in Abyssinia or Egypt has always been questioned. Many hold that it is a man-made breed from our native British Tabbies. It is a very beautiful cat, Foreign in type, with a long, lithe body, a long pointed head with large 'listening' ears, and almond-shaped eyes, green, yellow or hazel in colour. The feet are small with black pads, and black extends up the hind legs. The outstanding characteristic of this breed is the unique ticked coat, giving the cat a typical jungle appearance. Each hair has two or three distinct bands of colour, giving an effect similar to the coat of a hare; in fact, it has sometimes been called a bunny-cat or hare-cat. The colour of the standard or normal cat should be ruddy brown, ticked with black or dark brown. The inside of the forelegs and belly should harmonize with the main colour, preferably orange-brown. There should be no bars or markings on the body and legs or rings on the tail, but a dark spine line may be permitted. No white markings are allowed and a white chin is undesirable. It is an active, friendly cat and very intelligent. Not very prolific and somewhat of a rarity, it has been called 'Child of the Gods'.

There is a red variety, differing only in coat colour, which should be a rich copper red, with belly and inside of the legs a deep apricot. The nose leather and paw pads are pink and the dark extension up the back of the hind legs becomes dark brown. The spine line also is brown. The Red Abyssinian was given an official breed number in 1963. There is also now the Blue Abyssinian, officially recognized in England in 1974. Blue Abyssinians had been bred in California from normal Abyssinians in 1964 and, as with the Blue Burmese, was a surprise, not a planned introduction of a different colour. In England in 1963, Fairlie Mehesso and his brother Fairlie Menelic, both blue Abyssinians, were exhibited. In the fullness of time, Mehesso was mated to one of Mrs Evely's normal Abyssinian queens and a litter of two blue females, two blue males and a red male was produced, proving that the queen also carried the recessive blue gene. Here was the beginning of a new variety. No doubt there will be cream and lilac Abyssinian cats calling for breed numbers soon. To my mind, the beauty of the Blue Abyssinian is out of this world and I would dearly love to possess one.

The Abyssinian cat is devoted to its owner and somewhat of a one-person pet. I knew a male that

The Abyssinian. Although a superb creature, resembling his big cousin, the lion, this Abyssinian has faults — a white chin, white whiskers, and the faint markings of an 'M' on his forehead.

Left
A Blue Burmese.

Below left
The Red Abyssinian. In the United States, this cat is known as the 'Sorrel'. The type is very similar to the cats illustrated in Egyptian paintings and some people believe the Abyssinian may be a descendant of the sacred cat of Ancient Egypt. This cat is a good example of the type and the coat colour is true. Abyssinians are 'one man' cats; they talk a lot and can and will learn to retrieve objects thrown to them. As a general rule, they have small litters with seldom more than four kittens and more of them are male than female.

Right
An unusual cat – a Russian Blue or Chartreuse crossed with Siamese. This cat shows the wedged shape face of the true Russian Blue, and also the typical brilliant green, almond shaped eyes. A cat collar with the address attached is a wise idea if you live in a town or where the cat may stray or get lost. For cats living in the country, it is not so necessary and might even be dangerous if the collar catches on a branch and pulls the cat up sharply.

Left
A Blue-Cream dilute Cornish Rex cat. Notice how every hair is curly, even on the face and whiskers. Breeders have become increasingly fascinated by Blue-Cream cats. The Longhaired Blue-Cream cats are invariably female, and a definite formula has been worked out by the geneticists for breeding from Blues and Creams so that the offspring are predictable in colour.

Right
A Cream Cornish Rex cat posing half way up a tree. Rex cats have a devoted following and are generally hardy cats with very lively and individual personalities.

always swore most fiercely at me but was extremely gentle and affectionate with his owner. He was a hunter and would often bring home his kill, frequently a rabbit. Although given complete freedom, he always returned home on the dot for mealtimes.

The Russian Blue

The Russian Blue is a cat with a long body, graceful in outline and carriage, with a medium strong bone structure. The tail is fairly long and tapering. The head is short, wedge-shaped with a flat skull; forehead and nose are straight, forming an angle. Whisker pads are prominent. Eyes are vivid green, almond-shaped and set rather wide apart. The ears are long and pointed, wide at the base, set vertically to the head. The true Russian coat should be really short, thick and very fine, like plush. Any tendency to lie flat is wrong.

This breed has suffered much over the years from careless breeding and controversy. The cats have been known by many names—Archangel Blue, Spanish, Maltese, Foreign, Chartreuse, and American Blue. The worst damage to the breed was done when Siamese crosses were made, and a kind of self-blue Siamese was produced. A new standard of points was even drawn up in 1950 to accommodate the new Russian, and some of the cats pictured in current literature still show the results. Fortunately, however, in 1965 the standard was re-written, returning approximately to the old standard, and a real effort is being made internationally to get back the original kind of cat. The best Russians in England were bred by Marie Rochford and her Dunloe prefix is world famous. The Russian Blue Association, founded in 1967, is guiding breeders of this attractive cat, and it is hoped that we shall see increasing numbers.

The Russian Blue is a hardy cat, preferring an outdoor life. Somewhat aloof and rather silent, with a small voice, it is nevertheless good-tempered, affectionate and intelligent.

The Cornish and Devon Rex

In 1950, an unusual curly-coated kitten was born in a Cornish farm cat's litter. The owner, having owned Rex rabbits, called it a Rex cat, and with the help of progressive fanciers began to establish it as a new breed. As far as was known at the time, this exciting mutation was a unique occurrence in the history of cat breeding. The cat is of modified Foreign type with a wedge-shaped head, and can be bred in all coat colours.

Eleven years later, another curly kitten of uncommon Foreign appearance was born in the neighbouring county of Devon. Coming so comparatively soon after the emergence of Cornish Rex, it was assumed that the two events were related. Test matings, however, proved conclusively that they were the result of two separate genes, and both Devon Rex, as it came to be called, and Cornish Rex were eventually added to the list of recognized breeds.

Pedigree Breeding

Angela Sayer

Breeding pedigree cats is an interesting and absorbing hobby. The rewards, while rarely financial, are many. There is a sense of pride and achievement to be gained from breeding healthy kittens, and a great deal of happiness is derived from caring for young kittens and watching their progress. Later, success on the show bench and the development of a distinctive bloodline may be attained without too great financial strain.

Like any serious hobby, cat breeding should not be entered into lightly. The mechanics of breeding are fairly straightforward, and cats left to their own devices rarely seem to have any problems in growing to maturity and finding themselves a mate. Mongrel cats do not seem to have difficulties in producing and feeding their young, but it must be clearly understood that in unnatural, controlled conditions some problems can arise. Pedigree cats, selectively bred for generations to emphasize certain characteristics, may have reached the desired standards of conformation, but at the loss of other features, such as stamina and the ability to reproduce satisfactorily.

Before embarking on the serious business of cat-breeding then, the fancier must consider several points. He must want to breed cats for the right reasons, not for financial reward, but for personal enjoyment and satisfaction. He must have the facilities to confine his breeding stock and to rear the youngsters. He must have funds to feed and house them adequately, and enough knowledge and patience to care for his felines and to cope with any emergencies or problems which may arise.

To the novice fancier it may seem logical to start cat breeding by buying a pair of kittens, one male and one female and letting them grow up and mature. Then they would be allowed to mate and produce one or two litters each year. In practise this is quite unworkable for several reasons. The kittens would probably mature at different ages, the male rarely tolerates young or growing kittens, and the female will not tolerate a male near her young. An additional problem is that the entire male needs several queens to keep him satisfied.

The sensible way to start cat breeding for pleasure is to first determine the right breed. This is best done by visiting a large cat show, looking at all the exhibits and talking to exhibitors. Many books on cats and their breeding are available and should be read carefully. Some are out-of-date and so do not describe all the breeds of today, and some give biased information in favour of particular varieties. By reading a selection of books and carefully sifting the information, it should be possible to make a short list of breeds that would be suitable.

The Queen

When a breed has been carefully chosen, a female kitten should be selected from the stock of a reputable breeder. It is pointless to start breeding from a poor specimen, for breeders should always strive to produce kittens which conform to the standards of perfection that are laid down by the various governing bodies. A kitten wanted for eventual breeding purposes should be bought at about three months of age, when it should be possible to assess its potential. If an older kitten is available, so much the better. The kitten should be the best that the novice breeder can afford, but even if she is not of top show quality, she should have a first class pedigree, be officially registered and vaccinated.

Care taken in the selection of this first female kitten will pay dividends in the long run, for she will possibly be the foundation queen of a whole new line of show cats. It is better to buy one really good healthy kitten at this stage, than to acquire several cats from an unreliable source. Most breeders of note would agree that their happiest days were when they had their first pedigree queen.

Left
Two young champion
Seal Point Siamese.

129

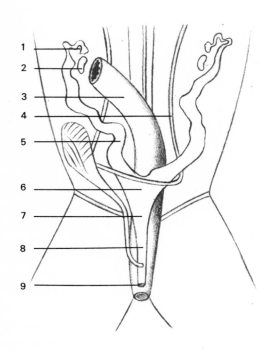
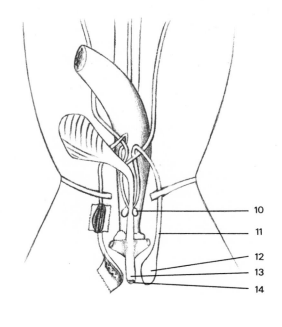

The reproductive system of the female (far left) and male (left) cat.

Female
(1) Fallopian tubes (2) Ovaries (3) Rectum (4) Ureter (5) Horn of uterus (6) Uterus (7) Cervix (8) Vagina (9) Clitoris.

Male
(10) Prostate gland (11) Spermatic cord (12) Testis (13) Penis (14) Glans penis.

Gestation Chart—(for cats mated between January 1st and June 30th)

January

Mated	1	2	3	4	5	6	7	8	9	10	11	12	13	14	15	16	17	18	19	20	21	22	23	24	25	26	27	28	29	30	31
Due	7	8	9	10	11	12	13	14	15	16	17	18	19	20	21	22	23	24	25	26	27	28	29	30	31	1	2	3	4	5	6

March   April

February

Mated	1	2	3	4	5	6	7	8	9	10	11	12	13	14	15	16	17	18	19	20	21	22	23	24	25	26	27	28
Due	7	8	9	10	11	12	13	14	15	16	17	18	19	20	21	22	23	24	25	26	27	28	29	30	1	2	3	4

April   May

March

Mated	1	2	3	4	5	6	7	8	9	10	11	12	13	14	15	16	17	18	19	20	21	22	23	24	25	26	27	28	29	30	31
Due	5	6	7	8	9	10	11	12	13	14	15	16	17	18	19	20	21	22	23	24	25	26	27	28	29	30	31	1	2	3	4

May   June

April

Mated	1	2	3	4	5	6	7	8	9	10	11	12	13	14	15	16	17	18	19	20	21	22	23	24	25	26	27	28	29	30
Due	5	6	7	8	9	10	11	12	13	14	15	16	17	18	19	20	21	22	23	24	25	26	27	28	29	30	1	2	3	4

June   July

May

Mated	1	2	3	4	5	6	7	8	9	10	11	12	13	14	15	16	17	18	19	20	21	22	23	24	25	26	27	28	29	30	31
Due	5	6	7	8	9	10	11	12	13	14	15	16	17	18	19	20	21	22	23	24	25	26	27	28	29	30	31	1	2	3	4

July   August

June

Mated	1	2	3	4	5	6	7	8	9	10	11	12	13	14	15	16	17	18	19	20	21	22	23	24	25	26	27	28	29	30
Due	5	6	7	8	9	10	11	12	13	14	15	16	17	18	19	20	21	22	23	24	25	26	27	28	29	30	31	1	2	3

August   September

The novice breeder should join a cat club that specializes in the chosen breed, and by attending cat shows, perhaps entering the new acquisition, he will learn more about cats, their care and breeding than he could sift from a library of books. Specialist Clubs and Societies normally issue leaflets and newsletters about their breed and the Honorary Secretary is usually happy to answer letters and queries from novices.

From the age of three months the young female must be allowed to live under fairly natural conditions. She should be fed a balanced, sensible diet and given facilities for plenty of exercise. Clean conditions and lots of fresh air are essential, and she should be given daily grooming sessions to keep her well-muscled and fit. Young cats kept in cramped conditions and overfed rarely prove to be satisfactory breeders. The kitten's first period of oestrus, or heat, may be noticed at any age from four months onwards, although it is rare to find such precocious kittens in most breeds. It is more likely to be about the age of nine months in Siamese and Foreign varieties, and twelve to fifteen months in Persian and Shorthaired breeds.

It is usual to observe the young female cat in her first heat and to keep her safely confined until the period of season diminishes, then she is mated on her next heat. The ideal time for her to be mated is between ten and twelve months of age so that she is over one year and fully grown before the kittens are born. Some little queens mature early and their periods of heat are repeated every three weeks. In this case it is sometimes advisable to mate them early as continual 'calling' without conception can cause breeding problems in later life. The veterinary surgeon should be asked to examine the kitten to make sure that she would be physically capable of producing kittens if mated, and his advice should be followed explicitly. The breeding problems which arise from holding back the young queen are produced because the cat is a spontaneous ovulator. Unlike dogs and humans, cats release ova from the ovaries only after the stimulation of mating. Continued production of ova which cannot be released can cause eventual sterility in the queen.

The female cat has two ovaries in which the ova develop gradually during her cycle, from the end of one heat until mating takes place. The stimulation of mating causes the ova to fall away from the walls of the ovaries. Two tubes lead from the ovaries to the uterus, which consists of a central body and two distinct horns in which the fertilized ova implant. From the base of the uterus, to the outside of the body, is the vagina into which the penis of the male cat

Gestation Chart—(for cats mated between July 1st and December 31st)

July

Mated	1	2	3	4	5	6	7	8	9	10	11	12	13	14	15	16	17	18	19	20	21	22	23	24	25	26	27	28	29	30	31
Due	4	5	6	7	8	9	10	11	12	13	14	15	16	17	18	19	20	21	22	23	24	25	26	27	28	29	30	1	2	3	4

Due dates begin in September and the 1, 2, 3, 4 fall in October.

August

Mated	1	2	3	4	5	6	7	8	9	10	11	12	13	14	15	16	17	18	19	20	21	22	23	24	25	26	27	28	29	30	31
Due	5	6	7	8	9	10	11	12	13	14	15	16	17	18	19	20	21	22	23	24	25	26	27	28	29	30	31	1	2	3	4

Due dates begin in October and the 1, 2, 3, 4 fall in November.

September

Mated	1	2	3	4	5	6	7	8	9	10	11	12	13	14	15	16	17	18	19	20	21	22	23	24	25	26	27	28	29	30
Due	5	6	7	8	9	10	11	12	13	14	15	16	17	18	19	20	21	22	23	24	25	26	27	28	29	30	1	2	3	4

Due dates begin in November and the 1, 2, 3, 4 fall in December.

October

Mated	1	2	3	4	5	6	7	8	9	10	11	12	13	14	15	16	17	18	19	20	21	22	23	24	25	26	27	28	29	30	31
Due	5	6	7	8	9	10	11	12	13	14	15	16	17	18	19	20	21	22	23	24	25	26	27	28	29	30	31	1	2	3	4

Due dates begin in December and the 1, 2, 3, 4 fall in January.

November

Mated	1	2	3	4	5	6	7	8	9	10	11	12	13	14	15	16	17	18	19	20	21	22	23	24	25	26	27	28	29	30
Due	5	6	7	8	9	10	11	12	13	14	15	16	17	18	19	20	21	22	23	24	25	26	27	28	29	30	31	1	2	3

Due dates begin in January and the 1, 2, 3 fall in February.

December

Mated	1	2	3	4	5	6	7	8	9	10	11	12	13	14	15	16	17	18	19	20	21	22	23	24	25	26	27	28	29	30	31
Due	4	5	6	7	8	9	10	11	12	13	14	15	16	17	18	19	20	21	22	23	24	25	26	27	28	1	2	3	4	5	6

Due dates begin in February and the 1, 2, 3, 4, 5, 6 fall in March.

enters to deposit sperms for fertilizing the ova. The tip of the penis reaches to the entrance of the uterus, called the cervix, through which the sperms are passed.

After copulation, the ova fall into the fallopian tubes leading to the uterus, where they are surrounded by large numbers of sperms. Eventually one sperm breaks through the outer casing of each ovum and reaches the nucleus where it fuses, and this phenomenon is known as fertilization. Once fertilized, the ovum attaches itself to the wall of one of the uterine horns, and gradually, implantation takes place. Many ova are shed from the ovaries, but a few implant after fertilization, the average numbering five.

The brood queen can breed satisfactorily for a number of years if she is maintained in good physical condition and not allowed to have too many kittens each year. Queens that start breeding at ten months or so, and are mated regularly, seem to breed successfully, if not allowed to rear large litters, until the age of about eight years. Lactating and feeding litters of five or more kittens seems to take more out of a queen than conception and pregnancy, and frequent lactations deplete a queen's calcium reserves very seriously.

For a cat to be termed a good brood queen she must not only produce even, healthy litters at regular intervals, but the kittens must live past weaning age and not fade out as do the litters of so many pedigree queens. She must give birth without difficulty, produce adequate milk supplies for her youngsters and enjoy rearing her litter.

Cats do not have a breeding season, but are in breeding condition for most of the year with peaks in February, at the end of April and August. It is interesting to note that queens kept indoors with longer hours of white light conditions will breed more frequently than those kept in a cattery, where the light conditions are completely natural. Kittens born between the months of April and August seem to be easier to rear and more robust than kittens born at any other time of the year. Spring and Summer kittens can spend much of their waking hours out of doors in the sunshine, and certainly seem to benefit from it. Unfortunately, some pedigree queens 'call' in the Autumn and Winter and have to be mated in order to settle them down. Thus, kittens may be born at inconvenient times and have to spend their first months of life confined in artificially heated conditions.

The signs of oestrus in the female cat have been described in a previous section of this book, so will not be repeated here. What must be emphasized however is the determination with which the queen will try to escape from the house in order to mate. Queens have been known to jump from very high windows, and from moving cars, and seem to have no thought for their own safety while in this aroused condition. Obviously, it is important that the queen should be

safely confined, for even if she does not become pregnant by a stray, non-pedigree tom, she may well pick up parasites or infection which could later be transmitted to the pedigree stud cat.

Some queens 'call' at regular, well spaced intervals, while others may seem to be perpetually 'calling' unless pregnant or lactating. There is no real hard and fast rule for cats in this matter, except that Foreign shorthairs and Siamese seem to 'call' more frequently than do the Persians and European Shorthairs. A few queens come into 'call' again although recognizably pregnant and will, if a male cat is available, be seen to mate. Some breeders, with their own males on the premises, have observed this mating and thought that the cat had missed conception in her previous season. Having altered the original dates and counted the 65 days gestation period from the second observed mating, they have been astonished when the litter has arrived on the earlier date. Those keeping cat colonies for research purposes have also observed this strange feline behaviour pattern, and it is now thought that mating while pregnant releases more hormone in the female cat's body, and helps with the processes of birth and lactation.

The same pattern of 'calling' may occur in queens which have just produced kittens, but they are

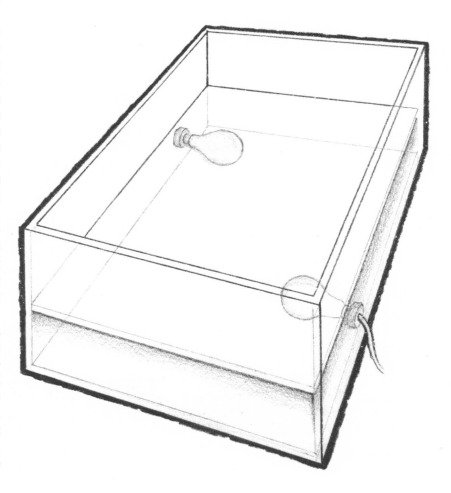

A hygienic kittening box moulded in fibre-glass and with a built-in heating element. This needs to be placed in a dark corner, however, or the queen may resent the lack of privacy and soon decide to move the litter to a new nest.

132

rarely seen to mate at this stage. In fact the scent of milk production appears to repel the male cat, who may spit at a lactating female, and give her a wide berth. The scent also repels other cats and older kittens who keep well away from the new litter. Even if a queen with a young litter does mate, conception rarely takes place, possibly because her hormones restrict the implantation of the fertilized ova.

In her first period of oestrus, the young queen must be treated tenderly, for this is a time of great stress to her and she may react in a number of different ways to the new feelings that she is experiencing. While she may be extra affectionate, she may also be hypersensitive to touch, and purring at one moment, may spin round and strike out at the next. She should be kept quiet, and not subjected to any unnecessary strain at this time, and this is another good reason for not taking her away from home to be mated on her first heat. This period of oestrus is best used to allow the queen to become accustomed to the strange new sensations within her body, without the additional strain of travel, new people and surroundings and the advances of a strange male cat.

A suitable stud cat is usually selected for the queen long before she has her first period of oestrus. Arrangements are made with his owner for the queen to be taken on her second heat. It is usual to telephone the stud owner when the queen has her first heat so that the approximate date of the subsequent season can be ascertained. When the female starts her second 'call', the stud owner is informed and she is taken to the stud on the second or third day. It is usually advisable to wait until the queen actually starts rolling as well as calling, for by this stage in the proceedings it is unlikely that the journey will put her off. She is usually kept there for at least three days and is served on each of these days. Some stud owners allow the queen and stud to live together after the initial, introductory period is passed. The male and female mate many times during this period if allowed to do so, and often curl up contentedly together in a box to sleep. Cats allowed to mate several times should be safely in kitten by the time they are returned home for, as we have seen, mating stimulates the release of the ova for fertilization. When the stud owner considers that the queen has been satisfactorily served, he contacts her owner so that she may be collected. On her return home, the young queen should be allowed to rest quietly for several days and given good, nourishing meals.

It is best to transport the queen to and from the stud by car if possible, for a long train journey can be fatiguing and cause emotional stress. She should be confined for the journey in a suitable, safe carrier, either of wood or plastic covered mesh. A wicker basket may be used but care must be taken to ensure that the lid fastens securely, and also that it is impossible for the queen to bite her way out. Wicker baskets and mesh carriers should be covered with plastic material or thick paper to keep out draughts during the journey.

Care of the pregnant Queen

It is not always easy to tell whether or not a queen is safely in kitten. Careful inspection of the nipples on the twenty-first day after conception may show that they are distinctly pink and slightly enlarged. While this is a hopeful sign it is by no means infallible. A queen that has had several litters does not exhibit this change. Her nipples will always be slightly enlarged after her first lactation, and will often appear pink in colour towards evening whether she is pregnant or not. In the maiden queen however, this sign, plus the fact that there is no appearance of a further period of heat, may be taken as a good indication that a litter is safely conceived.

At the end of the fourth week of pregnancy, a veterinary surgeon can palpate the queen and feel the tiny embryonic kittens in the uterine horns. Obviously, inexperienced breeders should not try this test for themselves, for the probing of inexpert fingers could cause internal damage to the queen. At the end of the fifth week, the queen's abdomen will be visibly swollen, giving her body a pear-shaped look, and, even in older queens, the nipples will show a definite enlargement.

The time from conception to parturition is known as the period of gestation, and in the cat this seems to be 65 days. Many books state different numbers of days for this period, but any breeder of standing will agree that the sixty-fifth day is the most common among his cats. Kittens have been born as early as 59 days after conception and survived, although this is extremely rare. Many queens go longer than the average, and kittens born on the sixty-seventh day are quite common. Here one must remember that conception occurs after mating, so it could be that these 'overdue' kittens were, in fact, to exact term.

Provided that the queen is eating well and shows no sign of distress, there is no need to get alarmed if the sixty-fifth day goes by with no sign of labour. It is not necessary to have the cat examined by the veterinary surgeon until the seventieth day unless she seems lethargic, hot to the touch, has no appetite or shows a vaginal discharge.

During her pregnancy, it is important to treat the queen as a normal animal, fulfilling a natural function, and not to coddle her or allow sentimentality to enter into the relationship with her. Queens which are over-humanized often prove to be extremely bad mothers and refuse to stay with the kittens unless their owners are prepared to sit with them. They sometimes resent the owner's interest in the litter and spend a lot of time carrying the kittens in and out of the nest box. If the queen usually has the freedom of the garden, she should still enjoy the exercise, and for the first four weeks of her gestation, she will not show any change in her normal agility. From the fourth week, the increase in her weight and its redistribution will cause her to take extra care in jumping up and down, and she will be seen to test the width of any space carefully before trying to squeeze through. The queen will not perform any movements at this stage which could injure herself or her litter, unless she is frightened. If she is chased by a dog, or otherwise very disturbed, she may run in fear, squeezing through palings and jumping up onto walls or high fences. Queens have been known to abort through straining themselves thus, and so they should be protected from this sort of danger whenever possible.

Halfway through her pregnancy, the queen's appetite increases, and her owner should provide an extra meal or two each day. This is preferable to increasing the size of the regular meals, for the enlarging of the uterine horns can restrict the stomach of the cat. At six weeks gestation, the queen exercises less, and appears obviously pregnant, even to the least observant of cat owners. She spends a great deal of time resting, and pays great attention to her daily grooming. Her diet should be of high protein foods at this stage, for she must not be allowed to accumulate fat and lose muscle tone.

From six weeks until the date that the litter is due, the queen's girth increases gradually in size, her coat takes on a bloom of health and she lives a quiet, contented life. Her grooming becomes even more meticulous and she pays special attention to her enlarging nipples. Her bowel movements must be watched carefully, for the pressure of the kittens on internal organs can cause problems. If she appears constipated, the veterinary surgeon will advise on a suitable form of laxative. Usually it is better to give oily foods, such as sardines or pilchards, to alleviate the problem, rather than a purgative medicine.

The queen is conscious of the kittens movements within her at the sixth week of gestation, and at this time she is seen to roll and stretch her body along the floor. In the seventh week, she may experience the first murmurings of the nesting instinct, and restlessly pace the house looking into drawers and cupboards for a dark corner in which to give birth. A large, dark cardboard box filled with newspaper is appreciated by the queen, who will go into it from time to time and rest. As her time of confinement draws nearer, she shreds the paper with her teeth, forming a comfortable pad on which to settle down.

During the last fortnight of the pregnancy, the queen should be encouraged to go into the kittening box, and discouraged from the rest of the house. She should be kept as quiet and calm as possible. Gentle grooming to remove all dead hair and to tone her muscles is appreciated, and if she is carrying a large litter, it may be necessary to sponge her anal regions clean. She will be unable to clean herself properly there now due to her bulky frame. The nipples should be examined and if they appear dry or cracked, a little vegetable oil can be applied and rubbed in gently. The queen's ears must be kept spotlessly clean at all times and her coat checked for parasites if she is free-ranging. Pest powders must not be used on pregnant or nursing queens. Prevention is better than cure, and combing daily through her coat with a fine toothed metal comb will ensure that she does not harbour any fleas or lice.

Some breeders have a special cat house in the garden in which queens are placed to have and rear their kittens. Most breeders, however, even if they have several queens, prefer the litter to be delivered indoors, so that progress can be watched at all times. It is important to be on hand during the confinement, for even with experienced queens, things can go wrong during the birth. Many people have special kittening boxes constructed, but it is better to use disposable materials for parturition, for there can be a build-up of low-grade infection from the birth and rearing of kittens which is not always controlled by normal household cleaning methods.

A large cardboard box is ideal for kittening. A round hole can be cut in one side, which enables the queen to get in and out without undue strain. This should be about six to eight inches from the floor, to prevent toddling kittens crawling out, and to shield the interior from draughts. The open top of the box can be covered with a large, flat sheet of cardboard, removable for easy access. The box itself should be placed on several thicknesses of newspaper to insulate from the cold floor, and several layers of newspaper placed inside. Even if the queen produces her litter elsewhere, the kittens can be transferred to this box soon after birth, when she will be happy to settle down with them. If the weather is cold and the room is not centrally heated, an infra-red bulb can be hung into the box from above. The advantage of using such a box and bedding for kittening is that its negligible cost enables it to be burned after the litter is toddling, which ensures complete hygiene.

Parturition
The normal processes of giving birth have been described elsewhere in this book (Cat Psychology), but it is sometimes necessary for the breeder to give a helping hand. An old terry towel cut into small squares, which have been sterilized by boiling and kept in a polythene bag, are useful for aiding delivery. A pair of blunt scissors and some astringent antiseptic lotion obtained from the veterinary surgeon should also be to hand, along with a roll of cotton wool, and a rubber or stone hot-water bottle.

When the maiden queen experiences her first stage labour, she will pace the house and may exhibit symptoms similar to that of 'calling'. She may vomit or go continuously to her toilet tray in a puzzled fashion. She may not go into the kittening box even when the first kitten is presented. More experienced

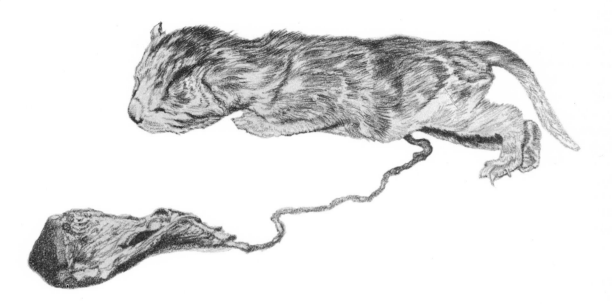

queens usually rest quietly in the kittening box right through the long, first stage of labour. The steady contractions which indicate that the first kitten is being pushed down the birth canal are quite obvious and accompanied by a break in the queen's steady breathing pattern. As she pushes, she may press her hind legs against the sides of the box. Some breeders place torn kitchen tissue paper under her haunches at this stage, as it is more absorbent than newspaper and soaks up the first copius birth fluids.

It must be emphasized that human intervention in the kittening process is only necessary if things go wrong. Too many breeders interfere, and do much more harm than good. Birth is quite natural, and most queens cope instinctively and well. The breeder should only be there to comfort and observe, helping only if an emergency occurs. Some queens insist that their owners are with them during kittening, and if left, will get out of the box and go to them, even with a kitten in a presented position.

Labour can vary· considerably in difficulty and duration, not only from queen to queen, but from kitten to kitten in the same litter. The kittens vary in size and position of presentation. The birth of a maiden queen's first kitten can be a very long and frustrating process, more so for the owner than for the queen, who seems to accept the situation in a calm, resigned manner. Only if the animal shows signs of anxiety or exhaustion need the veterinary surgeon be called. Sometimes a kitten is half-presented and despite all the queen's straining, appears to be stuck. A terry-towel square should be placed over the part of the kitten which is protruding, enabling a firm but gentle grip on the tiny, slippery body. Then as the queen strains, the kitten can be eased slowly and steadily downwards and round towards the queen's belly, until

free. It must not be pulled, and if a breech presentation, it may be necessary to slightly rotate the body in order to free the head.

The queen should immediately start to lick the newborn kitten, but if she starts labouring to expel the placenta, or the next kitten, she may well ignore it. In this instance, human assistance is vital. The kitten's head must be freed from the sac and the nasal passages cleared without delay, or it may inhale some of the amniotic fluid and drown. The face and nostrils must be wiped with cotton wool, then the kitten is placed on the palm of the hand, head down and rubbed gently from tail to head with a terry towel square. This action pushes the fluid out of the lungs and nostrils and enables the kitten to breathe. It is quite possible that the kitten's umbilical cord is still attached to the placenta inside the mother's body. If so, the cord can be gently pulled when the mother next strains, and the placenta will be expelled.

Placing the kitten and placenta near the mother cat's head may encourage her to clean the baby and to sever the cord herself. Most cats eat the placenta, then along the cord, stopping about one inch from the kitten's body. This is a natural function and should not be discouraged. Placing the cord across one of the queen's forepaws often triggers off the cleansing response. If the queen ignores the kitten completely, or is busy giving birth to the next one, then it is best to cut the cord. Blunt scissors, sterilized by placing in boiling water for ten minutes, are used. The cord is cut one inch from the kitten's body, the blunt scissors sealing the cut ends and preventing bleeding. Astringent antiseptic is applied to the end of the cord attached to the kitten. Experienced breeders can sever the cord by pulling with the thumbs and forefingers, but it is important to be shown how to do this by a veterinary surgeon, otherwise it could result in a hernia protruding from the kitten's navel.

The kitten should be rubbed with a towelling square until dry to stimulate its circulation, then placed on a well wrapped hot water bottle in front of the queen until she is ready to nurse it. If the queen is not interested in eating the placenta, it should be taken away. Even if the mother cat refuses to cope with the cleaning of her first kitten, she should be encouraged to deal with each subsequent kitten as it is born. Human interference as a matter of course can result in a queen becoming quite hopeless as a mother. Sometimes there is a period of hours between the birth of each kitten, sometimes they are born in pairs, sometimes in rapid succession. When the queen has finished, she usually turns onto her side and gathers the kittens to her, to nurse.

Abnormal births

Although most kittens are born normally, a breeder should always be prepared for things to go wrong. If labour is very prolonged or the queen turns violently from side to side in her box, it is essential to call the veterinary surgeon. If the queen is displaying uterine inertia, he will inject a substance to help her contract and expel the first kitten. If a kitten is delayed for too long in the birth canal, it may die, for there is a limit to the length of time that a kitten can survive before birth, after the placenta has become detached from the wall of the uterus. The movements of a live kitten help the queen to bear down, but dead kittens, whether they die before the onset of labour or during birth, usually present problems.

The queen finds it easier to expel a kitten presented head first, than one in the breech position, because the kitten's head provides a more suitable surface on which to exert muscular pressure. Often in a breech delivery the hind feet and tail are visible first, and are very difficult to grasp without damaging the the kitten. The most troublesome presentation is one where the kitten is turned so that the head is trapped near the cervix, the back of the head and the shoulders then block the entrance to the vagina. In this case the veterinary surgeon must carefully manipulate the kitten so that it may be pushed backwards, the head disengaged from its trapped position, and drawn down the birth passage. In an animal as small internally as a cat, it will be seen that this is a delicate and highly skilled procedure, not to be attempted by a novice cat breeder.

Some kittens which are abnormally presented are eventually delivered safely by the veterinary surgeon using forceps, but others may die during the long process of removal. In very serious cases, where the kitten is firmly blocked in the passage, there is no alternative but to perform a Caesarean section. Even when expertly carried out this operation can make subsequent litters difficult, if not impossible, to produce normally. Adhesions which change the shape of the uterine horns may follow the operation, making the passage of kittens into the vagina, extremely complicated. Most veterinary surgeons only decide to perform a Caesarean section as a last resort. It has been recorded quite frequently that queens have rested for long sessions between the birth of individual kittens, eventually producing the final ones with no ill effects even after periods as long as three days.

In carrying out a Caesarean section, great care is exercised by the veterinary surgeon in the choice and administration of the anaesthetic. As cats are poor subjects for anaesthesia at the best of times, it is particularly important that no ill effects are suffered during this type of operation, by either the queen or the kittens. The veterinary surgeon usually takes the queen to his surgery to deliver the kittens, but will often allow the breeder to go along to sit in the waiting room until the operation is over. The kittens are usually quite strong, unless affected by the anaesthetic, and are passed to the owner in an ante-room so that they can be rubbed dry and stimulated while the veterinarian deals with suturing the incision in the queen. Sometimes the breeder is allowed to take the queen home, but the veterinary surgeon usually keeps her under surveillance until she recovers consciousness. In any case, the cat does not want to be bothered with tiny kittens scrabbling for milk near her sore, tender incision area. The kittens are usually hand fed for a few days but later the queen accepts them and feeds them normally.

Abnormal kittens

Unfortunately, not every kitten that is born survives to become an adult cat. Some kittens die in embryo, some during birth and some shortly after. A very tiny percentage of kittens may be born deformed in some way and have to be destroyed. It is unfair to attempt to rear a kitten with a serious deformity, for it can never be anything but a freak. The unfortunate creature should be painlessly destroyed by the veterinary surgeon. Cleft palate is perhaps the most common deformity in some strains of pedigree cats. The kitten is born normally and seems content at first. After 24 hours however, it will be restless and noisy, nosing from one nipple to another searching for food. If closely watched, some milk may be seen to drip from its nose and a slight wheezing sound can be heard. Such a kitten will be found to have a cleft palate, because the bones across the roof of the mouth have not joined together. There are varying degrees of the extent of the cleft. In some cases it runs forward to the front of the jaw and the kitten cannot even suck. In other cases, it runs halfway along the roof of the mouth, and while the kitten can suck, it cannot obtain enough milk to satisfy its needs. These kittens must be humanely destroyed without delay. If the cleft is only partial, the kitten may survive with care and extra feeding by hand, but it must never be allowed to breed future stock if it lives to adulthood.

Kittens are sometimes born with twisted legs. Often the hind legs appear to have been put on the wrong way round and drag behind the kitten as it crawls. With careful exercising and manipulation, this condition can often be corrected, as long as the correct number of bones are present and the hips are not dislocated or deformed. The veterinary surgeon can determine whether or not there is any anatomical reason for destroying these kittens. If the bone structure is normal, it is merely the muscles that are causing the twisted condition and physiotherapy can produce a complete recovery. Again, it is advisable that such kittens are eventually kept as pets and not used for breeding.

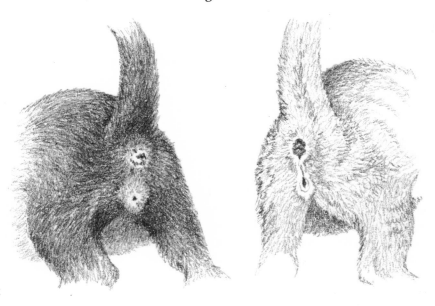

Sexing kittens is easy, even for the novice, provided that youngsters of both sexes are present for comparison. In the female (far right) both tiny orifices are close together and resemble an inverted exclamation mark. In the male (right), both openings are round and are well separated by twin swellings of the testes.

Now and again a kitten may be born with its eyes open, instead of being tightly sealed in the normal way. Until quite recently it was thought that such kittens would be blind, and so they were destroyed. Luckily, a few breeders decided to rear open-eyed kittens and it was found that in most cases they were perfectly normal. It is important to keep these kittens in very dim light conditions however, and in some cases the eyes close after 24 hours, to re-open along with the eye-opening of their normal littermates. Kittens born with serious deformities of the eyelids usually have other internal problems and fade away shortly after birth.

One of the most distressing deformities that is experienced, is that of an umbilical hernia which is so pronounced that the whole of the kitten's intestines are enclosed in a pouch of skin outside its body. Unfortunately, such kittens are strong and crawl to the queen's nipple to feed, but must be euthanised without delay as there is nothing that can be done for them.

There are a few minor deformities which occur in kittens which do not affect them unduly, so they may be reared. These include polydactyly, which is the presence of extra toes on the foot. This condition may vary from a simple extra toe on each forefoot to the presence of several toes. One cat exhibited in the household-pet section of a large British Championship show had double front paws and seven toes on each hind foot. He was appropriately named 'Boots' and although he plodded about in a rather stolid fashion, his enormous feet did not seem to present him with any serious problems.

Kinked, bobbed and bent tails are also common, although selective breeding has reduced the numbers one sees today. Originally, the Siamese cats first imported from the Orient had extremely short, kinked or knotted tails, and even today Siamese kittens are more prone to this deformity than those of any other breed. Occasionally kittens are born with their tails bent double and folded flat. As they dry out, the tail straightens but is left with a deformed joint where the bend occurred. Most kinks occur at the tail root. This deformity can cause serious problems as it often affects the base of the spine and the anal region. As the cause of these deformities is genetic, it is better not to breed further generations from stock which continually produces such kittens. An extreme case of tail deformity is seen in the Manx cat, where the tail is either greatly reduced until only a stump remains, or is missing completely.

Rearing kittens

Despite all the things that can go wrong, in most cases the cat will have a normal healthy litter without undue difficulty. After cleaning the kittens thoroughly and then cleaning her own legs and flanks, the queen will be grateful for some nourishment. The most acceptable food is two tablespoons of evaporated milk with one egg yolk, one level teaspoon of glucose and two tablespoons of boiling water. She will take this greedily before settling down to a good, long rest. It is best to leave her quietly alone for several hours until she stirs and leaves the nest to pass water or to stretch.

When the queen has settled down completely after the birth, her bedding can be tidied up. This is not essential from her point of view, but makes the owner feel better. A pad of newspapers are folded to fit the base of the kittening box and then covered with a disposable cot sheet or a piece of flannelette material. This pad is warmed, then the whole litter is quickly placed upon the pad while the queen is exercising herself. The solid papers and debris are lifted from the kitten box and the clean pad, complete with kittens, is tucked neatly into place. If the kittens squeak, the mother cat will come running in to see what is happening and may try to carry the kittens back into the box, so it is important to make the procedure as smooth and swift as possible. The soiled papers should be disposed of completely, preferably by burning, for if they are placed in an outbuilding, the queen may well decide to carry her kittens to that spot, attracted by the scent of her nesting material.

Sometimes a queen will remain in the box and have

to be lifted out if she refuses to leave her kittens. It is important that the queen is encouraged to take exercise and to use her toilet tray, and she should be taught to allow the breeder to handle and examine the kittens without showing resentment. It is best to stroke the queen with one hand, talking quietly and soothingly while lifting the kitten with the other hand. The navel of each kitten should be checked daily to make sure that no infection has entered the severed end of the cord. An infected navel looks sore and may have a greenish, raised rim where the cord enters the body. If this is noticed, the veterinary surgeon must be advised for he may wish to administer an antibiotic to the queen, which will be passed to the kitten through her milk.

Most queens enjoy having their owners examine the kittens and purr proudly while they are handled. Others resent it and carry the kittens around the house trying to find a safe place in which to hide them. This may also happen if dogs or small children are allowed to disturb and upset the nursing queen, and it can result in damage to the kittens. Too much carrying, especially by a nervous or inexperienced queen results in badly scarred necks and even in skeletal fractures if the tiny creatures are dropped.

For the first few days of its life, a kitten sleeps and feeds, its mother cleans its coat and stimulates it to evacuate its bladder and bowels by licking its anal regions with her rough tongue. Each kitten in a litter selects its own nipple soon after birth, and usually prefers to feed from that nipple only. In a large litter, the mother cat may feed some of the kittens, then, when they are replete, lick the others, waking them and encouraging them to feed. The queen, especially if she has eaten the placentas, does not seem to be hungry for the first 24 hours after the birth. Some queens are an exception to this rule however, and demand food almost straight away. The diet should be light at first, for it is very important that the milk flow is stimulated, and that the queen does not get diarrhoea.

If the queen can tolerate milk, this can be given. She may like cooked flaked fish, rabbit or chicken. It is best to avoid red meat at first, but some queens demand it. The breeder usually knows exactly what his own queen prefers and can feed her accordingly.

The queen's nipples must be examined on the day following the birth to ensure that the milk is flowing properly. Occasionally a queen may have one or more 'blind' teats. This may be caused by a blockage and the nipple must be bathed gently with hand-hot water before massaging. Olive oil can be worked into the nipple to make it supple, and eventually the milk should flow. If it does not, and the gland becomes hard and inflamed, veterinary advice must be sought. Some queens have one or more permanently 'blind' teats as no milk is formed in the gland behind them. These rarely cause trouble, but just means that there is one less teat from which the litter may choose.

Kittens vary in birth weight in much the same way as human babies. Persian kittens are quite large generally, weighing in at about four ounces, while Siamese kittens may weigh as little as two and a half ounces. A lot depends on litter size, also. Obviously if there are only three kittens in a litter they will weigh more, on average, than kittens in a litter of six. Kittens born with a birth weight of under two ounces rarely survive to adulthood, even if they are reared past weaning age. Queens with weakly kittens often reject them, pushing them to the back of the nesting box, and eventually these are found dead from starvation, or having been overlain by the queen. The kittens gain weight rapidly from birth onwards. A good guide to expected weight increase is to calculate that the birth weight will be added each week. Thus a Siamese kitten weighing into the world at three ounces should weigh nine ounces at three weeks. This weight gain will only be maintained if the queen is adequately fed however.

Novice breeders, and sometimes even experienced breeders, are anxious to determine the sex of the new-born kittens. It is often easier to tell the males from the females while they are still wet at birth. In longhaired breeds especially, once they dry, their sex is rather indeterminate. If both sexes are present in the litter, this helps the novice to decide which kittens are which. In the female the two openings, anus and vagina, are very close together, while in the male the tiny round anus is separated from the minute dot of the penis by the two small swellings of the testes. Comparing all the kittens in the litter should be a good exercise in sexing for the novice. Even experienced breeders make mistakes from time to time,

Kittens are naturally clean in their habits and are easily trained to the use of a sanitary pan. This must be kept clean at all times for the use of confined cats to prevent 'accidents'.

and this is no disgrace. Whatever sex they are, nothing can be done about it, so the litter should be left in peace to grow up a little. The veterinary surgeon can always confirm the sex of the kittens when they have their pre-vaccination examination, at ten weeks.

Sometimes it happens that a queen's milk is too acid, and this condition is almost always caused by faulty digestion or the wrong diet. Many litters have been lost because of the unsuitability of their dam's milk. If a queen is suffering from a digestive upset, diarrhoea or constipation, excessive fermentation in the bowels upsets the acid balance of the body. The kittens are restless and noisy if the queen's milk is too acid, and these signs in the kittens' behaviour should always be taken seriously. The veterinary surgeon will prescribe tablets to help the condition, and with careful feeding of the queen, the kittens will soon be seen to become relaxed and contented once more. Some breeders add sodium citrate tablets to one of the queen's meals each day as a matter of course, for this helps to alleviate any acid condition of the milk.

During the first week of life the kitten begins to open its eyes. In some breeds such as the Siamese and related varieties, the eyes open from the second or third day, while in most mongrel kittens, they do not open for eight or nine days. At first a tiny slit appears as the eyelids begin to part. Often one eye opens before the other, but within 24 hours they are both unsealed. It sometimes happens that the eyes water at first and become re-sealed with dried matter. This must be bathed away daily or infection may set in. A tiny drop of cod liver oil may be smeared along the eyelids. This has a two-fold purpose. It is healing and soothing to the eyelids of the kitten and also encourages the mother cat to lick at the area, helping to keep the eyes clean and opened. The eyelids of the kitten must never be forcibly opened but only bathed gently. At first, the kittens must be protected from strong light, as the structure of the eye is very delicate and can be injured at this stage of development. If the eyes appear very full of matter, even after bathing, then it is possible that an infection has been introduced and veterinary advice must be sought without delay. Neglected eyes in small kittens can lead to serious defects in later life.

During the first four weeks of a kitten's life, it makes progressively greater demands upon its mother, as its appetite and weight increase daily. If the litter is large, the mother cat will soon show the strain on her bodily resources, for she will become thin and weak unless she is fed correctly and well. The lactating queen should have four good meals each day, and fresh, clean drinking water should be available at all times. It is important to feed these small, frequent meals rather than one or two large ones. If the queen is allowed to become really hungry, she is likely to gorge herself at the next meal. This may lead to vomiting, diarrhoea, or both, and will make her ill. Meat takes several hours to digest, so is best fed at midday and last thing at night, with lighter meals of fish, cheese or milk products in the morning and early evening.

When the kittens are four weeks old, they may start to show an interest in the queen's food. From this age they will eat a little more solid food each day and so take less milk from their mother. Nevertheless, it is important to feed her well during the four to ten week period so that, by the time the kittens are fully weaned, she is still in good physical condition. Occasionally, queens become very thin while nursing despite excellent feeding and expert care. They make so much milk that their own resources are depleted. If this happens, the kittens should be weaned at the earliest possible time, and the queen rested, and fed small nourishing meals until she regains her normal weight and appearance. This emaciated appearance is due to a deficient metabolism, and is no reflection on the husbandry of the cat breeder. It can sometimes be righted by treatment with various vitamins and minerals, but this can only be done by trial and error until it is discovered just what element is lacking in the requirements of that particular queen and then provide it in her diet or otherwise.

The growing kitten

From the age of six weeks, the young, growing kitten takes much of its daily requirements in the form of solid food. Some breeders feed a great deal of cereal mixed with milk, and this does tend to put weight on to the young animal. Other breeders prefer to feed mainly meat and other protein foods, thus producing tough, wiry kittens. It is a matter for conjecture which is the best method. Perhaps feeding two meals of meat and two meals of cereal and milk might be the answer. Many books are written on the subject of animal diet, but it is up to each breeder to find the best methods of feeding his own stock. Only he will know which foods make his kittens thrive and which foods give gastric upsets.

To encourage a kitten to lap rather than suck, evaporated milk and water, mixed to a cream with some baby cereal, can be placed in a teaspoon. This is held in front of the tiny kitten's nose and lightly touched against its lips. Its natural reaction is to lick its lips and it then gets the taste of the cereal mixture. It is a small step from this stage to full scale lapping. After a few days of spoon feeding in this manner, the spoon is lowered in stages into a saucer of cereal, when the kitten will also lower its head. Before long it will be happily lapping from the saucer. A very shallow saucer must be used, otherwise the cereal mixture will be so deep that the kitten will dip its nose in too far and splutter. Pilchards and sardines have a strong odour which quickly attracts small kittens. The fish should be flaked up with a fork into little peaks and the kitten will quickly learn to nibble away at the solid food, often growling over it with delight.

Kittens eating solids for the first time must be watched carefully. Sometimes a lump of food becomes wedged inside the top of the mouth against the palate and causes great distress as the kitten cannot dislodge it. It will paw at its lips and become very frightened. A matchstick or the handle of a plastic spoon can be used to prise the food away from the roof of the mouth. Tiny chicken, rabbit and fish bones can also cause trouble to the young kitten in this way, and all cooked food must be carefully forked over to make sure there are no pieces of bone left behind.

As the kittens grow and their jaws become stronger, they may be given long, thin strips of raw meat to chew. This helps with teething and to develop healthy gums. The meat must not be fed in small cubes for these may be swallowed whole and become stuck in the gullet. Kittens pounce on strips of raw meat as if it is prey. They grip it with their forepaws while chewing on the end. If approached, they often growl ferociously and will strike out with one paw, claws extended, if any attempt is made to take the meat away.

The stomach of the young kitten is very tiny, about the size of a walnut, so small meals at frequent intervals are essential in order to avoid gastric upsets. Many kittens are lazy about drinking enough water, so wet meals can be given. If a kitten appears constipated, a little water can be stirred into canned food, or extra gravy added to cooked meat. A sprinkle of table salt on the food also increases the thirst and encourages drinking. Most kittens prefer warm food and drink at this stage. Cold water will definitely be refused, and freshly drawn water should be allowed to stand until it attains room temperature before being offered to the kitten.

While the kittens are fed only on their mother's milk, she cleans away every trace of their excreta. The moment they begin to eat solids, however, she expects them to make their own sanitary arrangements. Many queens actually encourage their kittens to use the toilet tray by nudging them towards it whenever they go to her to be relieved. Sometimes, if a kitten has an 'accident', the queen will clean it up, but will then carry the kitten to the tray and deposit it firmly on the litter. Most kittens quickly learn to use the tray by watching their mother, but sometimes are too small to climb into a tall or slippery sided tray. A sheet of newspaper should be placed under the toilet tray and a sprinkle of litter placed on it. Before long the kittens will get the idea and be happily using the right area.

Any form of litter can be used, depending on availability and disposal methods. People living in the country can easily use sand, earth or ashes. Those who can have bonfires can use sawdust, paper or wood-chippings. Those in town houses must use a proprietary brand of fuller's earth which can be disposed of by close-wrapping before putting in the rubbish bin for collection. Some kittens may eat cat litter and make themselves extremely ill. In this instance, torn kitchen paper is the best litter material being highly absorbent and disposed of easily. Whatever litter is used, the toilet tray must be kept clean with soap and water, and if disinfected, no phenol or cresol based products must be employed. Ordinary household bleach, diluted as recommended on the bottle, is safe for kittens. No cat or kitten will use a heavily soiled litter tray, and if the tray is allowed to remain wet or dirty, the animal will use some other area of the room. Most cats which are called 'dirty' are usually only those which have rebelled against using a dirty lavatory pan.

At eight weeks the kittens may be completely weaned from their mother if required, although she will be happy to feed them for another fortnight or so. It is probably better for the kittens to make a clean break away from their mother, and at this time she can have a period of rest and recuperation. The breeder usually settles the queen in an outdoor house for this period, for it is likely that she will come into season and mating is not advisable so soon after rearing her litter. The kittens do not seem to miss their dam very much. They are used to eating solids and lapping water and milk. They are quite capable of eating sufficient food for their bodily requirements at this stage. It is advisable to give a calcium supplement to the kittens and it is time to start a course of worming treatments. After two clear weeks have elapsed since they have ingested any of their mother's milk, the kittens may be given their first vaccination against Feline Infectious Enteritis. It may be felt preferable to wait until they are twelve weeks, and have them injected with a combined vaccine against FIE and Cat 'Flu. Only after their immunity is assured should the kittens go to their new home.

When a kitten is collected by his new owner, it should be sent off with a pedigree form correctly filled in and signed as being a true record of its particulars and forebears. If it is registered with a governing body, the necessary transfer forms should be completed and handed to the new owners. They should also be given the kitten's vaccination certificates and, perhaps most important of all, a detailed diet sheet and notes on the kind of care it has been used to receiving. The kitten may have dietary upsets, or teething problems at this age, but with understanding new owners and the excellent start in life given by careful rearing, it should grow quickly into a happy well-balanced and healthy adult cat.

Most cat breeders at some time may find it necessary to hand rear one or more kittens, if the mother cat is taken ill or dies. Orphan or rejected kittens are best reared by a feline foster mother whenever possible, but it is no easy task to find a female cat with small or newly-born kittens at the time of the emergency. If a suitable queen can be found, one or two kittens can be introduced carefully and, with luck, she will accept them and care for them as her own offspring.

To introduce kittens to a foster mother, the queen should be let out for exercise well away from her nest box. While she is away, one of her own kittens is lifted and its anal area wiped gently all over the body of the orphan kitten. This procedure imparts some of the nestling's individual scent to the newcomer and helps it to be more acceptable to the queen. The orphan kitten should be placed in the middle of the nest material and the other kittens heaped on top of it. When the mother cat returns to the house she should be given a good feed before being allowed to go back to her nest. She will know that something is amiss when she gets into the nest box. She will lick all the kittens and may then notice the newcomer. She must be watched very carefully in case she attempts to bite, or otherwise hurt the strange kitten. With luck, she will settle down to feed her litter and then the orphan can be put between her back legs to suck at a rear nipple while the queen is petted and fussed. After one good feed, the orphan should be accepted. If a queen is going to reject a strange kitten, she will do it immediately, not after having fed and washed it.

Rearing tiny kittens by hand is a long, tiring business and must not be entered into lightly. Unless one is determined to keep up the fostering for at least three weeks, it is kinder to have the kittens euthanised by the veterinary surgeon. This is more preferable than being forced, by fatigue, to take them along when they are ten days old. It must be remembered that the queen spends most of her day and night caring for the kittens, keeping them at a constant temperature, washing and cleaning, as well as feeding them. To take over the queen's role is no easy matter for a mere human.

The first essential is a warm box. If an entire litter is to be reared it is easier, for the first two weeks, if the kittens are kept in discrete compartments. To achieve this, a cardboard box should have small refrigerator boxes placed inside, each lined with cotton wool. The

When bottle feeding an orphan kitten it is imperative that the milk mixture is dispensed at the correct rate, otherwise the kitten may choke as the milk enters its windpipe and this could lead to the development of pneumonia and death.

size of the boxes is determined by the size of the kittens. They should fit snugly into the softly lined plastic containers. Obviously the lids are not used, but an infra red or similar heat source is suspended at just the right height above the kittens to keep them comfortably warm.

A thermometer must be placed in the box for the kittens need a constant temperature of 32°C (90°F) for the first 24 hours of life. During their first week, this is dropped to 29°C (85°F), and thereafter they can manage with a heat of between 22°–24°C (70°–75°F). In an emergency, an ordinary light bulb can be used, but this is not satisfactory once the kittens' eyes begin to open.

Other equipment needed for attending to the kittens should be stored close at hand. A stock of 5ml disposable syringes is ideal for feeding purposes, and bicycle valve rubber, cut into 2cm sections before being fitted over the hard nozzles, makes them more acceptable for the kittens to suck. A set of scales for weighing the kittens and a large stock of paper towels for cleaning purposes is essential.

The best method of feeding the kittens is to use one of the specially formulated milk products prepared by the larger pharmaceutical companies. These must be reconstituted strictly according to the instructions and fed as directed. Undiluted evaporated milk warmed to blood heat may be given; or plain cow's milk, two tablespoons heated, with one level teaspoon of glucose and an egg yolk is roughly equivalent to the content of cat's rich milk.

To feed the kittens, the washed syringes are filled with the warm milk mixture and the kittens are encouraged to suck. If the kittens are strong, they will usually suck greedily, kneading away with their forepaws. It is best to take each kitten in turn and put it on a pad of kitchen paper on the lap. As it sucks, the plunger of the syringe is depressed very gently. It is important that the liquid is taken at the correct rate, for if the kitten chokes and draws any milk into its lungs, pneumonia will set in and the kitten may die. Each kitten should take about 5ml of milk every two hours for the first day, then it may accept about 7ml at each meal. Practice improves the feeding technique for both the attendant and the kittens. The filled syringes should be kept standing in a jug of hot water and each kitten should have its own syringe so that a check can be kept on the quantity of food taken.

Kittens should be weighed before and after each meal, and a chart kept to show progress. The ones that are going to fade can be observed almost straight away from this chart. It is pointless to struggle on with very weak, sickly kittens, and far better to employ one's efforts to save the stronger ones. The two-hourly feeding must be continued day and night for the first three days at least, but after that the kittens can manage on three-hourly feeding during the day, giving the last feed at midnight and then leaving them until about 7.00am.

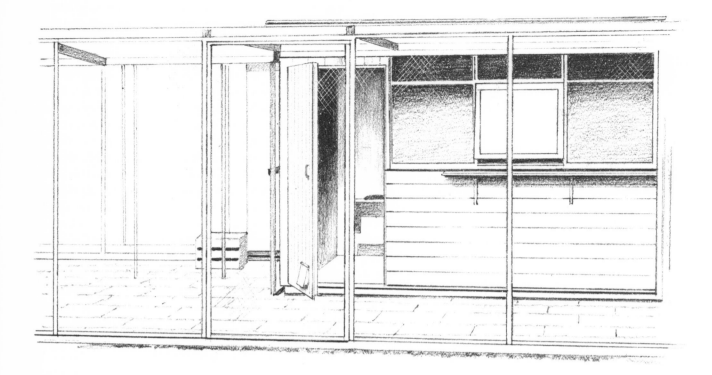

Equally as important as the feeding is the stimulation of the bladder and bowel movements of the kitten. After feeding, each kitten is turned onto its back and the genital regions are wiped with warm, damp cottonwool, simulating the actions of the mother cat's tongue. The kitten urinates slowly and the fluid is taken up by the cottonwool. Often solid motions are also passed at this time. The area is then patted dry and a dusting of baby powder helps to prevent any soreness developing. The face, eyes and mouth should also be cleaned after each feed, and once the eyes open, they may need extra bathing. Any soreness around the eyes, mouth or genital areas can be treated by the application of a smear of petroleum jelly.

At two weeks the kittens attempt to crawl out of their small plastic compartments and can be put together in a larger box. They will not disturb one another at this stage and need to become accustomed to their litter mates before play behaviour starts.

Hand-reared kittens should be taught to lap and eat solids at the earliest opportunity, and it is possible to have them eating suitable food at four weeks of age, with perseverance. Cereals are not recommended, as the kittens need to consume quite large quantities in order to ingest enough protein for their requirements. Creamed fish is excellent, and if built into tiny peaks on a spoon, the kittens soon get the idea of chewing and swallowing. Meat can be stewed in bone stock, minced finely, then returned to the stock and cooked until well reduced for two or three hours. When cool, this forms a thick, nutritious jelly which the kittens will eat with relish. Hardboiled and finely chopped egg is also popular with tiny kittens, but the bowel movement must be watched as this can cause either constipation or diarrhoea in some strains of cat.

One essential requirement of hand-reared kittens is Vitamin A. Each kitten requires 1000 i.u. added to its diet each day. For convenience, this may be given in the form of Cod Liver Oil, and it is important that the correct dose is given, not exceeded. A careful watch on the motions is a guide to the kittens' health. A normal motion is of the consistency of thick cream, greyish-yellow in colour. As solids are introduced into the diet, the colour gets darker and the consistency becomes firmer. Any deviations from this pattern should be discussed with the veterinary surgeon who can advise on any treatment or variations in the diet that are necessary.

Perhaps the biggest problem with orphan kittens is the fact that they have not received the benefit of the mother's first milk, or colostrum, which provides immunity against disease in their early weeks of life. Because of this, they are particularly vulnerable to infections of all sorts and so should not be exposed to many visitors, and no other cats should be allowed in the room reserved as their nursery. The veterinary surgeon will probably advise on vaccination of the orphans much earlier than would be considered wise in a normal litter.

Tiring and time consuming it may be, but to rear an orphan kitten or litter by hand successfully is one of the most rewarding exercises in animal husbandry. Once the kittens reach ten weeks of age, they are usually indistinguishable from normally reared kittens in size, but are often extremely fond of the human foster parent and make exceptionally loving pets.

As the stud male spends most of his life in confined conditions, his accommodation should be designed to provide him with adequate warm housing. A large exercise run is necessary for his health and well-being. It should be situated so that he has plenty of visual stimulation to prevent boredom.

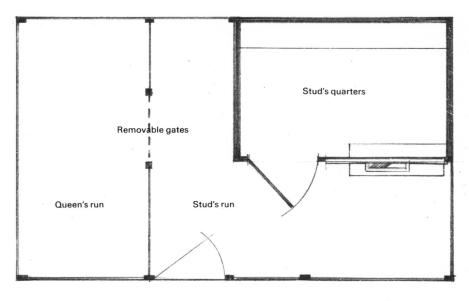

Removable gates

Stud's quarters

Queen's run

Stud's run

The stud male

The most important part of any breeding programme for the production of pedigree cats is the stud male. Whereas a brood queen is obviously important, for she will produce between 30 and 70 kittens in her own lifetime depending on her fertility, the male may sire hundreds of kittens to many different queens. It is obvious therefore, that a male cat used for stud purposes must be an exceptional specimen of his variety. The true quality of a male can only be assessed in his progeny, so it may be about three or four years before the worth of any male cat can be truly evaluated for his influence on the development of his breed.

In selecting a male for stud purposes it is usual to pick one that has had outstanding success on the show bench. Most experienced breeders recognize a kitten of promise and will often retain him, showing him as a kitten, to see how he develops as he grows up. He may then be sold as having stud potential, or kept on as a representative of the cattery and to perpetuate his line. As well as being a good representative of his breed and very beautiful, a male cat used at stud must have other qualities. First and foremost he must be robust and extremely healthy. He will come into contact with all manner of lowgrade infections at cat shows and from visiting queens, and he may well be faced with the challenge of coping with some of the serious cat diseases as well. His temperament must be equable, for he will have some difficult queens to cope with, and he must not resent their tantrums, or being picked up by his owner immediately after mating. Longhaired males must be particularly good tempered for they

have to endure long hours of meticulous grooming, to keep them in show condition at all times.

Keeping a stud male is not a job for the novice breeder. Only after some years of showing and breeding from one or two queens should anyone even contemplate owning an entire male cat. A knowledge of the animal's needs and psychology are essential to establish the correct relationship required between a working tom and his owner. Entire males are very affectionate and crave for attention. Unfortunately their malodorous habit of spraying on everything means that they have to be confined, away from the house, in their own specially built accommodation. This should not be tucked away at the very end of a quiet garden, however, for the stud needs company when he does not have a visiting queen. The stud house should be large enough for an attendant to stand upright in, and to give the cat plenty of exercise space when the weather is cold or wet. It must be constructed so that it is easy to clean otherwise it will soon smell of spray.

A wooden building about $3 \times 2 \cdot 5$m $(10 \times 8$ft$)$ makes ideal stud quarters and can be lined with insulating material covered by smooth hardboard or blockboard on the inside. Painted with vinyl paint, this provides a washable smooth and attractive surface. A wooden floor is warm but must be covered with an impervious material such as vinyl sheet flooring. Several shelves for sitting or resting can be fixed to the wall and one under the window is appreciated on wet days. Some form of pen to hold the visiting queen is essential. This must be constructed so that the cats can see, smell and touch each other without doing any harm. Wooden framing covered with $25 \cdot 5$mm (1 inch) square wire mesh makes a securely wired-off area across one wall and is quite adequate, otherwise a portable pen may be used. Some form of heating for cold weather should be professionally installed and if electric, must be well earthed. The run must be escape proof and as large as possible. Tree stumps and shelves all help to provide exercise facilities for the cat, keeping him fit and healthy. Although grass runs look pleasant when fresh and new, they soon become untidy and soiled. Paved runs can be regularly cleaned, and are especially valuable if any illness is introduced into the cattery, as the whole area can be washed down and sterilized.

The stud cat must be fed extremely well, but must never be allowed to grow fat. Daily grooming with a brush and comb for longhaired cats, and a chamois leather for shorthairs, is essential. After loosening and removing all the dead hair the body should be firmly groomed with strokes of the brush or pad, rather as one grooms a horse. The firm strokes tone up the muscles and most cats love this, leaning against the brush, purring with enjoyment. Some time for play should be allowed also each day. Even quite old stud cats will chase a feather or shuttlecock when there are no calling queens around to provide a distraction.

When the male is working he should be watched carefully to see that he does not lose too much weight. If he has several queens in succession, he must be rested and fed up until really fit again. He must also be checked very regularly to make sure that he has not picked up any parasites or infection from visiting queens. Most stud owners have a closed season for their stud males, during which time they are allowed to laze around and put on a little extra weight. This is an excellent time to repaint and maintain the stud's accommodation.

It is difficult to state a precise age at which a male cat may be said to be sexually mature. It varies from breed to breed and also among individuals. As in the females, the Siamese and Foreign varieties are more precocious than the Shorthairs and the Persians. It is not wise to hurry any male cat, and many established breeders keep several young toms together for company until they are fifteen or even eighteen months of age. They do not seem to want to fight each other at this stage and in most cases, do not spray. The best way to introduce a young male cat to the joys of sex is to wait until a suitable, older queen is in season. She is less likely to turn on a young male and will be easier for him to mate than a maiden queen.

The queen is placed in the pen in the young male's house and both cats are fed and settled down for the night. It is best to leave them for at least twelve hours undisturbed. The young male probably stays awake for the whole of this time, quite intrigued by the female's scent and posturing but also a little alarmed. The queen should then be taken completely away from the stud house and the young cat allowed to sniff the area of the pen in which she had been confined. He should be fed, then left alone for another twelve hours in which time he will get some rest. When the queen is returned to his pen he becomes very excited and after a suitable time for getting acclimatized again, the queen is let into his section of the stud house. The initial mating may take some time, for the male's technique will be understandably naive. Complete quiet must be maintained while the male attempts to mate the queen for his concentration must not be disturbed. The stud owner should not attempt to help the cat in any way, but be content to sit quietly and observe the proceedings. Most well-reared, well-grown young males will achieve a successful mating and can then be shut away from the queen while she rolls and growls. It is essential that she is not allowed to attack the young stud, or he may retaliate in his immaturity, and a fierce fight could ensue.

Having once achieved a successful mating, the young male's confidence grows steadily and he will soon perfect the technique of dealing with even the most difficult of queens. If the first mating is unsuccessful, the cats should be separated and another attempt made the following day. Should this also prove unsatisfactory, then the mating should be abandoned, and the male tried again some four or five weeks later. Some male cats never achieve keen sexuality and it is better that these are not kept for stud purposes. It is essential that a stud male is virile and gets his queens safely in kitten without delay. It is frustrating to the queen, her owner and the owner of the stud if the queen misses and has to be returned for a second service.

When using the services of a stud male it is usual to pay a stud fee. This is due to the owner of the stud cat when taking the queen to the cattery. The fee is for the act of mating by the stud male and is not a guarantee of a safely delivered litter. Sometimes, queens are taken to stud when they are not properly in season, and their owners are quite annoyed when they find that they are not in kitten. Most stud owners give a free return. That is, they accept the queen again for another series of matings if she comes into season, instead of proving to be in kitten. This is not obligatory however, and a stud owner does this out of goodwill only. The onus is on the owner of the queen to ensure that his animal is in breeding condition. The stud cat will mate any female in oestrus and a proven stud will fertilize any suitable queen. If conception does not take place, there could be many reasons. Usually it is a failure of the ova to implant. If a stud owner allows his male to give a second series of matings to a queen, it is a courtesy to at least offer to pay the extra expenses of feeding the cat during her stay.

It is also a courtesy, often neglected by owners of queens, to write to the stud owner and advise him of the number, sex and colour of the kittens born to the queen. Most stud owners like to keep progeny charts of their males, and welcome such information. Occasionally they are able to pass prospective buyers on to the owner of the queen, for many people will want sons and daughters of a famous sire.

Even famous cats lose their popularity as stud males when new Champions are made. It is always difficult to know what to do about a virile cat of about six or seven years, who just does not get enough stud work. It is possible to neuter male cats at any age, although there is a slight risk factor as they get older. Many famous studs have been neutered and spent their middle and old age happily as pets. The biggest problem in these cats is that they rarely lose the habit of spraying. Because of this they seldom make good house cats, but after a period of rehabilitation, they may often be given the freedom of the garden, being shut away in their house only at night. After neutering, a male cat that has been used for stud must have his diet carefully watched for he soon becomes grossly overweight, if overfed. After a while, his spray will lose its overpowering odour, and he will become less inclined to pick fights with other cats. He may occasionally decide to assert his authority and take his place as a feline patriarch. Most male cats neutered late in life are extremely fond of young kittens, and treat them rather like some benevolent old uncle.

Cats on Show

Grace Pond

The history of show cats really began thousands of years ago. Short-haired cats were worshipped in Egypt at the time of the Pharaohs and were kept as pets in other parts of Africa, in India, in China and in Japan. Much later, cats with longer coats were imported from Turkey and Persia. As a result of cross-matings over the centuries, cats were eventually produced with a wide variety of coat patterns and colourings. But it was not until the first cat show was held at the Crystal Palace in 1871 that people realized how truly beautiful the animals could be. More important still was the discovery that by careful choice of adult males and females it was possible to produce kittens that were replicas of the parents.

Cat breeding became the hobby of many in high society, even including royalty, and in due course others followed suit. One well-known breeder at the end of the nineteenth century owned as many as 80 cats and travelled far and wide through the British Isles with a retinue of servants, exhibiting and, of course, taking prizes at all the cat shows.

Many visitors came from overseas to inspect the cats and to take back kittens to their own countries, and soon shows were being held in many parts of the world, organized, more or less, along the same lines as British shows.

The format and rules regarding showing have changed little over the years. Briefly, a cat must be registered with the Governing body sponsoring the show, and must have been transferred to the exhibitor, if not bred by him, several weeks prior to the show. This regulation is sometimes overlooked and can lead to disqualification if not observed. Schedules giving details of classes, judges, times of opening and closing, fees and prize monies, and general rules and regulations, are sent out many weeks before the show.

Entry forms and correct money should be sent back to the show manager well before the closing date, since, more often than not, there is insufficient space

to pen all the cats eligible for entry. It is important to make sure that the details on the entry form are exactly the same as those given on the cat's registration certificate. Incorrect information may mean disqualification and forfeiture of entry forms. About a week prior to the show, the exhibitor will receive a vetting-in card and a numbered tally which, on the day, has to be attached to a piece of white tape around the cat's neck. The number on the tally is the same as that on the cat's pen.

The day previous to the show is one of feverish activity for the show manager. She has to supervise the preparation of the hall and to make sure that tabling and pens are all erected in time for the exhibits when they arrive in the morning.

At 7 o'clock on the morning of the show, all is quiet in the hall. The numbered pens, still empty, stand on the spotlessly white paper-lined tabling. Soon there are signs of activity. The officials and stewards begin to arrive, donning white overalls. So too do the veterinary surgeons, taking up positions behind the vetting-in tables, their stewards beside them with bowls of water, disinfectants and towels at the ready.

For an hour or more the exhibitors will have been queuing up outside the hall, their cats in baskets and boxes, for they are not allowed to arrive carrying the animals in their arms or on leads. At about 7.30 or 7.45 the doors open, and the vets begin the exacting task of examining each exhibit before allowing it to be penned. The whole atmosphere is very subdued, the exhibitors chatting quietly to one another, each secretly a little worried in case, for some unforeseen reason, their entry is turned down by the vet. Could a flea have been overlooked in the final grooming? Were the ears as clean as they should be? Has the journey perhaps upset the cat a little and raised its temperature? Will a small gum ulcer have appeared in a teething kitten? Will the cat that was so healthy

Following page
A Blue Tortie Point Siamese kitten with a cat-nip mouse. Tortie Points come in the four Siamese colours – Seal, Blue, Chocolate and Lilac and all Torties are classified as a single separate breed at the shows. The different Siamese colours are shown in individual classes.

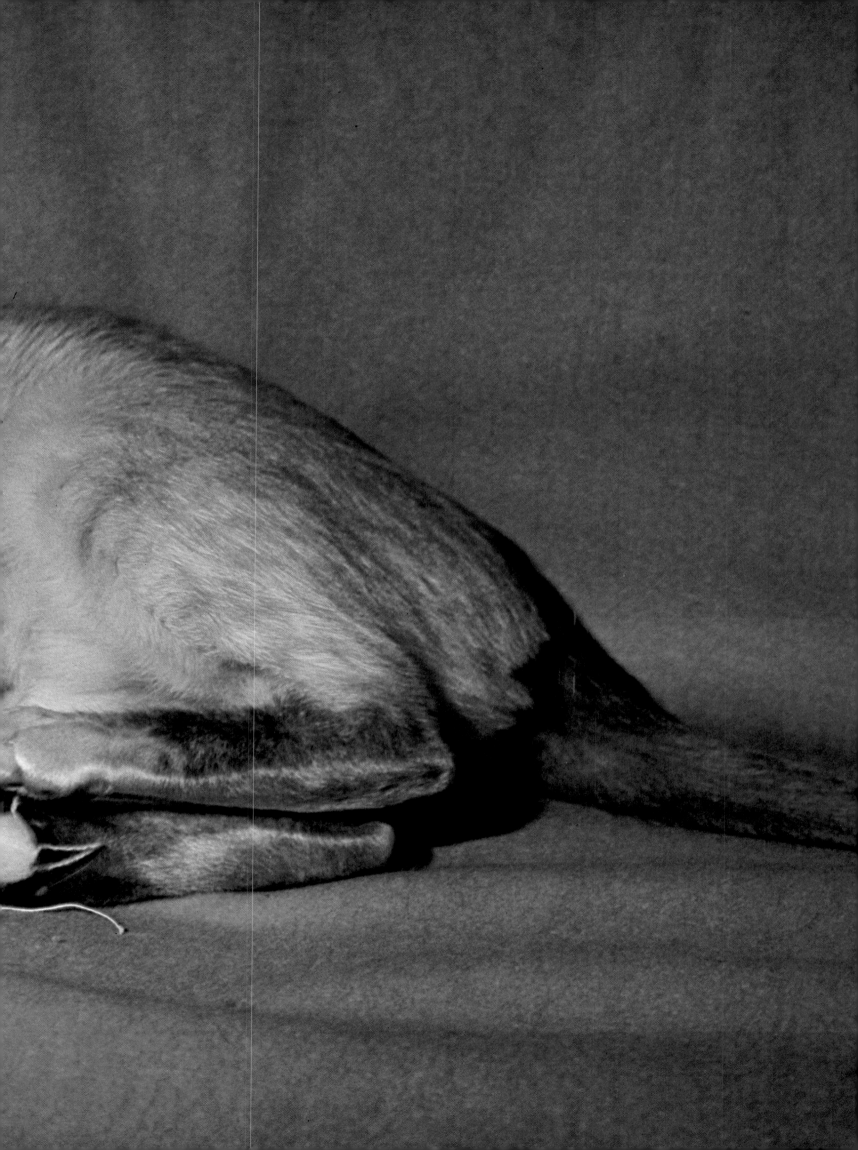

yesterday suddenly start showing signs of a cold or even a fever, thus being refused entry to the hall?

If there is the slightest doubt in the mind of the vet, he will insist on the animal being placed in an isolation pen in a separate room or—far more sensible—taken home. It may seem hard on an exhibit to be turned away for some trivial reason, but the vet not only has to consider the cat being examined but also the wellbeing of hundreds of other exhibits, any of which could pick up some infection. Most cats are now vaccinated against the potentially lethal feline infectious enteritis, but there are still other illnesses which may affect the animals, including pneumonitis, ringworm and several more.

Once the vetting-in is completed the successful exhibitors heave sighs of relief. Each cat's number is now marked off a large board and the exhibitor given a card with a large printed red 'V', to be displayed on the pen as proof that the cat has been vetted-in.

In the body of the hall, although exhibitors are now more relaxed, their main concern is to get the pen ready and to see that the cat is looking its best for the judges. There will be sufficient time later to greet old friends from last year's show and to exchange 'catty' news.

As a safeguard against infection some exhibitors wipe the wires of the pen with a piece of cotton wool dampened with a mild non-toxic disinfectant.

In Britain, the only articles that may be placed in the pen is the obligatory white blanket and a sanitary tray filled with peat (available in the hall) or, if preferred, with litter or torn-up newspaper. It does not matter if the cat decides to sleep in the tray rather than put it to proper use. No food dishes are permitted in the pens until after lunch time. It is in fact, just as well not to feed the cat when it first arrives in the hall. It should be given time to settle down. In other European countries, the pens may be decorated and furnished as the owner wishes, for there the cats are judged in separate areas of the show hall.

Whether or not a cat is a good traveller, it is strictly prohibited to give it a tranquillizer before the journey. It has been found that a cat may suffer a severe reaction when the effects of such tablets wear off, becoming quite neurotic and flying at the steward and judge if they try to remove it from the pen. At one show, before this rule came into force, the public became very alarmed at the sight of what appeared to be a dead cat in a pen. Even when taken out, the animal just hung limp, apparently lifeless; but on examination by a vet, it was found to be completely tranquillized, and even when removed from the hall, took hours to revive. Any cat now found to be suffering from the effects of drugs is automatically disqualified.

As time passes, more and more owners with their cats pour into the hall. The last pens are made ready, the final grooming done. Powdering is forbidden in the hall and any powder in the coat can mean dis-

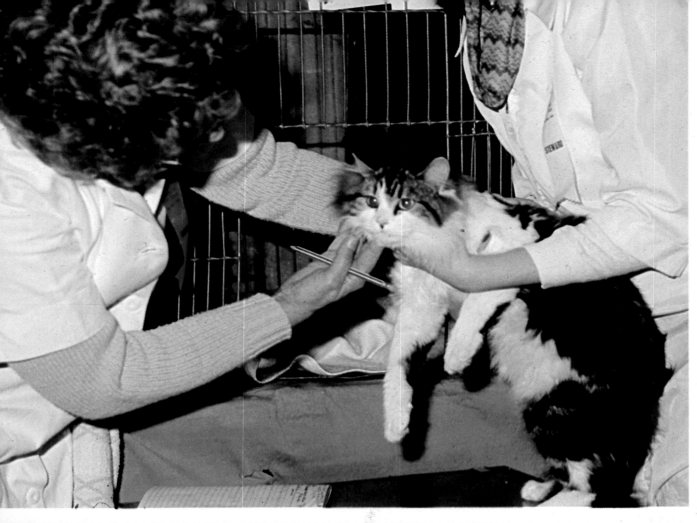

Previous pages
Above left
Two Seal Point Siamese.
Kittens can be shown
after three months in
Britain and after four
months in America. At
nine months (ten months
in America although the
large Societies allow
eight months) they are
eligible for the adult
cat classes.

Left
The Olympia National
Cat Show, 1974.

Right
A Tortie Colourpoint.
This is a magnificent
specimen and he knows
it. To some people the
Tortie markings are
more attractive on the
longhaired Colourpoint
than on the shorthaired
Siamese. Breeders have
had problems in achieving
a true dark blue eye
colour.

Above Right
Chinchillas are very
popular entries at all
shows.

Above Left
Judging a Tortoiseshell
entry in the Pets class of
the National Cat Show at
Olympia 1974. The
entries are judged on
their health, general
well-being and well-
cared for appearance.

Left
An odd-eyed white
Cornish Rex cat. The
curly Rex coat can be
transferred to a cat of
any colour and Rex cats
were recognized as a
listed Shorthaired breed
in 1967. Rex cats are
very lively, hardy and
individualistic, and are
rewarding cats to have
at home.

feited but, in the case of illness, provided a veterinary certificate is sent to the show manager at least a week before the show, half the fees may be returned. It is impossible to reimburse all those absent, as so much expense is involved before the show is held, including the printing of the schedule and catalogue, and the provision of a pen whether it is used or not.

In British shows, apart from the largest one in the world organized by the National Cat Club at Olympia in London, where the public are admitted throughout the day, the hall is cleared. Some halls, however, have galleries from which judging can be viewed. It is much easier for the judges to get on with their arduous unpaid task (in the United States they are paid) if there are no crowds milling around.

The majority of cats take things in their stride, sitting up in their pens surveying the scene with large, bright eyes, some obviously loving the attention they receive. The kittens, in particular, are usually very playful, showing off, dabbing at passers-by or climbing up and pulling down the numbered cards. Admittedly, there are a few who resent the whole business, turning their backs, ignoring everyone and even creeping under the blanket so that not a hair is visible. But most visitors are astonished at the good behaviour of the cats and how little noise they make.

The handling of the cat is very important. The steward has to lift the animal out of the pen and place it on the table for the judge's inspection. It must be held gently but firmly, never by the scruff of the neck. The majority make no objection to being brought out of the pen, but there is the occasional miscreant, defying with tooth and nail any attempt to handle it. Such a cat has to be passed over, otherwise the steward or judge may receive a bad bite or scratch. If a cat behaves in this way at a show, it is as well not to enter it again.

In Britain the judges start with the Open or Breed classes, in which all the cats and kittens are of the same variety. Wins in such classes are important. If the winner is an adult male, its success may be noted by the owner of a female (queen) as future mate; if a female, she may have her name taken as a possible breeder of prize-winning kittens.

Before judging begins, any exhibitor showing two cats should make quite sure that each is in its correct pen. It has happened that two exhibits have been reversed, the mistake only being discovered after judging, which is too late, for both cats will be disqualified. A cat may, in theory, be entered for a maximum of twelve classes, but this is really excessive, for if a number of judges are involved, it will have to be taken out and put back far too many times. A novice should only put a cat in a few classes to see how it behaves.

By lunch time the Open classes should have been judged and work will have begun on the Miscellaneous and Club classes. It is at about this time that the public are admitted and the owners allowed to

qualification by the judge. It is said that at one early show an exhibitor deliberately rubbed powder into the fur of a rival black cat so that her own pet could win!

It is nowadays obligatory for each cat to be placed in a pen but nearly a century ago there were ring classes at shows, very much as at modern dog shows. This practice was ended after an occurrence at one show, for while a group of elegantly clad Edwardian ladies were marching around the ring with the gaily beribboned pets in tow, one cat made a 'savage onslaught' on another, spoiling its show chances for ever! It is recorded that a Russian princess who was there to distribute prizes preserved a remarkable equanimity 'despite the screaming of several ladies' and the severe scratching of a gentleman judge who attempted bravely to separate the cats. At the same show, apparently, when the princess tried to caress a prize-winning Chinchilla, it made a most 'savage snap' at her fingers. There is no note of her ever attending another show.

After vetting-in, the judging commences. British shows are one-day affairs and the judges, accompanied by their stewards, start their mammoth task of visiting each pen in turn. They use a portable table and carry disinfectant and towels so that their hands can be cleansed after each exhibit has been examined. In other European countries, cat shows last for two days and the judges have the cats brought to them.

There may, for various reasons, be some absentees. A cat may have been turned down by the vet, have proved to be in kitten or have started calling; or an exhibitor may have been prevented by bad weather from reaching the hall. As a rule, the number of missing entries is very low. Such entry fees are for-

visit the pens to see their cats. If the judge is still at a pen, however, the owner should not approach while the cat is being examined. In due course slips showing the prizes awarded by the judges are put up on an award board and exhibitors flock around to see how their cats have fared. The actual prize cards start being placed on the pens shortly after lunch.

Cats are judged according to the standards set by the Governing Council of the Cat Fancy, with 100 points being allocated for the various characteristics required for what would be considered the perfect cat of a particular variety.

In Europe, the *Fédération Internationale Féline d'Europe* looks after the interests of its associated clubs in eleven countries by holding shows and issuing standards of points. Another group, the *Union Nationale des Associations Félines,* holds shows throughout France. The *Cercle Félin de France* also puts on shows throughout the country. The standards devised by the various governing bodies for the points of perfection in each breed are almost identical.

The climax of many shows is the award for Best in Show. This is decided by separate panels of judges, one for Short-hairs, one for Long-hairs and one for Siamese – the three sections into which most shows are subdivided. Each judge nominates one cat, one kitten and one neuter to be considered by the Best in Show panel. Such nominees must have come first in their respective breed classes.

In British cat shows, adult cats winning their breed classes may, if of high quality, receive a Championship Challenge Certificate. Winning three such certificates at three shows, and under three different judges

entitles the animal to be termed Champion. In European shows, Certificates of Excellence are awarded along the same lines, the procedure differing slightly according to the governing body's regulations. British fanciers are able to show their Champion cats against each other for the title of Grand Champion. European fanciers can go still further as their quarantine regulations allow them to exhibit their top cats in several countries to compete for the title International Champion.

American show procedure is very different from that of the British being more like the European. They have Open classes but no Miscellaneous and Club classes. The entrance system and the regulations are very similar, full details being given on a so-called premium list (equivalent to the British schedule), listing the prizes and cups which may be won.

Many of the American shows, like those on the continent, are two-day events, as against a single day in Britain. The hours of judging may also be longer.

The principal difference, however, is that the judging is done in rings and that a show may actually consist of four separate shows, sponsored by four clubs, with their own rings and judges, working simultaneously. The judge in one ring will not know the results in another ring, but a cat may be entered in two, three or even four of the shows, and perhaps win in each.

In an American show the judge sits at a long table, with a row of about ten pens behind her. On entering the show, each exhibitor is told approximately at what time her cat will be judged. When her number is called, she takes the cat up and places it in the num-

bered pen pointed out by the ring steward. Each judge has a clerk (with similar functions to a steward in Britain) who keeps a record of the judge's points for each cat and the award given. The judge herself handles the cat, replaces it in the pen, and, where applicable, awards the appropriate ribbon. In Britain a red rosette is awarded for a first place, but in America a blue ribbon is given to the winner, a red ribbon to the second-placed cat and a yellow ribbon to the cat coming third.

In America a cat that has never previously been entered in a show is classified as a Novice; and one that has already won a prize enters the Open class. Champions are entered in the Champion class and Grand Champions in the Grand Champion class. In Britain a cat can only become a Champion by winning three Open classes at three separate shows under three different judges; and having won three Championships under similar conditions, it can enter for the Champion of Champion classes. In the United States, however, it is theoretically possible for a cat to enter as a Novice and finish up as a Champion. A winning cat will be transferred to the next class up— from Novice to Open class and, if it wins this, to the Champion class. A red, white and blue ribbon is given to the Best Cat. If the Best Cat in Show is a male, the second-placed cat, should she be female, will be known as the BOX (Best Opposite Sex) Cat, and vice-versa.

As a rule, there are more prizes to be won in American shows than in Britain. In many shows, for example, there are special awards, rosettes and trophies, not only for the first three places but for fourth, fifth and sixth as well. Furthermore, the exhibits may also participate in a competition organized by *Cats* magazine, in which points are awarded and recorded for wins at every show. The cat scoring the most points throughout the show year is declared overall winner and receives a great deal of publicity as well as valuable prizes.

Whereas in Britain there may be as many as 60 cats or kittens of a particular variety in the Open or Breed class, all competing against one another, in the United States numbers are far fewer.

Since the American judges do not proceed to the individual pens, there is more latitude given to exhibitors who are allowed to hang coloured curtains inside the pens, choosing those which set off their cats to best advantage. Rosettes and ribbons previously won may be displayed and frequently the pens contain little beds, lace curtains and other forms of decoration. The overall effect is very festive and the public are freely admitted at all times.

Whatever the conditions and wherever the shows are held, the cats are always great attractions; and throughout the world the Cat Fancy has become virtually an international institution, with many long-lasting friendships being formed between people with a common love of cats.

Stars of Television and Film

Gladys Hayward

Left
A Shorthaired Cream of excellent type. Well bred kittens of this breed are quite hard to come by as it is difficult to breed out the tabby markings on the face, legs and tail.

Below
A Longhaired Cream Persian who might be a professional 'actor' but which has been cleverly caught by the camera as he rolls on his back.

How often, when watching your pet cat stretching comfortably in front of the fire, kicking a ball across the floor or pretending to be a tiger in the garden, you must have wished you had a camera at the ready to record the precious moment. If only you could capture all those changing moods—the characteristic expressions and actions which tell you quite clearly whether your cat is contented or angry or amused or just plain bored. What a natural actor the cat seems to be, but when it comes to the point—as any professional photographer will confirm—what a difficult subject it really is!

One of the most appealing things about a cat is that it will never do what *you* want, unless that action happens to suit its inclinations at that particular moment. You can't just pop it down on a cushion, ask it to look at the camera and click the shutter. In the case of, say, a child, it takes two—the subject and the photographer—to make a good picture. Where the cat is concerned, it takes three. Even the most skilled photographer can do little with an unco-operative subject. If the cat refuses to take part in the 'game', he might just as well give up. This is where the third member of the trio—the trainer or handler—comes in.

Delightful cats and kittens nowadays peer out from cards, calendars, chocolate box lids, magazine covers, newspaper pages and book jackets. They pose for television commercials and they appear in films with famous actors. Most of these so-called 'working' cats are especially trained for such a career. Breeding and training them is a full-time occupation and, like any job, it has its rewards, its occasional setbacks and its peculiar problems.

The making of a star

A future feline star can often be discovered when still a kitten. Beauty is, of course, important, but most cats fulfil that simple requirement. The crucial test of

a working cat is that it should be gentle, loving and tractable. It must be placid in temperament, display no sign of nerves, show complete trust in strangers and adapt to all manner of unusual circumstances. Because cats are such individualists few will combine all these qualities, so that potential stars are not born every day. Many cats, for example, may be ideal as far as colour and temperament are concerned, but still fail to pass the vital test of immunity to studio light, noise and bustle.

Selecting a star-to-be from a litter of kittens is largely a matter of observation and experience. Our method is to let them run freely about the garden and then entice them with titbits. If one of them responds to the call every time, whereas the others saunter up only now and then, this will be the one on which it is worth concentrating.

A kitten embarking on an acting career will probably begin with 'stills' for birthday cards, calendars and so forth. Although this is a matter of simple posing rather than performing, the kitten will gain valuable experience from the travelling involved and from the movements, sounds and flashing lights that make up the studio atmosphere. By the time it has done two or three sessions of photography it will have learned that posing for the camera can be great fun.

Having persuaded it to pose for a 'still', the next stage is what is known as an 'easy' shot, in which the cat plays a passive part in a scene. This will probably involve being held by an actor or actress, which gets it accustomed to remaining quiet and still when other people are performing.

Tricks of the trade

Even training a cat to this level requires long hours of patient love and care; but the real fun (and the headaches) begin when it is ready to progress further and launch out on an acting career in its own right. Basically this is a question of getting the cat used to

156

Far left
Two Silver Tabbies
posing perfectly for their
picture.

Left
The well-trained
Chinchilla who
advertises carpets.

Right
Cats are natural actors
and this Longhaired
Silver Tabby is posing
arrogantly in a chair
which matches his colour.
The beautiful cat below
is also posing but he is
dignified and aloof,
pretending to be unaware
of the camera's existence.

special and varied situations. Total obedience is naturally the main objective, but this can only be achieved by patience and kindness. The voice must never be raised in anger – calmness and tolerance are the golden rules. With a cat that enters into the spirit of the thing and takes positive pleasure in being trained, persistence and gentle encouragement will work wonders.

Sometimes a good deal of ingenuity on the handler's part may be entailed in order to attract the cat's attention, such as displaying toys, rattling keys and even lying flat on the floor, pretending to be another animal. Bribery, in the form of food, is essential to all training procedures. Offering a cat its favourite food is an obvious way of calling it, and this is an important part of any lesson. Getting it to sit or stand in a certain spot is basic training. This can be done by enticing it with a plate of food and encouraging it, by means of petting and talking, to stay still at the exact point you want. After a time the cat will get the spot fixed in its mind and stay put even when you remove the food, but you must, of course, reward its obedience with a titbit.

This is the way we train the beautiful Chinchillas that are required to pose on carpets for a well-known television advertisement. Once the cat has been persuaded to settle down in the right place, it is simply a matter of chatting softly and stroking her continuously, then gradually moving away. The whole procedure generally has to be repeated many times before she realizes what she is expected to do.

Confidence is all-important and the cat must have a familiar face around and, if possible, an easy bolt-hole. Provided it feels happy and contented, it will stay in one place for a lengthy period – as one of our pupils did with Peter Sellers in *The Wrong Box*.

For one advertisement a cat was required that was able to pick out the correct bowl of food – say the middle one of three – and for this we trained a tabby named Tib. After a few experimental tastes in each bowl Tib never made a mistake, and would go through the routine for the benefit of the camera time and time again. But having had enough, he would retire to his basket for a rest – a sign to the studio staff that the moment had come for their coffee break. Ten minutes later they would all begin again.

Training a cat to jump down from a high place to a given spot is also done by tempting it with food. The cat will be set on a ladder and a dish put on a table below. Gradually the distance between ladder and table is increased, and after several lessons the cat will be jumping freely from a height of six feet or thereabouts. Tib, although a large cat, specialized in high-jumping and did so in a number of films, as well as in a television series.

Teaching a cat to leap through a window is not nearly so easy, its general attitude being 'Show me what's on the other side first'. The handler can usually get results by showing a plate of food or a toy through the open window and then lowering it out of camera range. Hopefully, the cat's natural curiosity will get the better of its common sense!

Ins and outs of acting

As every owner knows, a household cat can only be trained up to a certain point, and its cleverness is

158

limited to actions that come naturally and in which it takes pleasure. As a rule, a working cat is not expected to perform tricks, but it may have to put on fancy dress for a particular advertisement or film sequence. A cat can be trained to wear a collar, a necklace, a tiara or even a hat, and still look cool and dignified.

Incidentally, studio training is not simply confined to the central character, the cat. A recipe for a disastrous day's work is an impatient director, an actress in flimsy clothing who hates cats, grabs your pet clumsily and complains that she has been scratched, and perhaps a small child who finds the cat too heavy to carry. Surprisingly few people know how to lift and handle a cat correctly. If the star is unaware of the proper way of picking it up and caressing it, this must be explained beforehand. Needless to say, the director's attitude is also important, and if he is patient and helpful, all will go well.

Some television commercials and films call for outdoor work and this is far more complicated than ordinary studio routine. It is not easy to find a cat that will work out of doors at any time, especially one that responds to the call and does not wander off the set between takes. This needs a great deal of patience on the handler's part because any shouting (and there is usually plenty of that) is liable to send a cat scampering off. A good method of training a cat to work outdoors is to simulate a film set in some open space, preferably close to a busy road with traffic. We are lucky to have a suitable field behind our home where we spend weeks on end, if need be, getting our cats accustomed to such conditions.

One of our successful outdoor actors was Bimbo,

Below
Chinchilla queen and kittens.

a Shorthaired Black, seen in a television film *Superstitions*. He was seen wandering freely through the streets of London—secure in the knowledge that just out of camera range was his basket, to which he could soon retire. Two of our Siamese, a Seal Point named Kye and a Lilac Point called Tuptin, were also trained to work outdoors in *Endless Night* with Hayley Mills. But perhaps our greatest triumph was in *Doctor Dolittle*, in which one of our cats was trained to jump onto Rex Harrison's shoulder and feed from his hand.

Stars and stand-ins

It is normal for a leading star to have one or more stand-ins, and this is true even for a working cat. Long studio sessions under hot lights can be extremely exhausting and it is important for the star not to look tired from overwork. Posing while lighting and camera focus are adjusted, or even racing across stage in long-shot, can be done just as easily by substituting another cat of the same size, colour and temperament. In this way work can proceed without interruption and when the moment arrives for the real rehearsal and takes, the star will appear fresh and fully rested.

The most difficult film sequences featuring a number of our cats were in *Diamonds Are Forever*, the James Bond thriller. The most demanding test of our star, a Chinchilla named Clarissa, was to walk down a broad staircase which had no back or sides. After hours of training we managed to get her three-quarters of the way down, but at that point she insisted on jumping through the back of the stairs to the ground. So we had to station one handler behind the stairs with a bowl of food that she disliked intensely, and another handler at the foot of the stairs carrying a dish of her favourite food. After two or three takes she gave a perfect performance.

Our problems for this film were not yet over, for other sequences required the same white cat to have a revolver fired close to her ear. No amount of training would have persuaded Clarissa to sit quietly while this went on. So we brought in one of her stand-ins, a Blue-eyed White Persian. Being stone deaf, like most cats of this type, she did not bat a whisker during the 'shooting', and all was well.

The climax of a working cat's career may come when, as a recognized star, it is exhibited at the National Cat Club Show at Olympia, reclining in a pen designed as a miniature film set or replica of a television advertisement, basking in the admiration of the crowds. But this glory and glamour are reserved only for a chosen few. Those that do not make the grade simply go back to being ordinary cats, unemployment being no great tragedy in the feline world.

For those of us who train cats for film and television work there are pleasures and rewards, to be sure, but do remember, if you are tempted to try it, that there can be no half measures. Love, patience, skill and dedication all amount to a life's work.

The Magical Cat

Angela Sayer

Since the earliest days of its domestication, the cat has been associated with magical and religious ceremony, and the subject of many superstitions and sayings. Although other animals have been venerated and feared through the ages, it seems remarkable that the cat alone has been chosen by so many civilizations throughout the ages, and throughout the world.

The eye of the cat, expressive and with variable pupil shape, gives the animal its enigmatic stare. Sometimes, if the pupils are wide open, the gaze is full and luminous with reflected light, while at other times, with the pupil closed to a narrow slit, the full beauty of the coloured iris gleams unblinkingly. Like the snake, the cat has the ability to gaze into human eyes, producing a mild hypnotic effect on sensitive people. A semi-precious stone, known as a 'cat's eye' is called this because it changes its lustre and shade, depending on the light conditions. The 'cat's eye' is made into brooches, pendants and rings and is worn as a lucky charm. Different cultures have formulated different beliefs about cats' eyes.

In Ancient Egypt, the cat was called *mau*, which means 'to see', and many cat-amulets of that time are engraved with an *utchat*, or sacred eye. In the great temple of Bast, the cat-goddess, at Bubastis, a wall relief shows the king presenting her with an amulet of the sacred eye. It is interesting to discover that the word utchat means 'to be in good health' and covers both physical and mental well-being. To the Ancient Egyptians, the changing shape of the cat's pupils was linked to the movement of the sun and moon in the heavens. The image of the cat and that of the eye were thought to possess great magical power, and if used in conjunction the powers were greatly enhanced. Utchats were often engraved with tiny cat figures to increase their protective powers when worn as amulets, and statuettes of cats often had collars, with pendant utchats, engraved around their necks.

Utchats were often carved from lapis lazuli, a

brilliant blue stone, with specks of gold on its opaque surface. A papyrus thought to have been used in human mummification rites was discovered, and is known as the Cat of Lapis Lazuli. It depicts an elegant, seated cat, drawn in profile, with a large scarab beetle, the symbol of resurrection, above it, and a rectangle enclosing the sacred eye below it.

The Chinese believed that the pupil size in the cat was changed by the position of the sun in the sky. They would lift the eyelids of sleeping cats, in order to tell the time. This belief is similar to another in which the pupil size was thought to echo the ebbing and flowing of the tides. At high tide the pupil would look full, and this would gradually change as the waves ebbed, so that low tide was indicated by a tiny, vertical slit.

The Celts believed that cats were supernatural, and that their eyes were windows, through which privileged men could look at the world of the fairies. Within the cats' eyes, the fairy world glowed with a luminous light, and the fairies could also look out, watching the activities of humans. This myth probably arose because of the disturbing effect of a cat's gaze. It is certainly true to say that looking directly into the contented gaze of a placid pet cat has a soothing effect.

Sometimes, the suspected magical powers of its eyes caused the cat to suffer torment or death. Those wishing to be given the gift of second sight would take the eyes of a black cat, roast them and grind them to powder; this was then mixed with human gall and worn in a leather bag as a potent charm. Cats' eyes were also used in strange rites to treat blindness in humans. In England, children were encouraged to play with tortoiseshell cats in order to receive the power of clairvoyance. The Jewish Talmud gave instructions that the placenta from a black cat's new litter could be burned to give a powder, which when rubbed into the eyes would endow the recipient with the perception of devils.

Left
An Abyssinian sunbathing. It is very difficult to catch the mood of a cat in the camera without disturbing it. When the cat is trained then it will enjoy being admired and watched but certain expressions can only be caught when the cat is unaware.

161

Edward Topsell, the naturalist, wrote of cats' eyes in 1607. He explained the changing shape of the pupils thus *'The male cat doth carry his eyes with the sunne, for when the sunne ariseth, the apple of his eye is long, towards noon it is round and at evening it cannot be seen at all, but the whole eye showeth through.'* To describe the changing luminosity of the eye which he attributes to the waxing and waning of the moon, he writes—*'They shine more fully at the full, and more dimly in the changing and the wane . . .'* He also quotes another writer—*'Albertus compareth their eyesight to Carbuncles in dark places, because in the night they can see perfectly to kill Rats and Mice . . .'*

Cat's cradle

A game known as 'Cat's Cradle' dates back for centuries. In it, string is wound in intricate patterns around the fingers, then passed to a partner. Such figures were used by tribesmen in the Congo to ensnare the sun and stop its blazing heat. Eskimos, on the other hand, used the strings to trap the sun cat, to try to keep it back from its long winter's rest. In New Guinea, after playing the game and weaving the patterns, the strings were unravelled and used for tying in the yam stalks. It was thought that the magic strings caused the yam plants to flourish and be more fruitful.

The rain-maker

Cats were used in rain-making rituals throughout the world, and indeed are still used in such ceremonies in a few countries. In Java, a cat is ducked repeatedly in a pool of water, having first been carried in procession with much chanting. In Sumatra, a black cat is used for rain-making, ensuring that the sky will darken with rain clouds. The cat is dragged into the middle of the river, then released so that it may try to swim to the bank, with many women splashing and chasing it. In Celebes, a cat was tied in a sedan chair and carried three times around each drought-stricken field, then splashed with water while prayers were chanted, invoking rain. To bring rain for Malayan crops a woman was chosen and an earthenware bowl placed, inverted upon her head. She set the bowl on the ground and filled it with water, then bathed a cat in it so thoroughly that it was almost drowned. In Britain, cats are not used in rituals to end drought, but are carefully watched during long, dry spells, for if they sneeze or pass a damp forepaw behind the ears, it foretells rain.

Cats and cornfields

Bast was an earth-goddess and has been identified with the Nordic sun-goddess Freya, portrayed by William Morris as:

Freya, thin robed, about her ankles slim
The grey cats playing.

Freya was the goddess of love and fertility, and rode in a chariot drawn by two grey cats around the harvest fields. Hoping to ensure good crops, farmers would leave offerings of milk in the fields to feed her cats. If she was pleased, Freya would bless the harvest, causing the seeds to swell. She would also hold bad weather at bay until the corn was safely gathered in.

Country children had old beliefs passed down to them, and were warned against playing in the cornfields for fear that the corn-cat would get them. The cat was the centre of festivities during harvest time at Briançon, France. Before the scything started, a cat was garlanded with ears of corn and ribbons laced with wild flowers, then carried in procession with the harvesters to the cornfields. It would be kept tethered on a long ribbon while the corn was cut and any reaper nicking himself on his scythe would insist that the wound was thoroughly licked clean by the harvest cat. When all the corn was cut and gathered in the cat had its decorations ritually removed, and was set free.

Elsewhere in France, the final sheaf to be cut and tied was called the 'cat's tail'. The reaper who cut it was given a tail of woven cornstalks to wear and called Tom Cat. He would choose a second reaper as a partner, called She Cat, and the two then chased all the other harvesters, beating them with their flails. In other mountain regions, the corn harvest itself was called 'the cat' and farmers would describe the crop as the fat cat or the lean cat depending on the quality and quantity of the grain. The reaper cutting the last sheaf here was called 'the catcher of the corn cat', and was presented with a small decorated fir-tree.

The Chinese *Book of Rites* describes the worship of a cat-god called Li Shou, to whom sacrifices of live cats were made after each successful harvest. In many countries, sacrificing a cat was believed to ensure a successful harvest the following year. The most usual method of killing the condemned cat was to tie it inside the final sheaf that was cut. Then it was ceremoniously beaten to death by the reapers, using the flails made for threshing the grain from the ears or corn. The original ceremony ended with cooking and eating the cat's battered body, but later, this gave way to the burial of the cat at the edge of the cornfield. In more recent times, the rite of killing the corn-cat consisted of beating the last sheaf, without an imprisoned cat, then carrying it home to the traditional harvest home feast which was called 'the cat'. In most fertility rites, it was felt necessary to kill a cat and the burial of the body in the cornfield was to ensure a good crop the following year.

Cat charms

Freya was also the goddess of lovers and it was thought that Friday, or Freya's Day was the most propitious for weddings, as was the presence of a cat at the wedding. Cats are thought to be able to foretell marriages. In Ancient Egypt, newly-weds would decide on the number of children they wished to have and find a cat amulet engraved with the same number of kittens. This would be worn by the wife as a pendant, or placed in the home as an ornament, and used as a ritual object during prayers to Bast, asking for the number of children to be granted.

Lucky cat charms are known thoughout the world, and certainly started their popularity in the days of the Pharaohs. In those times, the charms were mainly to ensure fertility, but as they were usually inscribed to the all-powerful Bast, they were also worn to guarantee long life, prosperity and health. Originally, the word 'charm' meant spell or incantation, but it gradually expanded to include any action or object believed to possess the power of the spell.

In China, live cats are used as lucky charms and are kept confined by long thin chains, fixed to leather

house, while light-coloured cats bring silver. In Europe, black cats are thought of as lucky, and in some countries brides are often given cat mascots as they leave the church after the wedding. In Scotland and Ireland, a tortoiseshell cat straying into the house portends good fortune, and in some areas, a cat with extra toes or claws is thought to bring health, wealth and happiness.

The most prolific of all cat charms must be the Maneki Neko or Beckoning Cat of Japan. This cat charm is modelled in a sitting position, its left paw raised to its ear, and a benign expression on its smiling face. The figure is a symbol of an ancient legend, and carries a popular belief that wealth and prosperity are drawn in by the beckoning paw.

An Egyptian bronze cat.

collars. It is believed that the uglier and older that these cats are, the greater luck they will bring. To let one of these precious animals escape would be to allow any chance of good fortune to escape with them. The Chinese also used cats for protecting their silkworms, mainly from rats, but if live cats could not be obtained, pictures of cats were fixed on the walls of the silkworm sheds to give spiritual protection. Clay pictures of sitting cats with staring baleful eyes were fixed beneath the eaves of Chinese houses and may still be found today. Buddhists believe that dark-coloured cats ensure that there will be gold in the

The legend tells of *Gotoku-ji*, a small temple, merely a tiny thatched hut, run by starving monks, headed by a master priest. This man had a small cat of which he was very fond, sharing with it the meagre scraps of his food. One day, six Samurai rode up on splendid horses and noticed that the cat was sitting up and beckoning to them with his paw. As they followed the beckoning cat into the temple the heavens opened and torrential rain poured down. While they sheltered, the Samurai talked with the priest and listened to his Buddhist doctrine. One of the Samurai was enchanted with what he had heard and later paid regular visits

163

to the temple to receive instruction from the priest. He caused the temple to become part of his family's estate and lavished great sums of money on it for improvements. To this day the temple may be seen, amid beautiful gardens, with avenues of tall trees. Pilgrims still go to visit the shrine in the grounds—the shrine of the Beckoning Cat.

Japanese shops and restaurants often have a Maneki Neko, made of clay, wood or papier-mâché, outside their doors to beckon to prospective customers. Sometimes, if a model is not available, a picture or even the name of the beckoning cat is written on paper, and hung, as a charm, on the wall. Occasionally, the Maneki Neko model will have one or more kittens, also beckoning, presumably to increase the chance of attracting good fortune.

The building sacrifice

Although other animals were occasionally used, it was the unfortunate cat, thought to be well endowed with magical powers, that was commonly chosen as a building sacrifice. During the demolition of an old building, the mummified body of a cat may be discovered in some cavity, such as between the floor boards or in the roof joists. In 1950, alterations were being made to a house in the Tower of London, and such a body was found between the floor joists of an upper room. It was dated at about 1700, and is now carefully preserved in the Department of Environmental Archaeology. Originally, such finds were attributed to natural causes, but as more and more cat bodies were unearthed, remarkably well preserved, it was concluded that each had been crudely mummified with smoke or chemicals after death, and deliberately placed in the buildings as some sort of talisman.

Building sacrifices were possibly made to protect the house from vermin. This is borne out to some extent by the attitude of the cat found within the walls of Hay Hall, in the north of England. It was placed in a standing position, with jaws open, and claws extended, facing a small bird. The cavity was obviously specially made to hold the cat when the Hall was built in the fourteenth century, for there was no way that the animal could have got in to it by accident. Another such tableau was found in a sixteenth century house in Southwark, London, where the cat was entombed with a rat in its mouth and another under its forepaws, and in a cathedral in Dublin, Ireland, a cat with a mouse in its mouth has been found walled in.

Though the idea of a building sacrifice is very ancient, and at one time the victim was human, the custom continued into very recent times. A wall built in 1879 in Gibraltar was found to contain the body of a cat, and the same custom was practised in Britain at least until 1890. It is recorded that during that year some builders in Cornwall refused to complete a house for their employer until he agreed that they could make a building sacrifice. In this instance, the rite was to

ward off the devil, and the workers were adamant. Eventually it was agreed that they should wall-in a dead hare, and so the house was completed.

The healing cat

The magical healing powers of the cat could have been the cause of the demise of thousands of the unfortunate creatures. Even in the days of the Roman Empire, Pliny recorded that the cat was used in medicinal rites and treatments, and so it has continued through the ages to the present time. Pliny, or Gaius Plinius Secundus, lived from AD 61–113 and was the author of a fine work on Natural History in which he explains that cat's dung was efficacious in treating many ills. Mixed with wine to a thick paste it would draw out thorns from the flesh, while added to oil of roses it would cure uterine ulcers. Made into a thick paste with mustard, it was used as a poultice for drawing ulcers of the head.

In 1607, centuries later, Edward Topsell recorded that a cure for bladder stones in humans was a medicine made from the dried and powdered liver of a cat. Fat, rendered from the cat's body was a cure for gout, and to help failing eyesight, the head of a black cat was burned to a cinder, ground down, and the resulting powder blown gently into the affected eyes with a quill.

The Japanese Maneki Neko cat is used as a good-luck charm. In one Tokyo temple a host of such cats, made of bronze, porcelain and paper, greet visitors.

164

Cat's fur was used in treating the extensive burns suffered by the people of London in the Great Fire of 1666. Many cats were killed and skinned, the fur being laid over the badly burned areas of the body. By insulating the wounds from the air, infection was warded off and the pain considerably eased. In Holland and other European countries, fresh cat skins were used to treat severe skin infections and sore throats. The Japanese relieved severe gastritis and even such conditions as epilepsy by placing a live, black cat on the stomach of the patient.

Just as the cat in Ancient Egypt was used to protect the home from snakes, so the cat through the ages has been considered able to heal by ridding the body of poisons. The cat-goddess was believed to be both nurse and healer, being able to draw poisoned wounds and destroy infections. In her animal incarnation, her tail was widely used in healing rites and a cure for blindness.

The tail, even today, is the part of the cat's anatomy thought to be most potent, both for healing and in magical exercises. In country districts of England it is thought that irritation or a stye in the eye can be cured by rubbing the lid with the tail of a black cat. In the south west of England in Cornwall, this action is accompanied by the invocation of a spell –

I poke thee, I do not poke thee

I toke the quoff that is under the eye

O, qualy way, O qualy way.

In the county of Northamptonshire, the swollen eyelid is stroked with a hair pulled from the tip of the tail of a black tom cat. This must be plucked on the night of the new moon and drawn nine times across the stye.

Whitlows are cured by passing the tail of a black cat down the back of the hand and through the fingers in a weaving movement. This must be repeated on three successive nights to take away the angry swelling. Warts are removed by rubbing with the tail of a tortoiseshell tom cat. As tortoiseshell tom cats are extremely rare, and the treatment is only effective if carried out in the month of May, it seems that other methods of wart dispersal should be sought!

As a cure for itching, a black cat was taken by a left-handed man, who whirled it three times around his head. Then three drops of blood were let from its tail and blended with the ashes of nine charred barleycorns. This mixture was applied to the itching area with a golden wedding ring, accompanied by the invocation of the Trinity. The tail of a cat, buried beneath the doorstep of the family home was thought to prevent any kind of sickness from entering.

Today, the healing powers of the cat are focused mainly on its use to mankind in the field of research. Thousands of cats have given their lives in laboratories for the direct benefit of humans and other cats, and the sensitivity of the animal's nervous system has revealed a great deal about the complexity of the parallel system in man.

The forecasting cat

Many superstitions and sayings arose following observations of the cat's responsiveness to atmospheric change. In the old days, when windforce sources and unusual weather patterns were unexplained, these conditions were often attributed to the works of witches and demons. Often these beings were thought to have assumed the form of cats before undertaking their mischievious tasks, or that they had employed cats in effecting the spells. In China, cats were said to wink an eye to signify the coming of heavy rain. Cats washing well behind the ears also heralds a downpour, while a cat sitting with its back to the hearth warns of a sharp frost.

A cat scratching at a table leg in Scotland would be watched with alarm, for this would presage gale force winds. If the cat raced wildly about the house, mewing, this would also announce the coming of a severe storm. Cats can quite definitely foretell a coming storm, and are nervous and very restless just before the weather breaks. One Slavic myth tells that cats' bodies are taken over by demons during thunderstorms. While great thunderclaps from the heavens bring forth the prayers of angels, they are mocked by the demons safely locked within the cats. The lightning is fired at the cats by the angels to try to cast out the devils they protect. This explains why in some countries cats are chased from the house when a storm threatens, in order to prevent them being struck by lightning.

Sailors and cats

Sailors have always been fond of cats, believing that they bring good luck and fair weather, as well as keeping the cargo holds of the ships relatively free of vermin. When a sailing ship was becalmed, the ship's cat was taken on deck and placed underneath a large, inverted cooking pot. This was called 'raising the wind', and it was hoped that before long the sails would fill and the voyage continue. If anyone was seen to throw a cat overboard in a fit of rage, especially if it was a black cat, the seamen would wait in apprehension, for this was thought to be a sure way of invoking a terrible storm.

Notoriously superstitious, seamen from many lands believe in cat magic, and many nautical terms have feline connotations. A light wind at sea is known as a 'cat's paw', and if the wind changes direction suddenly, and without warning, it is watched carefully, the men being instructed to 'see how the cat jumps'. Narrow walkways or bridges on board ship are called 'cat-walks'. Punishments at sea were meted out in the old days by whippings given by the bo'sun, wielding a lash called the 'cat-o-nine-tails'. This was made of nine knotted leather thongs plaited into a handle at one end. When wetted with sea water and applied with skill to the offender's back, the flesh was soon opened and bloody.

A small, single-masted boat used for going to and

from the ship was known as a 'cat-boat', and its rigging was called the 'cat-rig'. An anchor beam is known as a 'cat-head' and the method of securing the anchor to the beam is called 'catting the anchor'. A special piece of iron clamping the rope into place is called the 'cat-harpin'. Even the roughest of old sea salts would take the time to give a kind word, or a piece of food, to the ship's cat, hoping to bring favourable winds and fair sailing weather throughout the voyage.

Witch cats

Witches used cats in spells to control the weather, and many trials were held in which the hags were found guilty of bringing about violent storms at sea, and the destruction of many ships. In the Scottish Highlands, a witch would invoke a storm by drawing a cat three times through the flames of a blazing fire. In other rites, a cat was ceremoniously baptized, then cast into the sea to raise a tempest.

In one famous trial in Scotland, Agnes Sampson was accused of trying to wreck the fleet of King James and Queen Anne of Scotland, journeying home from Denmark. After terrible tortures, this wretched woman confessed to her crimes. She told the court that on All-Hallows' Eve she went to sea in one of a flotilla of sieves, in the company of about two hundred other witches. They took flagons of wine which they drank, then made land, where they sang and danced on the beach. At a later date, while the king was abroad, Agnes and her witch friends took a cat, baptized it, then tied to its body certain parts from the corpse of a man. The witches took the cat and set sail in their sieves, causing 'a tempest in the sea as a greater hath not bene seen'. A ship taking the same direction as the royal fleet foundered and almost sank, and Agnes admitted that the whole of the royal fleet would have sunk without trace, had it not been for the strong faith of the king and his retinue. For centuries, laws were made directed against those who invoked storms by magic.

During their trials, many witches told how they were able to transform themselves into cats. One French witch explained how she rubbed her body with a special black ungent in order to effect the change, then she was able to pass unseen through the dusk, in the form of a sleek black cat. A Scottish witch in 1662, recited a spell in the court, which, she said, if chanted three times over, would turn her into a cat. She admitted that she performed this ritual quite regularly, when she and her coven would range the countryside, causing trouble throughout the night. She said that it was only necessary to chant another spell to return to human form. Members of a coven were also able to turn one another into cats. If a witch in cat disguise met one in human form she would say 'The Devil speed thee and go thou with me,' then, immediately, the second witch would assume feline form and the two would trot off together.

Beware of the Cat, written by Baldwin in 1584 states that a witch could only take on the form of a cat nine times. It is said that the cat has nine lives, and nine is a mystical number for it is composed of a trinity of trinities. Taking one of a cat's nine lives could have serious consequences, for it is said that a cat will haunt anyone who takes one of its lives and seek vengeance for it.

Witches were often identified when they were found to have wounds known to have been inflicted on cats. A man walking alone in Strasbourg late one night was attacked viciously by three large cats. He fought them off and inflicted wounds on all of the animals. Later, he was accused of attacking and wounding three notorious ladies of the town. He denied the charges, but was astonished and horrified to learn later that medical examination of the women showed that they had injuries identical to those borne by the cats.

Another case was recorded of a Scottish laird who noticed that his fine stocks of rare wines were

In the Western World cats were regarded as evil creatures. Many fifteenth-century woodcuts of witches are full of fierce-looking black cats.

diminishing in his cellars. As there seemed no other reason, he put this down to black magic and decided to keep watch. One night, he stealthily crept down the cellar steps, armed only with a sword, and was immediately surrounded by an ominous throng of black cats. The cats crouched and sprang at him and he had to wield his sword vigorously about him for his own protection. In the battle one cat was mutilated, and eventually they all fled, squalling. The next day, one of the village women, already suspected of witchcraft, was found dying in her cottage, with one leg missing.

A similar case is that of the witches of Vernon, in France, who were said to gather, disguised as black cats, in an old castle. Four young men took a bet, and spent the night in the castle. At midnight they were attacked by hundreds of black cats and a dreadful fight ensued. One man was killed and the other three severely wounded, but they managed to injure some of the cats in return. The next morning, several local women were found ill, with bleeding wounds.

Basque farmers as late as the end of the last century claimed that witches assumed cat form and took the milk from their cows. One farmer, determined to discover the cause of his herd's disappointing milk yield, concealed himself in the cowshed at night. At midnight, several black cats slunk into the bier, at which the farmer sprang from his hiding place and attacked them. Putting them to rout, he went to bed. In the morning, he found a woman's ear, complete with gold earring, lying in the straw on the cowshed floor.

Witches could not only turn themselves into cats, they also kept cats as familiars, and took them along on

A procession of witches bearing a cat on a litter from a sixteenth-century woodcut by Ulrich Molitor.

their nocturnal excursions. These witches were said to have a third nipple from which their cat familiars could suck. The powers of the witch obtained from the Devil were shared by her familiar who also took part in magic ceremonies and rites. In 1579, a witch confessed at her trial that she had a cat-familiar which she fed daily on drops of her own blood mixed with milk. Some years later, at another trial in England, a witch told the court how her cat stayed with her at night and fed by sucking blood from her arms and body. Another witch described how her familiar sucked her body for blood, saying that the sensations caused her to enter a trance-like state. The witch would often prick her face, arms and body to produce blood for her cat, as a reward for having carried out her wishes.

In England at Lincoln in the year 1618, a witch was hanged after confessing to using her cat in rites performed to render heirless the Earl and Countess of Rutland. A glove belonging to the couple's eldest son was stolen by the witch, along with some feathers from the mattress of the Countess' bed. The witch performed spells on the glove then rubbed it ritually on the body of the cat before sending it off into the night. The eldest son was taken ill and soon died despite all possible care. Shortly afterwards, the witch performed similar magic with the second son's belongings, and he too, was taken ill and died. Then the feathers were subjected to magic and rubbed on the belly of the cat. The Countess, now childless, was made sterile by the spells and the couple were left without legal heirs.

Many amulets and talismans were made to protect ordinary folk against witches and their cat-familiars.

It was thought that a rowan branch shaken in a cat's face would cause it to vanish, and to protect babies, rowan branches were tied at the head of their cribs. The most potent defence against witches however, was to invoke the Trinity. One Scottish witch confessed at her trial that she and her friends were often thwarted in their attempts to work mischief on neighbouring farms, by fences of prayer and charms.

Gatherings of witches, known as Sabbats, usually took place at crossroads, on high mountains or in deep caves, and corresponded with certain phases of the moon. The Sabbats were ceremonial occasions, presided over by the Devil himself, often in the form of a black cat, and many strange rites were performed. At these ceremonies, novices were initiated and allocated their familiars. To show their allegiance to the Prince of Darkness, it was sometimes necessary for witches and wizards to sacrifice their own cat-familiars to him. Cat-familiars were also sacrificed to work very powerful magic, though it was usually felt preferable to employ the live cat for these tasks. The most potent of all sacrifices was that used to make a Dead Man's Candle. Grease and fat rendered from the witch-cat's body was moulded into a candle around a wick made from the hair of a corpse. The candle holder was made from the hand of an executed murderer, and had to be severed from the wrist during an eclipse of the moon. Anyone subjected to the light from this candle would become totally paralysed.

The victimized cat

Witchcraft trials started in Europe in the thirteenth century and in many, cats were involved as familiars. Thereafter, for some 400 years, cats were often persecuted and regarded with suspicion. Even the most innocuous, normal behaviour of the cat was misinterpreted. For example, one man, seeing a cat lift a door latch with its paw killed it instantly, believing it to be possessed of the Devil. Women were often accused unjustly of witchcraft if they owned cats. One was hanged as a witch after her pet cat was seen to jump, innocently, through her open window.

Most witch cats were said to be black, but it is more likely that they used tabbies, the most common of cat patterns. This would explain why tabby cats are so rarely seen in many rural parts. However, black cats were the victims of the terrible Taigherm ceremonies. Adapted from remote pagan rites, black cats were dedicated to the Devil before being put on a spit and slowly roasted to death over an open fire. The tormented creature would struggle and howl piteously before the release of death, and was then replaced by another victim, so that no break occurred in the continuity of the rites. The torture continued for at least four days and four nights, when the operator would feel worthy of a reward from the spirits, and usually asked for the gift of second sight. The location of the last recorded Taigherm, which took place in the middle of the seventeenth century, is marked on the Island of Mull.

A very similar ritual was performed at crossroads, when a large fire was built on which a generous pot of water was brought to boiling point. A witch would take a large black tom cat and drop it into the bubbling water. It was thought that the Devil would appear and ask for the cat, so that its torment would cease, and the creature was exchanged for whatever the celebrant most desired, which again was often the gift of second sight.

While in the Taigherm the cats were sacrificed to the Devil, other rites were performed in which the wretched creatures were offered to God. In Aix, France, on Corpus Christi, the area was searched for the finest male cat available. He was then tightly swaddled in fine linen and placed on exhibition in a beautiful shrine so that all could come and worship before him. Prayers were chanted and incense burned, until as the day drew to its close, the doomed animal was placed in a wicker basket and tossed alive into the heart of a huge bonfire in the city square. As it screamed in its agony of death, the priests began to sing an anthem and marched off in procession around the town.

Most of the ceremonies involving cats also included ritual burning, possibly as some sort of purification. In England at the coronation of Elizabeth the First, an effigy was made of the figure of the Pope. This was filled with live cats and burned on a street bonfire. As the screams of the dying cats echoed forth, the people were told that they were the cries of the devils within the body of the Holy Father. Papists tortured a cat by shaving its head like that of a friar, tying its paws together and dressing it in vestments, and it was then hanged on a gallows at Cheapside in London. At the same time in France, baskets of live cats were burned on St. John's Day each year, being tossed into the heart of hill-top bonfires amidst much ceremony.

Even at the end of the eighteenth century a similar custom was being followed and is described in Moncrif's *Lettre sur les chats*:

'*Every year a festival is held at Metz which is a disgrace to human nature. The city fathers go in solemn procession into the main square where a number of cats are exhibited in a cage. This is hung over a bonfire which is then set alight with great ceremony. When they hear the frightful shrieks of the cats, the people believe that they are once more torturing an old witch who, it is said, once turned herself into a cat when she was about to be burned.*'

Even a century ago, the unfortunate cat was still being tortured and killed. Sacrificed to God and the Devil, burned by witches and priests alike, it seemed that by his very nature the cat was doomed to perpetual persecution. Now, however, the tide appears to have turned in its favour, and each year the cat grows in popularity as a pet.

The Literary Cat

Angela Sayer

The elegance, natural grace and enigmatic personality of the cat have made it a favourite subject for authors and poets throughout the ages. Some have merely described the charm and pleasing habits of their pet cats, while others have delved into the depths of the feline psyche. Some writers have managed to explore the many facets of the cat's character with an almost uncanny perception.

An early European poem about a cat was penned in the eighth century by a young Irish monk. In it he tells of the mutual sympathy and trust between his white cat, Pangur Ban and himself. As the cat skilfully searched for mice to hunt, so his master hunted for the philosophical words he needed to complete his writings and reinforce his Faith. At the end of each allotted task, cat and man sat quietly together and found comfort in their companionship.
The poem's first verse read:

I and Pangur Ban, my cat,
'This a like task we are at;
Hunting mice is his delight,
Hunting words I sit all night.
and the last verse:
Practice every day has made
Pangur perfect in his trade;
I get wisdom day and night,
Turning darkness into light.

At the same time a poem was written in Arabic by a young man called Abu Shamaqmaq, who lived in such poverty that his poor home even lacked mice for his cat to eat. In his poem he remonstrates with the cat, encouraging it to leave him and to go to live in the nearby hotel where the pickings are so much better. Another Arabic poem, written a century later, chastised the cat for having met its demise, due to its irresistible urge for catching doves. Despite warnings, she climbed up to raid the dovecote of a neighbour,

who shot at her with bow and arrow, causing her to plummet to her death on the ground below. Ibn Alalaf Alnaharwany mourned her in his poem thus:

Why, was pigeons' flesh so nice,
That thoughtless cats should love it thus,
Hadst thou but lived on rats and mice,
Thou hadst been living still, poor Puss.

According to a popular legend, Dick Whittington was a poor orphan boy who heard that the streets of London were paved with gold. He travelled to the city, and was disappointed to find as much poverty there as in the countryside. After many vicissitudes Dick sent his only possession, a cat of whom he was extremely fond, in a shipment of goods for sale in Morocco, at the suggestion of his master, a rich merchant.

As it happened the palace of the Emperor of Morocco was plagued with mice, and Dick's cat soon had them under control. This so delighted the Emperor, that he paid a great price for the animal. When the ship returned to London, Dick received the money and used it to start in business on his own account. He prospered and eventually married the merchant's daughter. He was knighted and known as Sir Richard Whittington and was three times elected Lord Mayor of London in 1397, 1406 and 1419. The story has been enacted as a pantomime for many years and the part of the cat is at least as important as that of Dick.

Perhaps the greatest insight into the ways of cats was observed and recorded by Edward Topsell, in his History of Four-Footed Beasts and Serpents, first published in 1607:

'the root of the herb Valerian is very like unto the eye
of a cat, and wheresoever it groweth, if Cats come
thereunto they instantly dig it up for the love thereof,

himself with his Cat, and verily it may well be called an idle man's pastime. As this beast has been familiarly nourished of many, so have they payed dear for their love being requited with the loss of their health, and sometime of their life for their friendship: and worthily, because they they love any beast in a high measure, have so much the less charity unto man.'

In the works of William Shakespeare there are 44 references to cats, and none are truly favourable. The bard was obviously not a lover of cats. The nearest he comes to complimenting the cat is in *Merchant of Venice*, when Shylock refers to the animal as *'the harmless, necessary cat'*. Elizabethan audiences would have appreciated the pun in *Romeo and Juliet* when

*One of Edward Lear's limericks:
"There was a Young Person of Smyrna, Whose grandmother threatened to burn her; But she seized on the cat, And said "Granny, burn that! You incongruous old woman of Smyrna!"*

as I myself have seen in mine own Garden, and not once only, but often, even then when I had caused it to be hedged or compassed round about with thornes, for it smelleth marvellous like to a Cat.

The tongue of the Cat is very forcible and attractive like a file, attenuating by licking the flesh of a man, for which cause when she is come near to the blood, so that her own spittle may be mingled therewith she falleth mad. Her teeth are like a saw, and if the long hairs growing about her mouth (which some call Granons) be cut away she loseth her courage. Her nails sheathed like the nails of a Lion, striking with her forefeet, both Dogs and other things as a man doth with his hands.

Cats will also hunt Apes and follow them to the woods, for in Egypt certain cats fell upon an Ape, who presently took himself to his heels and climbed into a tree, after whom the Cats followed with the same celerity and agility: for they can fasten their clawes to the barke and run up very speedily: the Ape, seeing himself overmatched with the number of his adversaries, leaped from branch to branch and at last took hold of the top bough whereupon he did hang so ingeniously that the Cats durst not approach unto him for fear of falling and so departed.

It is needless to spend any time about her loving nature to man, how she flattereth by rubbing her skin against ones Legs, how she whurleth with her voice, having as many tunes as turnes, for she hath one voice to beg and to complain, another to testifie her delight and pleasure, another among her own kind by flattering, by hissing, by puffing, by spitting, in so much that some have thought that they have a peculiar intelligible language among themselves. Therefore how she beggeth, playeth, leapeth, looketh, catcheth, tosseth with her foot, riseth up to strings held over her head, sometimes creeping, sometimes lying on the back, playing with one foot, sometimes on the belly, snatching now and then with the mouth, and now with foot, apprehending greedily anything save the hand of man, with divers such gestical actions, it is needless to stand upon; as much as Coelius was wont to say, that being free from his studies and more urgent weighty affaires he was not ashamed to play and sport

Tybalt is called *'good king of cats'*, for Tybalt is the French form of the name Gilbert, the cat in the popular story, *Reynard the Fox*. Shakespeare usually shows the cat as a quiet, subdued creature, with sly and thieving ways. Falstaff says *'I am as melancholy as a gib cat or lugged bear'*, and later, *'I am as vigilant as a cat to steal cream.'*

George Louis Leclerc Buffon, the French naturalist, also disliked cats. In 1791 he described them as being very unfaithful creatures, perverse and treacherous of nature which became more defined with age. While admitting that kittens were pretty and charming, he considered that cats fulfilled only one important function in life, that of keeping vermin under control. The Jesuit Father Bougeant wrote of cats in an entirely different vein, describing contented, glossy tom cats, peacefully sleeping after a good meal, paws and whiskers occasionally twitching as, in their dreams, they happily pursued scampering mice.

An illustration from Boswell's "Life of Johnson" showing the famous cat Hodge asleep at his master's feet.

170

Goethe loved cats, and in his poem *Westlosthcher Divan*, he considered the animal as being one of the four beasts that would be favoured by admittance to Paradise. A literal translation of one of the final verses reads:

This cat of Abuherriras purred
About the Lord and coaxes
Since he is ever the holy beast
Whom the Prophet stroked.

A beautiful, colourful and pathetic poem is the one by eighteenth-century poet Thomas Gray, *On the Death of a Favourite Cat Drowned in a Tub of Gold Fishes*. The cat, Selima, was described as being a demure tabby, with emerald eyes, velvet paws and jet-black ears. She was fascinated by the brilliant goldfish and tried to hook them out of the water with her outstretched paw. Eventually, she over-reached and fell into the water, and though she mewed loudly, no-one heard her or came to her rescue, so she eventually drowned.

One of the most famous relationships between writer and cat is that of Dr Johnson and his pet cat, Hodge. James Boswell, in his *Life of Samuel Johnson*, recalls Hodge 'scrambling up Dr Johnson's breast, apparently with much satisfaction, while my friend, smiling and half-whistling, rubbed down his back, and pulled him by the tail; and when I observed he was a fine cat, saying, "Why, yes, Sir, but I have had cats whom I liked better than this"; and then, as if perceiving Hodge to be out of countenance, adding, "but he is a very fine cat, a very fine cat indeed."'

A Sienese painting of a cat.

In the eighteenth century, William Cowper translated from the Latin of Vincent Bourne a story of a game that went too far. It is called *Familiarity Dangerous* and tells how an old woman played with her little tabby kitten. The game became too rough and the kitten tore a deep wound in her mistress' arm, was thrown to the floor and threatened with a worse punishment. The poet remonstrates with the old woman for not having understood the rules of play with a cat:

But, Lydia, bid thy fury rest;
It was a venial stroke;
For she that would with kittens jest,
Should bear a kitten's joke.

During the nineteenth century, the cat inspired many writers to take up their pens. In France, the animal was portrayed in several forms. Gautier described his own cats in *La Nature chez Elle et la Menagerie Intime*, and also wrote about the rapport that Baudelaire had with cats of all sorts. Baudelaire himself wrote many evocative poems dedicated to cats. Felines remained popular subjects for literary works in France, and reached a climax in the famous, emotional stories of Colette.

The Kitten and the Falling Leaves by William Wordsworth is a word-picture of the antics of a small kitten, learning its hunting techniques through play. Withered leaves lightly fall from a tall elder tree, through the frosty morning air, spiralling excitingly as they float down. The kitten starts up—'*crouches, stretches, paws and darts, First at one, and then its fellow, Just as light and just as yellow;*' She leaps at one leaf, releases it, grabs another—'*Now she works with three or four, Like an Indian conjuror; Quick as he in feats of art, Far beyond in joy of heart.*' Leaping, scudding and pouncing, the kitten's pleasure is shared by her captive audience.

Surely the best-known and one of the most popular of literary felines is the widely grinning Cheshire Cat in Lewis Carroll's *Alice's Adventures in Wonderland*? Alice comes upon the Cat in the garden, where he is perched high in a tree. Although it looked good natured it was possessed of '*very long Claws and a great many teeth, so she felt it ought to be treated with respect.*' The Cat tells Alice that everyone in Wonderland is quite mad, so is Alice, or she would not be there. Alice found the most disconcerting thing about the Cheshire Cat was the way in which it would appear and disappear at will, and told him that this habit of his made her quite giddy. Then the cat grinned even more widely than before and started to disappear very, very, slowly, '*beginning with the end of his tail and ending with the grin, which remained some time after the rest of it had gone. 'Well! I've often seen a cat without a grin,' thought Alice, 'but a grin without a cat! It is the most curious thing I ever saw in all my life.*'

Although many nursery rhymes were written during the eighteenth century, most were amended and altered before being set down in print a century later. It was in 1871 that Edward Lear wrote his best known set of verses, *The Owl and the Pussy Cat*, who sailed away in a beautiful pea-green boat, to be married. This much loved tale has been set to music and recorded, and has also been adapted as a pantomime.

The cat story that most fires the imagination and captures the animal's unique spirit is *The Cat That Walked By Himself* by Rudyard Kipling. It tells of the old days when all creatures were wild and man lived in a cave, warmed by his new discovery–fire. The wildest of all the wild animals was the cat, who walked by himself and to whom all places were alike. Man tamed the animals one by one and drew them into his circle, feeding them in return for their labour or services. The horse, the cow and the dog all bowed to man and became tame. Eventually, even the cat was drawn to the warmth and shelter of man's habitat, but although it became more tame, it did not become servile, and to this day walks by himself. This very moving story manages to contain the unique relationship between cat and man in a few pages of compulsive prose.

Alice awakes after her dreams, back home with a clutch of kittens.

Many other writers have used the cat as a subject for their works, and in the English language one should particularly note the famous Beatrix Potter stories for young children, and also T. S. Eliot's Old Possum's Book of Practical Cats.

The role of the cat through the ages has changed much, and this has been reflected in its portrayal in poetry and prose. From the days of its veneration as the God of the Pharaohs to its persecution as a tool of the Devil, its mysticism, its role as hunter, its serenity, beauty and charming grace have all been observed and carefully written about. Today, the trend continues and all aspects of felinity are recorded in contemporary works. Anthologies, 'bedside' books, pocket-sized handbooks, massive encyclopaedias and colour illustrated 'coffee-table' editions are all eagerly sought and bought by cat-lovers throughout the world. Many collectors specialize in books on cats, and there are hundreds of titles in and out of print.

Chances are, as you, the reader, scan this page, you will have your favourite cat upon your knee, for this is a cat book, so you must be a cat lover. Reading, while stroking a cat is surely one of life's pleasures?

In *Through the Looking Glass* by the same author, Carroll described the antics of two young kittens and their mother, a cat called Dinah. The mother cat meticulously washed the white kitten's face while the black kitten got into considerable mischief with a ball of wool, turning it into a muddle of knots and tangles. Alice played and talked with the kittens, and it was obvious that Carroll had spent much time observing, not only the play fantasies of children but also the mannerisms of cats and kittens and their relationships with one another.

In popular Nursery Rhymes, the cat is seen in several different roles–the fiddling cat in *Hey, Diddle Diddle*, the cat who journeyed to London to see the queen in *Pussycat, Pussycat, Where Have You Been*, the Puss that ate the dumplings, the kittens who lost their mittens, Dame Trot's cat and the Puss that danced out of the barn. *Ding Dong Bell*, a lesson in verse for small children, tells how a cat was dropped down a well by one young man and then rescued by another; the rhyme moralizes, saying,

What a naughty boy was that
Who tried to drown poor Pussy Cat
That never did him any harm
But kill the mice in his father's barn.

This simple Nursery Rhyme remains a favourite:

I love little Pussy
Her coat is so warm,
And if I don't hurt her
She'll do me no harm.

Stately, kindly, lordly friend,
Condescend
Here to sit by me, and turn
Glorious eyes that smile and burn,
Golden eyes, Love's lustrous meed,
On the golden page I read.

From To a Cat   by Algernon Charles Swinburne
(1837–1909)

172

Cat Standards

Angela Sayer

Every breed of pedigree cat that has been officially recognized by a governing feline body is allocated a standard of points of perfection. The total number of points for each breed adds up to 100, but as will be seen, the allocation of these points varies considerably from one breed to another. The most important features of each breed are assigned the highest number of points.

For example, in the Chinchilla Longhair, it is the unique colouring of the coat that is considered to be its most important characteristic, closely followed by the type of the head. Therefore, in this breed, 25 points are given for overall colour, plus an extra fifteen points for coat and condition, while head-type receives another twenty points out of the total 100. In Shorthairs, the unique Manx cat is renowned for its taillessness, high rump and short back, and these features, as can be seen from the chart, account for 60 per cent of its points.

The points scores are published and revised from time to time as a different characteristic needs emphasis in a particular variety. If a general trend to poor coat colour or texture is noticed in a specific breed, then more points will be allocated for that feature. Cats with this defect will receive lower prizes at shows, and so breeders will be automatically encouraged to improve the coats in that variety. Breed societies keep a general eye on adverse trends within their pet varieties, and are quick to attempt to remedy matters in this manner. A meeting is called, representatives of the breed are examined and the matter discussed at length. Having decided on a revision of points, the matter is then passed to the governing body for ratification.

Judges are usually interested in the overall quality of the exhibits that they assess, but the points standards are always present in their minds. They are fully conversant with the allocation of points for the breed of cat in which they specialize, and judge the class accordingly, arranging the cats in order of merit. It often happens that two or more cats in a class of high quality are equal in a points score, and then it is the experience of a qualified judge that enables him to place the first prize on the cat with the best, overall presence.

Few judges actually write down the points score of each cat as they handle it. They make only mental notes and place the cats on general overall appearance. Although the judge can get a good idea of the placings by looking at the cats in their show pens, it is only after handling and examining each one individually that faults are found, and the final assessment can be made. Often a very promising cat is found to have a defect which immediately takes several points off its total score.

A study of the comparative points allocated to the Longhaired breeds will soon show the reason why it is impossible to judge on points alone. All the varieties have a number of marks allocated for coat, body, head and eyes, some have no marks for condition or tail, and a few, although they have high scores for coat, are not required to satisfy standards for colour. Judging solely on a points score then, would enable a black Longhair of good colour, with a fine coat, body, head and eyes to score 100 per cent, even if he was in bad condition and missing his tail! Other varieties that could win, even without their tails, appear to be the Whites, Red Self, Cream, Tortie, Blue-Cream and the Brown and Red Tabbies.

Obviously, this situation could not arise, for no judge would place a cat with a fault such as a missing tail, but it does indicate the failings of such a points system.

Different countries of the world have differing standards of points, even for the same breeds. A typical case is that of the Blue-Cream Longhair. In Europe these cats must have beautifully intermingled coats of blue and pale cream. Any sign of clumping

173

of the colours is considered a show fault, and many show reports point out that a certain exhibit would have gone higher if it had not shown, for example, a solid cream or blue foot. In the United States, the Blue-Cream Longhair must be distinctly patched all over with clear areas of blue and cream. An intermingled cat would not gain a winners ribbon.

These anomalies may be accounted for quite simply. Most standards of points are drawn up by a specialist breed society in the early days of a new variety's development. The group of breeders inter-ested in the progress of the variety discuss its merits and problem areas. They draw up a description of the desired, perfect specimen and allocate high points for the features most difficult to breed in, and low points for those features that are already present in the foundation stock. Early specimens of new breeds are in demand in different countries of the world, and exports are made before cats of high standard are produced. The stock arriving in new countries is bred from and a new gene pool arises. From this, breeders devise their own standards of points for the judges

Comparative Points Standards for Longhaired Cats (GCCF)

Variety	Colour	Condition	Coat	Body	Head	Eyes	Tail	Total
Black	25		20	20	20	15		100
White	25		20	20	20	15		100
Blue		10	20	15	25	20	10	100
Red Self			50	15	20	15		100
Cream	30	(20	)	15	20	15		100
Smoke	40		10	15	20	10	5	100
Silver Tabby	40	(15	)	10	20	10	5	100
Brown Tabby/ Red Tabby			50	15	20	15		100
Chinchilla	25	(15	)	15	20	15	10	100
Tortie			50	15	20	15		100
Tortie and White			50	15	20	15		100
Blue-Cream	30	(20	)	15	20	15		100
Colourpoint	10	10	15	10	25	20	10	100
Birman	(20	)	25	20	20	5	10	100

Comparative Points for Shorthaired (British or European)

Variety	Colour & Eyes	Legs & Feet	Head & Neck	Body & Tail	Ears	Coat	Condition	Total
All (except those below)	50 (25/25)	5	10	10	10	10	5	100
Cream	(35/15)	5	10	10	10	10	5	100
Blue-Cream	(35/20)	(		40		)	5	
Bi-colour	(20/5) Markings—	5 25	10	10	10	10	5	100
Manx	Colour— } Markings— }	5		Roundness of Rump 15				
				Depth of Flank 10				
	Taillessness	15		Double Coat 10				
	Height of Hindquarters	15		Head and Ears 10				
	Shortness of Back	15		Condition 5				100

In the United States, the Havana Brown cat (left) has a distinct head shape. In profile, there is a sharp stop at the eyes and the whisker pads are full, giving a 'puppy-dog' expression. In contrast, the Havana cat of England (right) is built on Siamese lines, with the typical long marten face and straight profile. Originally, the Havana was exported from England to the US and the illustrations here show how diversity occurs in isolated gene pools.

to use in assessment. Winning cats are always in demand for stud purposes, and so completely different forms of cat, of the same root stock, may appear in different countries.

Burmese cats were developed in the United States from a small brown cat called Wong Mau, taken by a retired ship's doctor from Burma to America in 1930. The doctor, Joseph Thompson, started a psychiatric practise in San Francisco and in his treatments he often used the gift of a pregnant cat as an aid to curing neuroses in his wealthy women patients. This demand for cats encouraged Thompson to breed extensively from Wong Mau and her descendants, and it is from her stock that the Burmese breed became well established. Today, in the United States, the Burmese is a thickset cat, with a large roundish head and full, golden eyes. The first Burmese to be sent to Britain were rather Siamese-like in appearance, much finer in bone structure and with a greenish-yellow eye colour. American breeders continued to strive towards their own ideal in Burmese, and now they have achieved the results they desired, while in Britain and other European countries, the standards were set to idealize a quite different animal.

The present descriptions of the head shape alone shows the difference between American and European cats of the same breed:

USA *Pleasingly round and without flat planes when viewed from front and side. Face full with considerable breadth between eyes, tapering to a short, well-developed muzzle. In profile there should be a visible nose break. Ears medium in size and set well apart on rounded skull. Alert, tilting slightly forward, broad at base and slightly rounded tips.*

UK *Head slightly rounded on top and with good breadth between ears, having wide cheekbones and tapering to a short, blunt wedge. Jaw wide at hinge and chin firm. Muzzle pinch a bad fault. Ears medium in size, set well apart on skull, broad at base with slightly rounded tips, the outer line of the ears continuing the shape of the upper part of the face. Profile: the ears should have slight forward tilt, distinct nose break and strong lower jaw.*

Discussing Burmese eyes, the US standard calls for 'Set far apart and with round aperture . . .' while the UK standard says 'Round or Oriental eyes a fault . . .'

A similar situation exists in another brown shorthaired breed, the Havana. This variety was developed in Britain and exported to the United States, the reverse of the situation with the Burmese. Today, the American Havana Brown is a small foreign cat with a puppy-dog expression, having a short wedge head and indented profile. Its eyes are full and its tail is medium in length with a blunt tip. The Havana cat of European countries is streamlined and elegant, a self-brown of extreme Siamese type and conformation. In profile his head is long and almost Roman-nosed and his tail is whip-like.

Nowadays, with speed and ease of travel, cats are exported from various countries to others without any problems, and it is probable that the various breeds will eventually become standardized throughout the world. Perhaps this is a pity, for beauty is truly within the eye of the beholder, and each country should be entitled to develop varieties pleasing to its inhabitants.

The Foreign Shorthairs, including the Siamese, are basically similar in body shape, but the various standards call for refinements in head shape, ear and eye placements and, of course, colouring. All Foreigns have short, smooth coats. The differences in standards of points does not allow this to be shown in chart form so the requirements for show specimens of the various breeds will be set out below:

Abyssinian This cat must be slim and dainty, never large or coarse, and has a ruddy brown coat ticked with bands of black or dark brown on each hair. Bars and tabby markings are considered faults, and the presence of white areas on the lips, throat, chest and belly are undesirable. Abyssinian cats have medium wedge-shaped heads, large ears and large expressive eyes of green, yellow or hazel.

Red Abyssinian cats are similar in type but the body colour is a deep copper red ticked with darker colour. The tail tip is dark brown and this colour surrounds the pads of the feet and extends up the legs. The scale of points for both normal and red Abyssinians is the same:

		Body, tail etc	20
Body Colour	30	Condition	10
Ticking	20		——
Head & Ears	15		100
Eyes	5		——

Burmese come in a wide range of colours—Brown, Blue, Chocolate, Lilac, Red, Cream, and four sorts of tortoiseshell. They must be of the same basic type whatever the colour. The head has been previously described, and the body must be medium in size, elegant but not as svelte as a Siamese. The large, lustrous eyes are set wide apart and may be any shade of yellow.

Green eyes are a defect in this variety.

Body Colour	25	Eyes	15
Body Shape & Tail	25	Coat	10
Head & Ears	15	Condition	10
			——
			100
			——

Havana cats are lithe and sinuous, with short, close-lying coats of rich chestnut brown, quite different in shade to any other variety. The eyes are bright, clear green. The Havana has a long wedge-shaped head, fine muzzle and large pricked ears, wide at the base. The elegant shape is finished off with long slim legs and oval paws, plus a long whipped tail.

175

Coat	30	Eyes	10
Head	15	Condition	10
Body	15		—
Legs	15		100
Tail	5		—

Colour	15	Ears	10
Coat	25	Eyes	10
Body & Tail	25	Head & Neck	15
			—
			100
			—

The *Foreign Lilac* and *Foreign White* are similar in build to the Havana, the former having a coat of silvery lavender and deep green almond shaped eyes, while the latter is pure white with sapphire blue eyes. The *Korat* is a foreign cat of less extreme type being rather cobby in stature with a heart-shaped face. The ears are large and rounded and the eyes full and luminous, brilliant green or with an amber cast. The colour of the Korat is silver-blue all over, tipped with silver, causing the coat to shimmer.

Head	20	Condition	5
Eyes	15	Body Colour	20
Body	25	Eye Colour	5
Coat	10		—
			100
			—

Rex Cats are produced by two quite separate genes giving two sorts of curled cats, the *Cornish Rex* and the *Devon Rex*. Cornish Rex have medium wedge-shaped heads with flat skulls, in profile. The eyes are oval and medium in size, of a colour consistent with the coat. The tail is long and tapering, the body hard and muscular. The coat is dense and very fine, forming waves over the entire body, with the exception of the head, legs and paws where it resembles short plush. Eyebrows and whiskers are crinkled. These cats may be of any recognized colour or coat pattern.

Devon Rex are quite different in body structure, having short heads with full cheeks, the muzzle showing a pronounced whisker break. Large, rounded wide-set ears set off the comical face with its slanting, oval eyes. The hard, muscular body is ideally covered in short, dense waves, and as in the Cornish, the whiskers and eyebrows are crinkled. Any colour or pattern is allowed and the eyes must complement the coat colour.

	Cornish Rex	Devon Rex
Coat	50	45
Head	5	10
Eyes	5	5
Body, neck, legs	25	25
Ears	10	10
Tail	5	5
	—	—
	100	100
	—	—

Russian Blue cats have a very distinctive coat, which although short, is thick and plush to the touch in a good specimen. It is a silver-blue in colour with a silky sheen. The skull is flat and narrow and the face and neck are long, giving a sinuous appearance. The body, legs and tail are also long, the whole cat lithe and elegant in build. White markings, tabby stripes and a square head are all serious faults in this breed.

Siamese cats, like Burmese, come in a whole spectrum of colours. From the original Seal, Chocolate and Blue varieties came the Lilac Point, followed by Red, then Tabby Points in seven shades, Tortie Points in four shades and the elusive Cream Point. To many, Siamese are *the* cats, and it is true to say that once you have been owned by a Siamese it is very difficult to live without one in the home.

In conformation all Siamese must be the same. The body is of medium size, long and svelte. The legs are slim with the hind legs slightly longer than the fore-legs, and with dainty oval feet. The body, head, legs, feet and tail must all be long and slim and in proportion, giving the cat an overall elegant, graceful appearance. The short soft coat is glossy and close-lying and the tail is tapered without any sign of a kink. The head is long and wedge-shaped, with a straight profile and a strong chin. The oriental eyes must not squint and must be quite definitely blue in colour, the shade varying in intensity to complement the points colour. Siamese cats have colour restricted to the 'points' or extremities of the body—mask, ears, tail and paws. The varieties are known by the colours of the points. The Seal-Point has dark, seal-brown points, while those of the Chocolate-Point are a lighter, brighter brown. Blue-Points have slate coloured tips and Lilac-Points are barely tinged with dove-grey. Red-Points have extremities of bright, copper-gold in a good specimen, while Cream-Points are delicately tinged with pale apricot. The Tabby-Points are strikingly pencilled on their points and have boldly thumb-printed ears. They may be seal, blue, chocolate, lilac, red, cream or tortie Tabby-Points, their markings coloured accordingly. Tortie-Points are exotically patched on the points, and may be seal, blue, chocolate or lilac, all mixed with cream.

Standard for Seal-Point Siamese:

Type:		*Colour:*	
Head	15	Eyes	15
Ears	5	Points	10
Eyes	5	Body	10
Body	15	Texture/coat	10
Legs & Paws	5	Condition	5
Tail	5		
	—		—
	50		50
	—		—

Note: The Seal-Point was the Royal Cat of Siam. The original standard of points was written for the Seal-Point. As other variety of colours developed, breeders aimed to produce cats to Seal-Point standards. The only difference in standards is in the colour.

176

Eastern Magic

Olivia Manning

Siamese cats were rare in the seaport town where I grew up. Few people had even heard of them. My father had never forgotten two Siamese kittens he had known in the Orient a long time before. He had joined the Royal Navy in the days of sail and when very young, was sent to the Far East. Somewhere among all those places that came into his stories – Hangchow, Kowloon, Borneo, the Celebes – someone presented a pair of Siamese kittens to his ship. They were wild little creatures that chased one another up the rigging, leaping like flying foxes from rope to rope, then rushing down to roll on the deck in mock battles. When they were exhausted, they slept in each other's arms. They were the delight of the sailors.

One day the admiral's wife came on board and she, too, was amused by the kittens. She told the Captain she simply must have one of them and at once it was passed down to the leading seaman that the men were required to present – quite voluntarily, of course – a kitten to the Admiral's wife. So one kitten was taken away and the other was left to play alone. A day or two later a message came to the ship that the kitten ashore was pining for its companion and could the second kitten be sent to join it? So both kittens left the ship and the sailors could no longer watch in wonder as they leapt overhead and fought their mock battles round the deck. For all I know they fared much better in the admiral's house than they could ever have done among shipboard rough and tumble, but the story filled me with rage against authority and I felt their loss as much as did the sailors. Not that I ever did lose them for in my imagination they still play among the rigging against the flamingo and persimmon colours of a tropical sunset. And because of them I longed to have one of these kittens for my own.

Owl from the Orient

Our first Siamese kitten would sit looking at us with blue, owl-like eyes. Owl became her name but as no-

one can comfortably call 'Owl, Owl, Owl,' we called her Hibou (Siam having once been a French possession) and this became Siamesed into Eebou.

Just as there is never another baby like the first, so there is never another Siamese like the first. Every one that comes after is a sort of analogue of the original. We have had kinder and more worthy cats, but Eebou had a magic of her own. As a kitten, she was a wonder among kittens. Her successors had the disadvantage of being male. The inventiveness and engaging coquetry of Siamese kittenhood is concentrated in the female, for the female, that needs the courage of the lion and the cunning of the fox to rear her kittens in the jungle, is far more astute and inventive than the male.

Eebou was intelligent and extravagantly charming. She would claim my attention by sitting like a fur slipper on my foot. Her white breast curving over my instep, she would stare into my face with her round, unblinking, owlish eyes. When she wanted something, she demanded it with howls. Sometimes she cried for horse-meat, sometimes whale, sometimes rabbit (this was during the war). She would starve rather than eat one of these when she had a whim for another. During the time she lived with us she must have eaten her way through a dozen horses and whales, and a hundred rabbits, yet she remained a small cat, very slender and sinuous, whose poses had a ballet-dancer's flow and certainty. At night she would sometimes sleep with my husband, sometimes with me. As she crept, smooth and cool, into one's arms, she would purr so the bed seemed to quiver with her purring. When we returned after an absence from the flat, she would welcome us by flinging herself in ecstasy at our feet and would lie there, pretending to be comatose until one of us picked her up. If I came in with my arms full of parcels so I could do no more than step over her, she would hurry on in front of me and fling herself down again until I was free at last to pick her up and make a fuss of her. Then her purring became a little smug as though a

Left
A Seal Point Siamese running in typical Siamese fashion, maybe in fun after the end of a game or maybe in alarm, before jumping up a tree. Leaping down later rarely presents problems to a Siamese; they are particularly agile and graceful cats. If you encourage Siamese to play and retrieve their toys they will learn to chase after them again and again and amaze you with a dance of ever-increasing speed and skill.

Right
A Tabby Point Siamese also enjoying a garden. However, he seems to have little patience for a small, but brave kitten who is in his way.

tiresome situation had righted itself in a proper fashion.

There was one chair she had decided to tear to ribbons. We could only hope she would be content with it. We were furnishing at the time and when any new piece of furniture arrived, she would rush at it with outstretched claws rousing me to squeal in protest, at which she would streak off, tumbling over herself with inward laughter. Preparations for visitors put her into a frenzy of excitement so she would bolt about the rooms like a clockwork car, but when the visitors arrived she would sulk under a chair or show sudden, unreasonable jealousy that could be savage. One evening, when we were all too absorbed in conversation to notice her, she sat at my feet staring into my face then, rising with a sudden upward movement, she lunged at my eyes. Afterwards she was contrite, knowing I had had a narrow escape.

Mother and kittens

As she grew out of kittenhood, that sweet time, a new fierceness grew in her. Then a terrible thing happened: she was, as D. H. Lawrence put it, 'crucified into sex'. We were all crucified, for she howled day and night and nothing would take her mind off her frenzy.

Of course we should have had her spayed but we listened to stories of cats who lost interest in life after the operation, cats who ceased to wash themselves and cats who died, and we hoped for the alternative of Eebou transformed by the serenity of motherhood. With this vision in mind, I took her again and again to a stud-cat that lived on the outskirts of London. These journeys resulted in a phantom pregnancy that collapsed with dramatic suddenness when we moved house. At last, after heaven knows how many lovers'

meetings, Eebou produced two kittens that seemed to be dead and had to be coaxed to life on a hot-water bottle.

Eebou in the part of devoted mother, becoming more anxious as the kittens became more adventurous, was a delightful interlude that had been reached by such an ordeal of uproar, uncertainty—slow trains to the suburbs, delivering her one day, returning for her the next—of failure, of starting again, to say nothing of the cost, that it was scarcely possible to contemplate a repeat performance.

Meanwhile there were the kittens and the exquisite respite of Eebou's absorption in them. She hid them to begin with in the lowest drawer of a chest of drawers. As soon as they were old enough to climb out, she begged for the drawer just above to be opened and carried them up there, a journey for each, and purred with content when they were again under her paw. In a day or two they would find their way down from the second drawer and have to be carried up to the next. Soon there was no height they could not negotiate and as they swung down from drawer to drawer in the first wonder of independent existence, Eebou watched, and gave little mews of concern and looked at us, pleading with us to restrain them. She was so absorbed in her anxious happiness, how could we ever deprive her of this natural condition?

As soon as they began to develop, the kittens became known as the Big Kitten and the Little Kitten. Both were males. We had to sell one of them and the young man who came to look at them at once chose the Big Kitten.

The Little Kitten was such a pathetic scrap of a thing we decided there was nothing to do but keep him. We named our kitten Faro after the cat in a novel which I published about that time. The fictional cat was a portrait of Eebou and a female, but Faro accepted the name without complaint.

The kittens were no age at all when Eebou started calling again. Her high penetrating cry that scarcely stopped day and night had got us into trouble the first time it started up. In Bloomsbury she had sat in the window and screamed so appealingly at the passers-by that people put notes in the letter-box accusing us of leaving her locked up alone to starve. One woman offered to give us advice on the care of Siamese cats, saying she had had two, one of which died by jumping out of a window and the other had pined and died while she was staying with her father. So we had not only to suffer Eebou's ceaseless cries but somehow to keep them hidden from the neighbourhood.

In the new flat matters were worse. The man who had an office below us did not care if Eebou were locked up or starving, but he was furious about the noise she made. He complained to the landlord. We were warned.

Things could not go on as they were. Apart from the complaints, the sleepless nights were telling on us.

We decided at last she must go to the country and return to us when we found a flat or a house where a cat could have freedom and call to her heart's content.

Here the story grows sad and tragedy enters. Eebou's two-kitten-triumph produced in her a feverish desire for more and more kittens. Production-line quantity, rather than quality, became her aim, so she would break out from any stronghold and entice to her purposes the shabbiest toms. She did not take to the rigours of country life. She would sneak into the homes of rich neighbours, seeking comfortable solitude away from the other cats and dogs among which she now lived, and curl up on silken counterpanes. Her new guardians thought her a selfish, moody, difficult cat but, unfortunately, kept this opinion to themselves and politely pretended they were pleased to have her. Then one day they gave her away to a kindly woman who knew nothing of the habits of the female Siamese and was shocked when she gave forth her uproarious jungle call. At last I discovered that Eebou had changed her home and was unwanted everywhere; I asked that she might be returned to me. She had with all her faults, a beauty, a quality of magic which makes lovable so many selfish and difficult creatures, humans as well as cats.

It was arranged. She was to return to us, but, alas, we never saw her again. It was sex that finished our poor Eebou. A few days before her arranged departure, she broke out of the house and took her last ride on the non-stop streetcar named 'Desire'. She was, per-haps, like so many modern heroines, a doomed creature from the start.

Crossing a main road in darkness, she was struck by a car. We can only hope she was killed at once. By morning nothing remained of her beauty. The flow and certainty of her movements were lost for ever.

Faro—a study in contentment

Faro was a problem kitten from the beginning. He had been a victim of his brother, Big Kitten, who was now christened Butch. Butch had grown twice as fast as Faro and had soon become a fat bully who badgered his little brother unmercifully. There was enough milk for both of them but Butch believed it was all meant for Butch alone. Whenever Faro settled down for a feed, he was pushed aside by his dreadful brother and as a result, developed an enduring sense of deprivation and the hardness of life.

Despite his magnificence, Butch did not last long. His new home was a flat and like all pent-up cats, he was curious about the world outside. One day, when by accident flat door and street door were open together, he made a bolt for it and met his death beneath the wheels of a passing taxi. Faro was to out-live him for twelve years or more.

Once the overwhelming figure of Big Kitten left his life, Faro started to grow and when he reached maturity, he was the classical Siamese, of normal size and strongly shaped like his champion sire. Except for his pale eyes, he seemed to have inherited nothing

Siamese cats . . . The appeal of the kitten, the devotion of the mother and the character of the wise old cat.

from his sleekly elegant little mother. He had none of her vitality or the sense of delight in life that made her death all the more painful to us. We remembered her as an Ariel, all caprice and sweetness, and forgot how our adored little friend had changed into a fiend, impatient of us and everything else that had once made her world.

As for Faro, he went early to the vet, and if he were deprived of the excitements of sex he was also saved from its miseries.

Faro developed into a comfortable teddy-bear cat. Though he lacked Eebou's grace and sparkle, he had unusual strength of character. What he wanted, he had to have. There could be no compromise. He would not let the matter drop. Humour was not his strong point. There had been times when Eebou seemed to be rolling about with laughter, but the most to be expected from Faro was a murmur of contentment when all was well. I soon learnt not to make fun of him. Once or twice when he was disgruntled because of the weather or some other hardship beyond my influence, I bent over him, commiserating in a suspect tone, and received a belt with a paw that soon put an end to that

sort of joke. Although poor Butch had gone so early to the Elysian fields, his shadow overhung Faro's life. Otherwise it was not an eventful life. Faro was a good cat, a devoted cat, but like an old bachelor of indefectible behaviour, he expected the world about him to be indefectible, too. Its shortcomings made him peevish and he had often to be cosseted back to good humour. His chief needs were warmth and comfort; not, as one might suppose in view of his infantile trauma, food. He was very difficult to feed. Those who imagine that any cat will eat if it is hungry, have never experienced the obstinacy of a fastidious Siamese. The owner is at a disadvantage not only because he loves the creature but because he hates to see so much good food go to waste.

'You spoil that cat,' said the butcher, a fat jolly fellow who was known to keep the best cuts for himself: 'Give 'im lights—'e'll eat 'em if 'e 'as to. Starve 'im till 'e does eat 'em, that's my advice.'

At first I was not greatly interested in Faro, accepting him as Eebou's son but seeing him a more sedate and less engaging creature. He was also something of a problem for we were moving to a St John's

Wood house and we had arranged to be abroad for a month before the move. He had to stay with my mother for two months and she was not enthusiastic about such long responsibility for someone else's pet. On our return to England, with the move hanging over us, I paid my mother a weekend visit. Faro was sitting in the hall. I picked him up. Purring, he passed his cold, small nose over my face then gave several crowing cries of joy, more intense and intimate than the welcoming barks of a dog. When I put him on the floor he rushed up and down stairs in a fury of rejoicing, loosening stair-rods and scattering rugs.

'He knew you were coming back,' my mother said. 'He would not go into the garden. He sat all day in the hall watching the front door.'

How did he know that I was coming? My mother's bustling expectation may have alerted him—yet to argue from it that someone was expected, and the person must be I, called for no small reasoning power. It is easier to see it as a case of thought transference.

Faro, though lacking his mother's insouciant charm and flights of fancy, had the confidence of belief in his own virtue. He led a quiet life. I can only twice remember his getting into a fight so furious that he came back torn and slept for hours, exhausted. He was not really a fighter. My Burmese, Miou, goes out looking for trouble but Faro was too near the human avatar for that. One tended to think of him as a human being—a gentle good-tempered old boy, not assertive

but, at the same time, not lacking in quiet self-esteem.

The Blue Point and the Burmese
After Faro died we adopted a Blue Point Siamese named Choula. He was a staid cat, lazy and greedy, and it must have seemed that in possession of an untroubled home where meals were regular and plentiful, he had nothing more to worry about. We thought so, too. We could not have imagined that by giving him a charming, loving little companion we would break his heart.

I was offered a Brown Burmese kitten which I found impossible to refuse. Choula had been with us so short a time, we supposed he would accept another cat as part of the established order of things. He did nothing of the sort. When I brought the little creature in, he stared at it, aghast.

The kitten, whose registered name was Ngo Ah-Miou, was a creature of delectable prettiness. His silken coat was the colour of snuff; he had a seal-dark line down his spine and a seal-dark mask; his eyes were topaz. He was most lovable and because we loved him so much ourselves, we were sure that very soon Choula would love him, too. We were wrong.

On the first day, as the kitten explored the house, Choula stalked it, keeping at a safe distance, occasionally sitting down, the better to observe its every movement. He seemed possessed by an intent interest, but not more than interest. He may have seen the

A Brown Burmese and Blue Point Siamese. Cats often seem to demonstrate that they have an aesthetic sense – they choose to sit and pose in places which match their colouring. Blue to match blue eyes, orange flowers to match a marmalade cat, white to offset rich burnished brown. And cats dance, and listen to music – sometimes – and can sit for hours, their ears twitching at sounds and sights unperceived by humans.

kitten as merely a temporary intruder, like a bird or a mouse. But in the evening, when we were sitting by the fire, Choula, on my knee, stared down at Miou playing on the hearthrug and seemed to realize that the kitten had come to stay. Suddenly, he gave a long drawn cry, agonized and angry. I put my hands on him to soothe him and felt his body tremble. He gave another cry, then another and another. These hoarse cries seemed to come from his very bowels.

Miou stopped and watched Choula, surprised but not alarmed by the terrible noise. Having just come from his mother, he was used to the presence of a large, furry protector; he seemed to see Choula as a similar, perhaps even identical, figure. As one cry followed another, Miou sat alert, delighted by the uproar.

What were we to do? We loved both cats and could only hope they would learn to live together. The problem was made more difficult by Miou's deep affection for Choula. Whenever he tired of playing Miou would nestle against Choula and lick him to show friendliness. Choula, unnerved, would shy away, leaving Miou bewildered by the rebuff.

Miou's vitality was a source of wonder and horror to Choula. Eebou had been vivacious enough but Miou was frenzied. He had the ability to rise directly from the ground. If in his play, he came upon some unexpected trifle—a button, a pea-pod, a feather—he would fly up to a height of four or five feet and seem to pause there in astonishment.

Miou the mischief-maker

The Burmese is the wildest of all kittens, climbing anything that can be climbed with a flash-speed that defeats the eye. Miou was not only likely to be 'surprised by joy' but life so elated him that he spent all his waking hours tearing up and down curtains, springing on to shelves and cupboard tops, and taking whole flights of stairs at a bound. Watching in dismay, Choula obviously regarded the whole exhibition as deplorable.

One day Miou found he could unroll the lavatory paper. Standing upright and spinning the roll with his paws, he would get a heap of paper around him, then cavort about in it, bringing down more and more paper, until the whole roll would be on the floor in ribbons. When we began to put the rolls out of reach, he looked for new entertainment and found a pound packet of cotton wool. I returned home to find the bathroom floor white with the torn-up cotton wool and Miou rampaging about in it like a little dark fiend. Choula, safe on the top of the clothes basket, gazed with the incredulous hostility of middle-age scandalized by the antics of lawless youth. He turned his head when I entered and looked at me as though to ask, 'How long can this go on?'

Not long. The cat's entrancing infancy is brief. Time subdued Miou's ebullience and slowly restored Choula to peace of mind. Though he would not tolerate Miou on the bed, he began to tolerate him as a sleeping companion on the sofa or before the fire. This intimacy

Left
A full-grown healthy Brown Burmese with a gleaming, shiny coat.

Below
A young Burmese kitten showing the fluffy lighter coat that will later develop into the sleek and darker fur of the adult cat.

A Blue Burmese, a Red Point Siamese, a Blue Point Siamese and two Brown Burmese kittens.

Following page Chocolate Point Siamese up a tree.

established, Choula submitted to be licked and one day began to lick back. This began the game of licking and counterlicking: two tongues travelling busily from coat to coat, so neither cat knew whether he licked his neighbour or himself. The game, that usually began after meals, was partly social and partly practical, for a good hunter must be odourless. When, as sometimes happened, Choula did not want to be licked, he would lick back in urgent protest, his gaze raised, intent and pleading, too polite or too nervous to stop Miou with a blow. At other times, asserting himself as though taking action against his own timidity, Choula would pin Miou down and wash his face with determined thoroughness, Miou submitting like a kitten beneath its mother's paw.

As Miou matured, his coat darkened. His belly fur kept its rich snuff brown but the rest took on the colour, as well as the lustre, of the darkest mink. One evening as he ran past us on the stairs, a visitor asked: 'Why is that cat more black than other black cats?'

'Because he is brown,' I said.

Miou undoubtedly is an 'all over seal' cat. In sunlight the maroon of his fur has the glint of copper. He is not only the colour of those sealskin coats our grandmothers wore, he has the same texture. I have never known a cat with such delicate fur. He is now so dark that he can easily hide in the shadows beneath sofa or bed, but his eyes, of topaz gold, give him away as they gaze out with the fearless innocence of one who has always been loved.

His dark paws have the feel of velvet, his touch the delicacy of a feather. In the morning, wanting to get the day started, he gives my face a brush with the fur round his pads. I refuse to wake—he brushes me again. And again. Each time it is the merest breath of a touch, yet it is more effective than an earthquake. I despair. I sit up. At once he flirts away, delighted by the promise of breakfast and the excitements of out-of-doors.

By now the reader may be saying, 'This is ridiculous. She writes of cats as though they were humans.' But are they so very different? The fact is that when an animal, any animal, enters one's home, it becomes something more than an animal. The change is brought about not merely by human fantasy and human need: the animal itself is drawn out of its animal world and advances to meet our wider understanding. In this way, Oriental cats, more sensitive and imaginative than other animals, come very close to those who love them. It is easy to accept the Hindu belief that they have souls and are now very near the human avatar. If this is so, we may hope that our love advances their development.

When they die—and even in these days they leave us all too soon—they live on in the mind, as individual as any human friend. That may be their only immortality, but who can tell? If we survive death, and no-one can say for sure we do not, would we not have them with us? Eebou, Faro, Choula, Miou—without their company, I would find Paradise so much the less.

Index

References in italics are to illustration captions.

Abscess, 60
Abyssinian, 6, 10, *31*, *54*, 113, 122, *122*, *161*, 175; Blue, 122; Red, 122, *125*, 175
Acinonyx, 33
Advertising, cats in, 155–60
Alice's Adventures in Wonderland, 171
Amulets, 161, 162, 167
Angora, 40, 41, 97
Arthritis, 96
Australia, quarantine rules in, 28

Baskets, 28, 133
Bast (Bastet), 37, 161, 162, 163
Bathing, 93, 94
Baudelaire, Charles, 171
Behaviour, 81; disorders, 94–6
Benzoic acid, 94
Birman, 97, 105, *106*, 116, 118
Blood circulation, 44
Bobcat, 33
Boswell, James, 171
Bougent, Father, 170
Bourne, Vincent, 171
Brain, 45, 82; development of, 76, 78, 82, 88
Breeding, first recorded, 39; of pedigrees, 18–19, 84–5, 129–44
Breeds, characteristics of, 22, 97, 118; compared, 10, 76, 97, 106; origins of, 113; *see also* names of individual breeds
Bryant, Doris, 116
Bubastis, 37, 161
Buffon, George Louis Leclerc, 170
Building sacrifice, 164
Burmese, 10, *76*, 113, 116, 118, 119, 175; Blue, 6, *6*, *117*, 118, *125*, *188*; Brown, *116*, 118, *185*, *187*, *188*; Cream, *117*; Sacred Cat of Burma, 116
Burmese/Siamese hybrid, 116, 119
Burmese Cat Club, 119
Burmese Cat Society of America, 118

Caesarean section, 136
Caffer cat (*Felis lybica*), 34
Calling, 14, 18, 56, 84, 85, 131, 132
Cameo, 106, *106*
Cancer, malignant, 62
Caracal, 33
Care of cats, 9–20
Carroll, Lewis, 171, 172
Cat, etymology of word, 38
Cat that Walked By Himself, The, 172
Cat Fancy, 152, 154
Cat-flap, 12, *24*, 25, 26
Cat 'Flu, 140
Catatonic state, 95
Catnip plant, 46
Cat's Cradle, 162
Cat's eye, 161
Cats, in old age, 96; introduction to Britain, 38; shipboard, 41, 165–6; worship of, 37, 38, 162
Cats magazine, 154

Catteries, 26, *54*, 56
Celts, and cats, 161
Central nervous system, 82
Cercle Féline de France, 152
Championships, 152, 154
Charms, 162, 163
Cheshire cat, 171
Cheetah, 33
Chinchilla, 10, 72, 98, *101*, 102, *150*, *157*, 158, 159, *159*, 173; Blue, 105; Shaded Silver, 102
Chinese beliefs, 161, 162, 163, 165
Chocolate gene, 105
Civet, 34, 35
Claws, 12, 25, 33, 35, 43, 44, 49, 60
Cleft palate, 136
'Colette', 171
Collar and lead, *26*, 28, 29, *54*, *125*
Colour, sensitivity to, 45
Colouring, 10, 41, 48, 98, 102, 104, 105, 106, 113, 115, 118, 122, 173
Colourpoint, 10, 105, *150*; Seal, *53*
Communication, 13, 47, 49, 78, 89
Conjunctivitis, 59, 60
Corneal ulcers, 59–60
Cornfields, and cats, 162
Cowper, William, 171
Cystitis, 62

DDT, 54
Deafness, 45, 95; 98, *101*, 109
Diarrhoea, 11, 16, 47, 56, 62, 138, 139
Digestive process, 46
DINICTIS, 35
Direction finding, 81
Disinfectants, 54
Dislocations, 43
Domestication, 21, 36, 37, 38, 41, 83
Dreaming, 92

Ears, 45, 46; attention to, 15, 134; health of, 55; health signs to look for in, 11
Egypt, Ancient, cat in, 36–8, 161, 162–3, 165
Egyptian Mau, *120*, 122
Eliot, T. S., 172
'Elizabethan collar', 50, *50*, 93
Erxleben, 34
Evolution, of cat, 34–6, 40, 41
Exercise, 54, 106
Eyes, *21*, 41, 45, 88, 137, 161; after birth, 137, 139; colour of, 10, 45, *97*, 98, *98*, *101*, *102*, 104, 105, 106, 109, 111, 113, 121; health signs in, 11, *59*, 59–60, 139

Familiarity Dangerous, 171
Fédération Internationale Féline d'Europe, 152
FELIDAE, 34
Felis, 33, 34, 37; *F. catus*, 34; *F. chaus*, 33; *F. domestica*, 34; *F. lybica*, 34; *F. ocreata*, 34;

F. sylvestris, 34
Fertility rituals, 162, 163
Fertilization, 132
Fighting, 85
Filming, 155–60
Fleas, 11, 14, 15, 25, 60, 61, 62, 93, 134
Flehman reaction, 68
Food and feeding, 15, 16, 54; calorie requirement, 18; diet, 43, 46, 47, 61, 84, 96, 134, 138, 139, 144; in old age, 96; in pregnancy, 43, 84, 134; of kittens, 11, 54, 139, 142; of mother, 19, 131, 138, 139; of stud, 143, 144; tinned, 11, 16, 18; when sick, 53, 62
Foreign cats, 72, 76, 113, 131, 132, 144, 175; Black, 122; Blue, 122; lilac, 121, 122, 176; Tabby, 122; White, 121, 122, 176
Fossil remains, 35, 36
Fostering, 86, 140–41
Fractures, 43
France, Mrs Lilian, 118
French, Mrs, 116, 119
Freya, 162
Fungal infections, 60
Fur, 11, 15, 44, 60; fur balls, 14, 47; *see also* Grooming

Gautier, Emile, 171
Gestation period, 18, 48, 56, 133–4; charts, 130, 131
Gingivitis, 46
GLOVED CAT, 37
Goethe, J. W., 171
Grass eating, *31*, 98
Gray, Thomas, 171
Greece, Ancient, cats in, 38
Grooming; by cat, 46, 47, 93–4; by owner, 10, 14, 15, *16*, 25, 54, 60, *60*, 96, 98, 106, 109, 143; excessive, 95; of queens, 86, 131, 134

Harvest rituals, 162
Havana, 119, *119*, 175; Brown, 175
Haw, 45
Hearing, 45, 92
Hernia, umbilical, 137
Herodotus, 37
Himalayan, 105
Himalayan factor, 48, 104, 105
Hodge, *170*, 171
HOPLOPHONEUS, 35
Hunting; cats used in, 34, 37; instinct, 72, 76, 82, 90, 91
Hygiene, 11, 25, 98, 140

Illnesses, 44; *see also* specific complaints
Incontinence, 94, 96
Independence, 25
Infectious anaemia, 62
Infectious enteritis, 26, *54*, 55–6, 62, 140
Infectious peritonitis, 62

Inoculations, *see* Vaccinations
Insecticides, 54, 60, 134
Intelligence, 81, 82

Jacobson's organ, 46
Jaguar, 33
Jaguarundi, 33
Japanese, and cats, 39, 163–4, 165
Jaundice, 44, 45
Johnson, Samuel, *170*, 171

Kidney disease, 62, 96
Kipling, Rudyard, 25, 172
Kitten and the Falling Leaves, The, 171
Kittens, *21*, *23*, *26*, 87–9, 132; abnormal, 136–7; and children, 23, 88, 95; and other animals, 23, 24, 25, 88, 95; bed for, 11; birth of, 19, 86, 134–6; Burmese, *187*, *188*; buying, 10, 11, 54; colouring, 98, 113; communication, 78; feeding, 11, 54, 88, 139, 140, 141; grooming, 14, 15, 25, 88, 93; hand-rearing, 141–2; hazards for, 11, 12, 23, 28, 29, 31, *50*; health signs, 11; introduction to home, 23; neutering, 56; Persian, 138; playthings for, 13, 23, 88; predatory instinct in, 90; rearing, 11, 137–9, 140, 141–2; determination of, 138; Siamese, 113, 138, 139, 177, *180*; sleep pattern, 92, 93; training, 11, 12, 25, 28, 87, 88, 139, 140; weaning, 11, 87, 139, 140; worming, 61
Korat, *120*, 122, 176
Korat Cat Fanciers' Association, *122*

Lactation, 84, 86, 132, 139
Lant, Miss, 118
'Language', 78
Lear, Edward, 172
Leopard, 33
Lice, 60, 61, 62, 93, 134
Linnaeus, 34
Lion, 33
Literature, the cat in, 169–72
Long-hair (Persian), 40, 41, 60, 68, 76, 97–8, 131, 132, 138, 143, 144, 145, 173, 174; Bicoloured, 104, *105*, 111, 112; Black, *81*, 98, 102, 104, *152*; Black Smoke, *105*; Blue, 10, 98, *98*, *102*, 104, 106; Blue-Cream, 10, 102, *102*, 104, 173, 174; Blue Smoke, 102, *105*; Brown Tabby, 98, *101*, 173; compared with Short-hair, 10, 76, 97, 106; Cream, *97*, 98, *102*, 104, *155*, 173; development of type, 41; Red Persian, 98, *101*, 104; Red Tabby, 98, 173; Self, 98, 173; Silver Tabby, 98, *157*; Smoke, 48, 102; Tabbies, 98, *158*; Tortoiseshell, 102, 104, *150*,

173; Tortoiseshell-White, 102, *102*, 104; White, 10, 98, 101, *159*, 173
Lymphosarcoma, 62
Lynx, 33, 35

Magic, cats associated with, 161–8
Manx, *9*, 10, 112, 137, 173
Margay, 33, 34
Maternal instinct, 19, 59, 65, 66, *68*, 86–7, 93, 134
Mating, 18, 48, 84–5, 131–3, 144
Medicine, administering, 53, 54
Merchant of Venice, 170
MIACIS, 34, 35
Mice, control by cats, 37, 39
Military excema, 61
Milk, *see* Lactation
Minerals, 54
Mites, 46, 60
Moncrif, 168
Morris, William, 162
Moulting, 44
Mouth, 11, 46
Musculature, 43

National Cat Show, *150*, 151, 159
Nature chez Elle et la Menagerie Intime, 171
Nephritis, 62
Nervous systems, 82, 83, 165
Neurons, 83
Neutering, 14, 18, 31, 48, 54, 56, 62, 68, 96, 144
Nose, health signs in, 11
Nursery rhymes, 172
Nursing, 53–4, 62

Ocelot, 33, 34
Odd-eyed cats, 98
Old Possum's Book of Practical Cats, 172
On the Death of a Favourite Cat Drowned in a Tub of Goldfishes, 171
Oestrus, behaviour in, 14, 47, 48, 84–5, 96, 132, 133; *see also* Queens
Oriental breeds, 113, *120*, 122, 176
Owl and the Pussy Cat, The, 172

Panther, 33
Panthera, 33
Parasites, 44, 60, 62, 93, 134, 144
Parasitic otitis, 55
Parturition, 19, 134–6; abnormal births, 136
Pasteur, Louis, 41
Pedigree cats, compared with cross-bred, 9; breeding, 18, 84, 85, 129–44; universal standards, 41, 173–6
Pens, *24*
Play, playthings, 13, 23, 25, 68, 69, 72, 91, 143
Pliny, 38, 164
Pneumonitis, 45
Pocock, 41
Polydactyly, 137
Potter, Beatrix, 172
Pregnancy; behaviour in, 84, 86; care of queen in, 133–4; mating in, 132
Preservation of wild species, 33

Puma, 33
Purring, 13, 47, 65

Quarantine rules, 26, 28
Queens; at and after parturition, 19, 65, 66, 135–9; choosing 129; in pregnancy, 19, 133–4, 135; mating, 18, 131, 132, 133

Rain-making rituals, 162
Rats, control by cats, 37, 40, 41
Red gene, 106
Reproductive system, 48, 131, 132
Respiratory infections, 62, 94
Reynard the Fox, 170
Rex; Cornish, *126*, 127, *150*, 176; Devon, 127, 176
Ringworm, 60
Rochford, Marie, 127
Rome, Ancient, cat in, 38, 164
Romeo and Juliet, 170
Russian, 106; Blue, 122, *125*, 127, 176; Blue Chartreuse, 122

Safety measures, 29
Scent, 68, 84, 85, 89; scent glands, 89
Scratching, scratching post, 12, *12*, *14*, *24*, 25, 98
Serval, 33
Sex determination, 138
Sexual cycle, 56, 84
Shakespeare, William, 170
Short-hair, 40, 106, 131, 132, 144, 174; Blue-Cream, 109; British, 106; British Blue, 10, *19*, 106, *109*; Calico cat, 111; compared with Long-hair, 10, 76, 97, 106; Cream, *108*, 109, *155*; Red Tabby, *108*; Spanish, 111; Spotted, 112; Tortoiseshell, 111; Tortoiseshell-and-white, 111; White, 106, 109
Shows and showing; American procedure, 152, 154; classes, 151, 152, 154; Croydon, 119; Crystal Palace, 113, *145*; judging, 151, 152; National Cat Club, 119; points, 97, 104, 106, 112; preparation for, 145, 148; regulations, 145, 148, *150*, 151; Siamese Cat Show, 116, 119; standards, 152
Siamese, 10, 43, 45, 47, 48, *53*, *56*, 69, 72, *74*, 96, 104, 105, 106, 113, 131, 132, 137, 138, 144, 159, 175, 176, 177–89; Blue, *59*, 105, 176; Blue Point, *113*, *113*, 115, 122, 176, *180*, *183*, *185*, *188*; Brown, *119*, Brown Tabby, *54*, *110*; Chocolate, 113, 115, 176; Chocolate Point, *59*, 105, 115, 176, 188; Cream Point, 113, 176; Frost Point, *113*; Lilac Point, *24*, 65, 105, 113, *113*, 115, 176; Pastel Tabby Point, 113; Red, 176; Red Point, 105, 113, 176, *188*; Royal Cat of Siam, 113, 176; Seal, 176; Seal Point, *10*, *18*, *19*, 105, 113, 115, *129*, *150*, 176, *179*, *180*; Silver Point, 115; Smoke, 113; Tabby Point, *12*, 113, *114*, 115, 176, *179*; Tortie Point, 105, 176;

Tortoiseshell Point, 113, *114*, 115, *145*; White, Odd-Eyed, *59*, 106, *109*
Siamese Cat Club, 119
Silver gene, 98, 102, 105
Skeletal structure, 42–3; defects, 43
Skin, skin diseases, 44, 60–61, 93
Sleeping, 91–3
Smell, sense of, 46
SMILODON, 35, 36
Snow Leopard, 33
Societies, 118, 119, 122, 127, 152
Spaying, 14, 31, 56
Spraying, by male, 14, 48, 89, 143, 144
Stud, 143–4; choosing, 133, 143; quarters for, 143; 'stud tail', 93–4
Survival, keynote of psychology, 82, 83, 91
Swinburne, A. C., 172

Tabbies, 39, 41, 48, 110; Short-hair Brown, *110*; Short-hair Red, 111; Short-hair Silver, 110, *111*, *152*; Silver, *157*
Tabby markings, 41, 98, *101*, 110, *110*, 111
Talmud, and the cat, 161
Taste, 46
Teeth, 35, 42, 46; health, care of, 11, 46, 59, 96
Television, cats on, 155–60
Territorial sense, 66, 68, 89, 90
Thompson, Dr J. C., 116
Through the Looking Glass, 172
Tibetan Temple Cat, 40
Tiger, 33; sabre-toothed, 35
To A Cat, 172
Tongue, 46, 93

Topsell, Edward, 39, 162, 164, 169–70
Travelling, 28, 29, 81, 91

Union Nationale des Associations Féline, 152
United States; health rules, 27, 28; show standards, 175
Urolithiarsis, 62

Vermin, control by cats, 37, 38, 39, 40, 165
Veterinary treatment, 49, *49*, 50, 53, *53*, 54, 55, 59, 62, 96, 131, 133, 134, 135–8, 142
Vibrissae (whiskers), 44
Viral infections, 62
Vision, 45
Vitamins, 16, 54, 142
Vocal chords, 13, 47
Vomiting, 56, 60, 61, 62
Von Ullman, Miss, 119

Washing, *68*, 93–4; *see also* Grooming
Watson, Mr and Mrs V., 118
Weaning, 11, *56*, 59, 66, 139, 140
Weather forecasting, 165
Weir, Harrison, 113
Westlosthcher Divan, 171
Whiskers, 44
Whittington, Sir Rd. ('Dick'), 169
Wildcats, 33, 34, 91
Witches, and cats, 166–8
Woodiwiss, Major, 119
Wool-eating, 96
Wordsworth, William, 171
Worms, 11, 47, 56, 61; worming, 54, 56, 61

Young, Mrs Herbert, 119

Acknowledgments

The publishers would like to thank the following individuals and organisations for their kind permission to reproduce the photographs in this book:

A F A (G Kinns) 68–9; Animal Graphics 17 below, 101 above left, 112, 146–7, 155; Ardea Photographics (S Gooders) 183; Barnaby's Picture Library 4–5, 50 below, 69 below, 101 above right, 180; Bavaria Verlag 79; S C Bisserôt 100, 102 above, 121 left; Bruce Coleman (Jane Burton) 19, 64, (A J Deane) 71 above; W S Crawford's (Kosset Carpets) 156 right; Anne Cumbers 10, 13 below, 16 above, 24 below, 25, 30, 52, 54 left, 102 below, 104 above, 104 below, 108 above left, 108 above right, 108 below, 110, 117 above, 127, 128, 148 above, 148 below, 149, 150 above, 152–3, 154, 156 left, 157 below right, 159; Daily Telegraph 114 above, (Kirkwood) 61; Robert Estall 66; Mary Evans Picture Library 166; Glasgow University Library 167; Robert Hallmann 1, 2–3, 103, 158; Louise Hughes 57 above, 57 below; Jacana 22 below, 23, 49, 54 right, 59 above, 77, 114 below, 125, (Labat) 28–9, 72, (P D O'Treppe) 20, (Soyamoto) 73; Keystone Press Agency 8; Mansell Collection 169, 170 right, 171, 172; Pierpont Morgan Library, New York 170 left; N H P A (S Dalton) 14, (M Davies) 157 above; Octopus Books 50 above, 50 centre, 51, 53 left, 53 right, 55 above, 60 left, 60 right; Pictorial Press 97, 115 below, 120; Spectrum 12, 15, 16 below, 17 above, 21, 24 above, 26, 32, 59 below, 67 above, 70, 75, 116, 157 below left, 181, endpapers; Sunday Times 151, 182 below; Syndication International 71 below; Sally Anne Thompson 7, 9, 13 above, 18, 22 above, 27, 31, 55 below, 56, 67 below, 74 above, 74 below, 76, 80, 99, 105, 106, 107, 109, 111, 115 above, 117 below, 118, 119, 121 right, 123, 124 above, 124 below, 126, 150 below, 153 below, 160, 178 above, 178 below, 179 above left, 179 above right, 179 below, 182 above, 184 above, 184 below, 185, 186, 187, 188 above left, 188 above right, 188 below, 189, 190; ZEFA 58, 63, 101 below.